UNDERSTANDING

MAINLAND PUERTO RICAN POVERTY

UNDERSTANDING

MAINLAND

PUERTO RICAN

POVERTY

Susan S. Baker

Temple University Press
PHILADELPHIA

Temple University Press, Philadelphia 19122
Copyright © 2002 by Temple University
All rights reserved
Published 2002
Printed in the United States of America

♾ The paper used in this publication meets the requirements of American National
Standard for Information Sciences—Permanence of Paper for Printed Library Materials,
ANSI Z39.48-1984.

Library of Congress Cataloging-in-Publication Data

Baker, Susan S., 1945–
    Understanding mainland Puerto Rican poverty / Susan S. Baker.
        p. cm.
    Includes bibliographical references and index.
    ISBN 1-56639-969-6 (cloth : alk. paper) — ISBN 1-56639-970-X (pbk. : alk paper)
    1. Puerto Ricans—United States—Economic conditions. 2. Puerto Ricans—United
States—Social conditions. 3. Puerto Ricans—United States—Statistics. 4. Poverty—
United States. 5. Poverty—United States—Statistics. 6. United States—Economic
conditions—1981–2001. 7. United States—Ethnic relations. I. Title.

E184.P85 B35 2002
339.4'6'097295—dc21

                                                                            2002020513

To my parents,
Eileen Strickland and
the late George Strickland,
with thanks for their
unconditional love and support

Contents

Preface

leven-year-old Jorge heard the shot, ran into the corner bar and found his father, Miguel Velez, on the floor, dead. Miguel had just killed himself. Jorge, the youngest of five children, was in shock. His mother had died from an illness just two years before. Now, his father had left him and his brothers and sisters all alone. Why?

Miguel had always worked. He had a job in a manufacturing plant in Chicago that made equipment for the tool and dye industry. Then, early in the summer of 1985, he was laid off. For a full year he tried to find a similar job but could not. He was the sole support for his family, and the longer he went without work, the more he worried about how he could meet the needs of his children. He went into a deep depression and finally convinced himself that they would be better off without him. One Saturday night he gave each of his children a piece of jewelry that had belonged to their mother or to him, and then, with no warning, he walked to the corner bar and shot himself.

Luis Aviles was forty years old. He sat on the stoop of his Bronx apartment building with a beer in his hand trying to make sense of what had happened to his life.

Luis's parents had come to New York City before World War II. His family did not always have a lot, but his parents had always worked—they were never on welfare. Shortly after he and his wife Benita were married, they had a son, José, and life looked good. He was supporting his family from his job in the garment district and had even received a promotion to manager of a warehouse.

In the late 1970s, after two years in his new position, Luis was told that business was getting slow, and he was laid off. He tried to find new employment, but all he could find were jobs that paid way too little to support his family. He had been brought up knowing that he was responsible for meeting his family's needs, but now he could not. He was frustrated, and the tension was hurting his family. He and his wife were having conflicts, and family life was deteriorating.

His wife eventually was able to find a job as a teacher aide in the public school system. This helped take care of some of the basic needs in the home but also caused further damage to Luis's self-image. After all, he, not his wife, was supposed to support his family. The arguments and tension increased until divorce was inevitable. Luis felt hopeless and lethargic and began to drink heavily. Now he was alone and so psychologically paralyzed that he was unable to even interview for a job. Why was all this happening?

How do we understand these stories? Were Miguel and Luis at fault for not finding new jobs or possibly even for losing their old jobs? Both these men were Puerto Ricans who had made their homes in major U.S. mainland cities—Chicago and New York. Are they exceptions within the Puerto Rican community? No, not at all.

According to the 1990 census, the official unemployment rate for all non-Hispanics across the United States was 6.0 percent. For all Hispanics taken together, it was 10.4 percent. But when we look at only Puerto Ricans, the rate goes up to 12.4 percent, and this does not include those "discouraged workers" who are no longer even a part of the labor force. A logical question might be: If things are so bad here, why don't they go back to Puerto Rico? Well, also in 1990, the official unemployment rate on the island was 20.4 percent, and the unofficial unemployment rate was close to 40 percent! Census estimates in March 2000 (before the decennial census was taken) indicate some improvement across the board. Unemployment for non-Hispanics was 4.1 percent; for all Hispanics taken together, it was 6.8 percent; and for Puerto Ricans it was 8.1 percent (U.S. Bureau of the Census, 2001a).

The reflective question *Why?* requires us to investigate what is going on, but where do we start? And how does unemployment affect the general well-being of Puerto Ricans in the United States, especially in regard to the issue of poverty? We could start by looking at the individuals who are unemployed and try to determine whether they are lazy, whether they lack job skills, or whether they are uneducated or undereducated. We could start by looking at Puerto Rican culture to see how it affects Puerto Rican work ethics, how it views education, or how Puerto Rican family structure affects their well-being. Or we could start by looking at U.S. society to determine how economics and politics affect local job markets, how labor needs can affect educational outcomes, or how an ethnic group can be manipulated and relegated to second-class status.

Although this book touches on all these areas, we will use the societal or structural area as our starting point. As C. Wright Mills said:

> When, in a city of 100,000, only one man is unemployed, that is his personal trouble, and for its relief we properly look to the character of the man, his skills, and his immediate opportunities. But when in a nation of 50 million employees, 15 million men are unemployed, that is an issue, and we may not hope to find its solution within the range of opportunities open to any one individual. The very structure of opportunities has collapsed. Both the correct statement of the problem and the range of possible solutions require us to consider the economic and political institutions of the society, and not merely the personal situation and character of a scatter of individuals. (1959, 9)

The Puerto Rican situation definitely falls into what Mills calls a societal "issue."

Troublesome Trends

In doing any type of sociological study, we need to look at how the area of interest has been studied in the past. Major historical methods for studying an issue can guide us as we approach mounds of data. However, they can also trap us into thinking a particular way and thus blind us to alternative explanations. I believe that three particular trends have hindered researchers from understanding the nature of Puerto Rican poverty. The first trend is that all Hispanics often are lumped together for research. This means that the experiences of immigrants/migrants from as many as twenty-three different countries, including Mexicans, Cubans, Puerto Ricans, Ecuadorians, Peruvians, Dominicans, and even

Spaniards, are all averaged together. Their different histories and back-grounds are overlooked. Many researchers (e.g., Bean and Tienda 1987; Portes and Truelove [1987]1991; Aponte 1991; Aponte 1993) have been challenging others to recognize the importance of looking at each national group apart from the mix, and I agree with this approach.

The second trend is that the studies that have been done on Puerto Ricans usually either combine all U.S. Puerto Ricans, regardless of where they live in the United States, or they single out New York City as a case study. A few studies have looked at Puerto Ricans in other cities, but there has been a real lack of research that compares the experiences of Puerto Ricans in different areas of the United States.

The third trend is that theories regarding adaptation of immigrants/migrants and poverty have primarily been designed to explain the experiences of either white European ethnic groups at the turn of the century or African Americans. Other nonwhite groups are "forced" to fit into one mold or the other. This was explicitly stated by Douglas Massey (1979) when he published his first national study on Hispanic residential segregation. We believe that studying Puerto Ricans (or any other group that is neither white European nor African American) using models that were not designed for their experiences results in inaccurate conclusions.

My Approach

This book is laid out in three major parts, each one corresponding roughly to one of the three troublesome trends. The first part responds to the first trend. By reviewing the historical experiences of the major U.S. Hispanic national groups—Mexicans, Cubans, and Puerto Ricans—and then comparing their situations in 1990 and 2000 wherever possible, we document the importance of separating Hispanics by national group for study and also address how Puerto Ricans fare compared with the other Hispanic groups.

The second part responds to the second trend. We show the importance of separating the experiences of Puerto Ricans by regions, and even by metropolitan areas within regions, by drawing comparisons that clearly show that not all areas of the country provide the same opportunities (or lack thereof) for Puerto Ricans. We also look at the possibility of Puerto Ricans moving to a new area as a strategy for trying to locate better opportunities. We then look at two significant pieces to Puerto Rican economic attainment: residential segregation and special issues dealing with Puerto Rican women.

The third part responds to the third trend by attempting to develop a truly Puerto Rican explanation for what is happening. Our approach in this section is to describe the effects of changing labor market dynamics using case studies of various areas of the country.

After these three major parts, we provide a concluding chapter that synthesizes the results of the three parts and introduces possible policy ramifications.

Underlying Themes

Throughout this book references are made to certain underlying themes. The first of these themes is the importance of New York City. Not only is New York important as the historical location of choice for Puerto Ricans coming from the island (and it still contains, by far, the largest Puerto Rican community on the mainland), but also its changing structure has perpetuated moves within the United States that affect the development of Puerto Rican communities across the country. The vast majority of U.S. Puerto Ricans trace their roots through New York City.

A second underlying theme is that although the situation is different in Puerto Rico from what is in mainland cities, the experiences of the two areas are intertwined. This book is concerned with the circumstances of Puerto Ricans on the mainland, but it is impossible to understand their situation adequately without drawing connections to the development of the island.

A third underlying theme is that although Puerto Ricans, even on the island, are U.S. citizens by birth, their citizenship has not been an asset when confronting U.S. labor markets. Labor structures in many U.S. cities are leaning more toward incorporating cheap new Hispanic and Asian immigrant labor, rather than finding room for another politicized "native minority." Throughout this book the framework is laid for recognizing the second-class status of Puerto Rican citizenship.

The final underlying theme requires recognition of the special circumstances of Puerto Rican females. Whether reviewing the rise of female-headed families, looking at the effects of welfare, or trying to understand the high percentage of females who are not in the labor force, we must acknowledge the importance of understanding the economic role of Puerto Rican women.

Keeping in mind the three major research trends we want to confront as well as the underlying themes just mentioned, we are ready to begin our journey of discovery into the Puerto Rican experience on the U.S. mainland.

n the mid-1960s my husband and I moved into the Puerto Rican barrio of Humboldt Park, Chicago. For twenty-one years we lived, worked, and raised our four children there. During those years we were struck by the paradoxes we found. On the one side, we learned to appreciate a gracious and gentle people who took the words *mi casa es su casa* (my house is your house) to heart. Never did we enter the home of a Puerto Rican family where we did not feel welcomed. Usually we were invited to share in whatever was cooking in the big pots on the kitchen stove. Hospitality was natural to them, as was caring for each other. When a family was going through a tough time and needed assistance, a brother, sister, cousin, or *padrino* (godparent) was always there to help. The extended family went beyond bloodlines to include others in the community as well. Family, community, hospitality—all these combined with an enjoyment of the beautiful things in life. We often sat on our stoop while neighbors with guitars and other instruments played the old songs from the island. However, this serene, somewhat idyllic image was only one side of the picture.

The other side of the community was a rough one. More than forty street gangs caused the deaths of so many teenagers that one year the community earned the unenviable label of being "the most violent community in the U.S." Welfare was becoming a way of life. The effective dropout rate at the main high school servicing the community was close to 75 percent. Drugs and alcoholism were commonplace.

How could such a caring, community-oriented people get caught up in violence and other behaviors that could cause only destruction and pain to their families and community? How do we reconcile this paradox? The easiest approach is to blame the people: They should be staying in school, learning a trade, and getting a job. But I found this to be too simple an explanation.

Being a part of the community allowed us to experience the structural discrimination and indifference Puerto Ricans on the mainland must face. Shopping in the same local supermarket, we had to carefully sort through the graying meat and the wilted and browning lettuce. Supermarket chains sent the "good" meats and produce to stores in other areas of the city—areas that were not inhabited by people of color, brown or black. Raising our children to play on the same streets meant warning them to stay clear of policemen, who would beat up teenagers in front of their mothers or take gang members to an opposing gang's "turf" and let them out of the squad car to see if they could make their way home safely on foot. Sending our children to community schools as well as being an advocate for many of the community children opened our eyes to a system that explicitly or implicitly made it clear that Puerto Rican children came from an inferior culture and were not worth the effort needed to properly teach any child. Attempting to find jobs for people who were out of work gave me a glimpse of a job market that primarily offered part-time jobs at minimum wage and with no fringe benefits, yet with hefty deductions for union dues.

This immersion into the everyday life and culture of a Puerto Rican community provided the impetus for me to more systematically research what was actually at the root of the frustrations and anger I saw each day. My experiences convinced me that Puerto Rican culture was not the problem. To adequately understand the causes of the distress in Humboldt Park, I had to look at how the city embraced or did not embrace different people groups. I witnessed discrimination on many institutional levels, from the city council's manipulation of ward maps to eliminate, or at least minimize, Puerto Rican representation, to the school board's requirements that Puerto Ricans take an English test to be certified to teach, even when they had been born and raised solely on the mainland. This test was so difficult that many of the Anglo teachers would not have been able to pass it (but of course they were not required to take it). Some changes have taken place, for example, in the mid-1980s the federal government forced the city to redraw its ward boundaries to allow for more representation from minority areas.

The underlying current of discrimination, however, has not changed—
it has only taken different forms.

When our family moved to Philadelphia in the late 1980s, we again
gravitated to the Puerto Rican community. We began learning about it
and spending time there with the people. In comparing the barrios of
Humboldt Park in Chicago and North Philadelphia, we found many
similarities, but we also found many significant differences. Attempting
to understand why these differences existed led me to view those communities within the dynamics of their host cities, especially in terms of
the interactions between the barrios and the institutions of those cities.

This book is the culmination of the lessons I learned and the experiences I have gone through since those early days in Chicago. It is an
attempt to look at the plight of the Puerto Rican people in the United
States, primarily in our urban centers. Its focus is to try to disentangle
the many dynamics affecting the status of Puerto Rican Americans to
determine what is behind their high poverty and low employment rates.
Guided by my discoveries of the importance of local contexts, this
research has a dual focus. First, I will attempt to share my understanding of the Puerto Rican mainland population as a whole in terms of relationships between the United States and Puerto Rico. Second, I will
review how Puerto Rican socioeconomic conditions have developed
within local (metropolitan area) contexts. I recognize that this work may
result in more questions than answers, but my hope is that it will point
the way toward a uniquely Puerto Rican explanation of poverty.

In my journey toward discovery, I have been fortunate to receive
guidance and support from several people. Dr. Manuel Ortiz, my friend
and colleague of twenty-eight years, encouraged me to do the research
found in this book, and he reviewed and critiqued all my findings. Dr.
David Bartelt and Dr. William Yancey, both of Temple University,
taught me the skills to make this research possible and guided my analysis as I faced piles of data. Doris Braendel, Janet Francendese, and Peter
Wissoker of the Temple University Press editorial staff gave me invaluable assistance in how to approach the organization and writing of this
book. My gratitude goes out to each of them. Finally, my deep appreci-
ation goes to my husband, Randy, who had to deal with my long hours
of work and mood swings as I alternately became excited about findings
and then worried about seeming barriers to completing this work.

Viewing Puerto Ricans as Hispanic

1

Hispanics in the United States

When we think of Hispanics in the United States, our minds often turn to a particular national group, depending on our backgrounds. For example, people living in the Southwest might immediately think of Mexicans; those from southern Florida might think of Cubans; and those from major cities in the Northeast would probably turn their attention to Puerto Ricans. If people from each of these areas were to provide a general description of Hispanics, they would give us very different pictures. Those from the Southwest might describe Hispanics by bringing up issues of "illegal aliens" (more properly referred to as "undocumented immigrants") and the low level of wages maintained for menial positions because Mexicans are willing to work for so little. Those from Florida might bring up the business acumen of Cubans and then complain about how they are "taking over" Miami and indeed all of Dade County. Meanwhile, those from the Northeast might complain about the large numbers of Hispanics on the welfare rolls.

Yes, all these descriptions are stereotypes, yet they clearly show us that the groups listed under the Hispanic umbrella are not homogeneous. Each group faces different issues. Sure, there are commonalities among the groups—they all use the Spanish language, have a religious orientation with roots in Spanish Catholicism, and were subjected to Spanish

3

colonialism (with the exception of those from Spain itself), to name a few. However, the groups are different from each other in more ways than they are alike. How, then, did they get lumped together as a "minority" under a Hispanic (or Latino) label?

The Hispanic Label

The Hispanic label, as with most labels, was not created by the national groups encompassed by it. Lucas warns us about the label's use: "This lumping together of national groups into a 'minority' is an artificial convenience" (1978, 2) for those in positions of power. He calls the label an "administrative convenience" (1981, 6). Portes and Truelove explain that "[*Hispanic,* until recently,] was essentially a term of convenience for administrative agencies and scholarly researchers. . . . The emergence of a Hispanic 'minority' has so far depended more on actions of government and the collective perceptions of Anglo-American society than on the initiative of the individuals so designated" ([1987]1991, 402).

Although sometimes the Hispanic or Latino label is used by a combination of national groups to provide solidarity on common issues (e.g., bilingual education) (Padilla 1985, 3), the people overwhelmingly prefer to call themselves and be referred to by their national origin, such as Mexican, Cuban, or Puerto Rican (Institute for Puerto Rican Policy 1993, 2).

Hispanic National Groups

We have been referring to the Hispanic national groups, but who are these groups and how large are they? Close to 22.5 million Hispanics were counted in the 1990 census (not including the more than 3.5 million residents of Puerto Rico). By 2000 that number rose to over 35 million (again, not including the 3.8 million residents of Puerto Rico). According to Aponte, "Hispanics are the nation's fastest growing minority in absolute terms. Indeed, the best available evidence indicates that Hispanics (Latinos) will almost certainly surpass African Americans in numeric strength by 2020, if not sooner" (1993, 527). The 2000 census figures show that 12.5 percent of the population was Hispanic and 12.9

percent was black (or black and another race) (U.S. Bureau of the Census 2001b, 1). Considering that many Hispanics identify their race as black, the two minorities are very close in size at this time, and the number of Hispanics may surpass that of blacks by the next census in 2010.

The three largest Hispanic national groups are Mexican, Puerto Rican, and Cuban (see Figure 1–1). Although the "Other Hispanic" group is actually the second largest group, it is a mixed group that includes (1) highly skilled Latin American immigrants; (2) refugees of the professional class; (3) Central American economic refugees (e.g., from Nicaragua, Guatemala, and El Salvador); (4) part-Hispanics, comprising those who have one Hispanic parent and one non-Hispanic parent; (5) mixed-Hispanics, which includes those whose parents are both Hispanic but are each from different national origin groups; and (6) Hispanos, who are descendants of the European-Spanish stock primarily found in New Mexico who never intermarried with indigenous Indians or with Anglos (Hispanic Almanac 1984, 49). Also included in this group are an increasing number of low-skilled Caribbean Hispanics, especially those from the Dominican Republic.

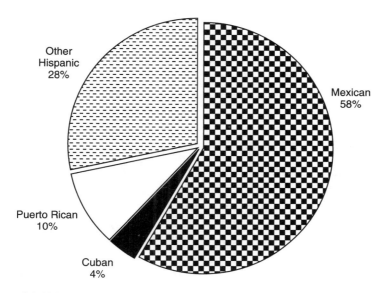

Figure 1-1: U.S. Hispanics, 2000

The "Other Hispanic" group increased from being 23 percent of all Hispanics in the United States in 1990 to 28.9 percent in 2000. This proportion indicates the importance of current immigration policies, which are discussed later in this chapter.

To understand just how diverse the Hispanic population can be, let's review the national origins of Hispanics in our two largest cities, New York and Los Angeles. Selecting those national groups that had a metropolitan population of at least 20,000 in 1990, we find eleven distinct Hispanic national groups in New York and ten in Los Angeles. In New York, where not too long ago *Hispanic* was almost synonymous with *Puerto Rican*, the close to one million Puerto Ricans make up only half the Hispanic population. More than 330,000 Dominicans, for example, were living in New York at the time of the 1990 census.

Small numbers of many Hispanic groups have lived in the United States for some time. If we look at the timing of entry for national groups, however, we find that most of the groups are relatively new. Mexicans are the major exception; large numbers of Mexicans have resided in what is now the United States since before the Southwest was annexed by the United States. Puerto Ricans have technically been part of the United States since the island was "won" in 1898 at the end of the Spanish American War, but their major influx to the mainland began just after World War II. Cubans were a relatively small group until Castro's takeover in 1959, which caused huge waves of refugees into the United States. The other Hispanic national groups, for the most part, did not gain prominence until the 1970s and 1980s. To understand why, we need to review the history of immigration legislation in the United States.

Immigration Policy and Hispanics

Initially, immigrants from a number of countries, including Spain, France, and England, settled in the United States. Individuals came to escape religious or political persecution; they came as prisoners or indentured servants; and they came to seek adventure and a new chance in life economically. Apart from the Immigration Act of 1882 (which barred immigration of criminals, mentally incompetent individuals, those who were seriously ill, and Chinese) and the "gentlemen's" agreement of 1907 between the United States and Japan to stop the flow of Japanese into this country (McCoy 1987; Reischauer 1989), immigration was "virtually unrestricted" (Reimers 1981, 2) until the National Origins Act of 1924. From 1882 to 1924, Caribbean Hispanics (including Mexicans) generally were treated positively. In fact, "in 1904, the U.S. Congress exempted immigrants from Cuba and Mexico from paying the 'head tax,' legislated the year before" (Pastor 1987, 243).

The National Origins Act of 1924 was based on discriminatory principles aimed not only at the Chinese and Japanese targeted by earlier policies but also at Southern and Eastern Europeans. The "avowed purpose of the law was to maintain the 'racial preponderance [of] the basic strain of our people' " (Pastor 1987, 245). This act established annual immigration quotas for each country based on the number of persons from that country already residing in the United States in 1890. Because the Southern and Eastern European immigrants were relative latecomers, their numbers were small in 1890, so their quotas were small too.

This act had an interesting effect on Hispanic immigration. All Caribbean colonies had to be counted as part of the quota of their "mother country" before entering the United States. This process was difficult and time-consuming, so little immigration activity took place. Puerto Rico, of course, was not affected because it was already a part of the United States. Mexico and other Caribbean countries that were not colonies were exempt from quotas and were allowed unlimited immigration based on "political considerations" (McCoy 1987, 228). These regulations affected the U.S. Hispanic population in a way that promoted the predominance of Mexicans and Puerto Ricans. No other subgroup had any numerical significance.

Although there was subsequent legislation, no major changes were made in the direction of U.S. immigration policy until the Immigration Act of 1965. This act was a thorough overhaul of immigration policy. It did away with the old quota system and set up qualitative standards based on occupation (to limit the number of low-skill workers entering the country) and family reunification. However, these two standards at times worked against each other. Family reunification allowed for the immigration of parents, spouses, and children of both U.S. citizens and immigrants with permanent residence status. This policy actually encouraged further immigration of low-skill workers. The 1965 immigration law also stipulated immigration limits for both the Eastern and Western hemispheres. This law, in effect, opened the door for a stream of immigrants from numerous Hispanic nations.

The final important piece of immigration legislation was the Refugee Act of 1980. Before that legislation was enacted, the U.S. refugee policy was a product of the Cold War and was primarily designed to assist individuals fleeing communism. The 1980 act brought U.S. guidelines more in line with United Nations protocol, which was much more inclusive.

To better understand this concept, we should recall the large numbers of refugees fleeing from oppressive governments in El Salvador and Nicaragua before this act became law. These people were regarded as undocumented immigrants and were not accorded refugee status because the government from which they were fleeing was not communistic. Therefore, they were subject to deportation if caught. Private "sanctuary" movements tried to assist these people, who often lived inside U.S. churches on arrival in the United States. Under the new guidelines, if these same people were to flee to the United States today, they could be considered refugees and could legally obtain the work and assistance they would need.

Although this act included a method by which the president could determine the number of refugees to be admitted annually (with the advice of Congress), the reality has been that many more refugees have entered the United States than were technically allowed. In terms of the U.S. Hispanic population, the large numbers involved in the 1980 Mariel boatlift from Cuba presented an immediate and almost insurmountable problem because of this legislation. The number of refugees was too large for U.S. structures to easily handle. Also, because many individuals entering with this group were criminals or had mental problems, the United States faced special needs with which it was ill-equipped to cope.

Although reviewing immigration policy might be an interesting undertaking, the next question should be: What difference does immigration-migration history make in terms of how national groups thrive or falter once they are in the United States?

Importance of Immigration Histories

Immigration histories include several factors that affect a group's well-being in the United States. Here we briefly review the reasons for migration, timing of migration, regional choice of settlement in the

United States, the attitude of the U.S. general public (hosts), and the importance of these issues for a group's overall incorporation into U.S. economic structures.

Reasons for Migration

We alluded earlier to a number of reasons that people immigrate, including low-skill laborers looking for work, professionals seeking better opportunities, family members of earlier immigrants who want to be reunited as a family, students, refugees fleeing oppressive governments, and economic refugees fleeing a catastrophe in their homeland (e.g., Irish immigrants escaping the devastation of the potato famine). These reasons can affect a group's adaptation in at least two major ways—their ability to enter U.S. labor markets and the capital (material and human) they brought with them.

Low-skill laborers have traditionally entered U.S. labor markets through the agrarian sector as farmhands, the industrial sector as factory workers, or as domestics. Farmworkers who wanted to advance usually left the farm to move to the nearest urban area and join the industrial low-skill labor pool. The industrial sector not only provided jobs but also offered avenues for advancement through on-the-job training. A worker could go from a low-skill assembly line position to a skilled position and then advance to foreman, supervisor, manager, and maybe even an owner. The service sector has become increasingly important as a supplier of low-skill positions. However, advancement is limited at best. At the risk of giving an absurd example, a hospital janitor has no built-in avenue of advancement to neurosurgeon. Low-skill service jobs tend to be dead-end.

Another issue involved in low-skill labor immigration is that the immigrants bring very little capital with them. If they had been able to accumulate material capital, they probably would have acquired skills that would remove them from the low-skill classification. Having low-level skills is a hindrance because it limits options available to the immigrants. Low skills generally indicate low educational levels as well. It could be that a strong desire to work (and work hard) may be the only human capital these immigrants bring with them.

Professional-level immigrants present a different story. They may have to enter the labor market at a lower level than they occupied in their home country (primarily because of language and professional

certification constraints), but their education, professionalism, and perhaps material/financial capital are assets that can open doors for earlier
advancement. In time they could exceed the opportunities offered in
their homeland, and certainly their children could benefit.

Refugees can be suffering from poverty or be among the elite (as
were the initial immigrant waves from Cuba and Vietnam). They would
enter the labor market in the same manner as economic immigrants but
do present some differences. First, they have suffered a trauma from
the situation that caused them to flee their homeland. These people
would not necessarily want to live in the United States—they were just
forced to leave oppressive situations. Second, even if they had wealth
in their homeland, they may have had to leave it all behind when they
fled, as happened to Cuban immigrants after the Bay of Pigs fiasco.
Third, the Refugee Act provides certain types of relocation assistance
to them that is not available to regular immigrants. In summary, refugees have additional burdens but also additional assistance.

Timing of Immigration

Timing refers not only to when a group first entered the United States
but also to the number of years the major immigration flow spanned.
The European immigration of the late nineteenth century usually
marks the starting point for U.S. immigration studies. At the turn of the
century, the United States was in the throes of industrialization, and it
attracted large numbers of immigrants from European nations to fill the
need for a growing pool of industrial laborers. However, the major European immigration spanned only forty years (1880–1920), and then it
slowed to a trickle, allowing the immigrants to settle into an assimilation
pattern.

Hispanic migration (apart from the annexation of large numbers of
Mexicans through war and the purchase of land as well as the acquisition
of Puerto Rico and its inhabitants at the end of the Spanish-American
War) began in the early twentieth century with Mexicans. It increased
after 1942, both in numbers and diversity, and has remained relatively
strong ever since and probably will continue to do so. This steady immigration level has affected the well-being of the Hispanic groups in a couple of ways. First, with the exception of the early waves of Mexicans,
most Hispanic groups entered the United States at a time when its economic structure was moving from an industrial to a service-oriented base.

Most Hispanics, therefore, did not enter a labor market with the same opportunities afforded Europeans. Second, because Hispanic immigration has not stopped, there is still a growing first-generation population, which tends to reinforce the ethnic identification of national groups and slow down the assimilation process.

Regional Choice of Settlement

As mentioned earlier, the three major U.S. Hispanic groups have chosen different regions in which to settle. Reasons for selecting a particular region vary among the groups, and each region presented a different opportunity structure to its newcomers.

Mexicans were living in the Southwest long before the United States acquired that area. It was natural for them to stay there. Also, because of the Mexican-United States border, the Southwest was closest to home and therefore more attractive to the many laborers who planned to return to Mexico. These workers were incorporated into the agricultural economy and were also experienced in work on the railroads. Those desiring to try their hand in the industrial sector made their way to more northern cities, especially Chicago. The majority, however, stayed in the Southwest.

Puerto Ricans were drawn to the industrial complex of the Northeast, especially New York City, through purposeful recruitment, an original pre–Spanish-American War base, and low airfares. Unfortunately, industry was already declining, so they entered a labor market that did not provide them with security, let alone advancement.

Cubans came to Miami primarily because of its proximity to Cuba. Many fled Cuba when Castro came to power, but few believed that he could maintain control for very long. They did not want to go too far from Miami so they could easily return to Cuba when Castro's regime was overthrown. Miami was not industrial, but many of the early Cuban refugees were professionals and were not looking to industry for their livelihood. They were able to utilize their skills and abilities along with their large numbers to develop an ethnic enclave within the greater economy.

Attitude of Hosts

We do not often think about it, but doors can be opened or closed depending on how the hosts look at newcomers. Because Cubans were po-

litical refugees fleeing communism and represented the elite of the island, not only were they widely accepted but also they were aided
through U.S. refugee policies. This treatment was in stark contrast to
that afforded Mexicans and Puerto Ricans, both groups that generally
were looked down on and viewed as exploitable, cheap labor to be used
and then let go according to the needs of the greater economy.

Attitudes of the hosts cannot be discussed without touching on the
topic of race. Race is a complex issue and is even more complicated as
it relates to Hispanics, so we next review Hispanic racial classification
in more detail.

Hispanic Race

When the U.S. census divides the population according to race, no classification exists for *Hispanic*. This situation is difficult for many people
to understand. The problem in Hispanic racial classification is a by-
product of the historical development of Hispanic peoples. Hispanics
are a mixture of indigenous Amerinds, Europeans, Africans (who had
been imported into Hispanic countries as slaves), and Asians. This mixture has not produced a uniform new race (although some Hispanic
groups speak of a *nueva raza,* or "new race"). Instead, we find individuals with skin tones ranging from extremely white to very dark and with
facial and other features that betray one or another of the source groups.
Because of these variations, the U.S. Bureau of the Census has determined that Hispanics must choose a racial identification from among
white, black, American Indian and Aleut, Asian and Pacific Islander, or
other.

This confusing categorization makes doing Hispanic research difficult, although the census does ask other questions regarding Hispanic
origin and then provides census data in tables that represent only Hispanics. The real problem arises when trying to make comparisons. As
an example, let's say we want to compare the experiences of Hispanics
and blacks. There is no way to tell from the printed tables which blacks
are Hispanic and which are not. The problem is obvious: Hispanic
blacks would be represented in both comparison groups. They would
be in the black tables as blacks and in the Hispanic tables as Hispanic.
However, they would be only a part of the groups listed in both tables,

because the black tables would also include African Americans, immigrants from Africa, and blacks from non-Hispanic West Indies areas and the Hispanic tables would include not only black Hispanics but also Hispanics who identified themselves as white, American Indian and Aleut, Asian and Pacific Islander, or other. Yes, this system is confusing, and it is precisely the problem that has made Hispanic research such a difficult task.

Where Do We Go Next?

This book's introduction stated that Part I should be viewed as a response to our concern that so much Hispanic research has been done using all the Hispanic national groups clumped into one group. This chapter has laid out some differences between the various national groups in very general terms. Chapters 2 and 3 review the immigration histories of the three major U.S. Hispanic groups in greater detail to provide a more in-depth understanding of their different experiences.

A second goal of Part I is to determine how Puerto Ricans fare when compared with the other two major groups. Therefore, Chapter 4 draws comparisons of several indicators, with the goal of leading the reader to an understanding of social and economic mobility patterns among these groups.

2

The Journeys of Mexicans and Cubans

The three major Hispanic groups in the United States are Mexicans, Cubans, and Puerto Ricans. This chapter focuses on the journeys taken by Mexicans and Cubans as they have claimed their place among the many nationalities of the United States. These two groups, although both are included under the Hispanic label, have extremely different stories. They came to the United States at different times, settled in different regions, had different reasons for immigrating, and were greeted differently by the Anglo majority making up the U.S. people and government.

The focus of this book is on Puerto Ricans, but we believe that understanding the differences in the journeys of the Hispanic peoples will help highlight the unique factors in Puerto Rican incorporation into the United States. What is common to all the Hispanic groups? What is unique to each of them? How do the differences in their stories affect their well-being in the 1990s? We start our quest for understanding by looking first at the Mexicans and then at the Cubans.

The Mexican Journey

Mexican Americans are both the largest Hispanic group in the United States and the oldest. Having been part of what is now the U.S. Southwest long before it was annexed by the United States, Mexicans encompass many generations of both legal and illegal immigrants. Unlike most European immigration, the flow of Mexicans has not subsided. Therefore, a continuing flow of first-generation immigrants must be absorbed into established Mexican American communities in the United States.

Citizenship figures can be deceptive. Mexican Americans who are second generation or beyond are U.S. citizens by birth. The first generation, the immigrants, has exhibited reluctance to being naturalized as citizens. Later in this chapter, we begin to determine the reason behind this stance.

To understand the development of this population, and later to make sense of similarities and differences when comparing Mexicans to Puerto Ricans, we must trace the history of Mexican immigrants and their internal U.S. migration patterns. We need to focus both on the migration dynamics per se—including settlement site choices, timing factors, and Mexican American community development—and on Mexican–U.S. relationships including policies, perceived benefits, and trust issues.

Events Leading to Annexation

We think in terms of Mexicans immigrating to the United States, but the first immigration relationship was actually the other way around—immigration from the United States into the section of Mexico that is now Texas. During the early nineteenth century, U.S.–Mexican relationships were friendly. Mexico actually patterned its constitution on the U.S. model, and the two countries developed an economic interdependence. Although Mexico encompassed what is now California, Texas, Arizona, and New Mexico, these areas were only sparsely populated with small Mexican settlements scattered across the area and isolated from each other.

When U.S. immigrants (primarily Germans) recognized the potential of Texas land, they continued their migration trek and settled there. Mexico approved of this activity as long as the U.S. immigrants abided by Mexican laws, became Catholic, and paid taxes (Gann and Duignan 1986, 14). By the 1830s, however, the U.S. immigrants greatly outnumbered the Mexican citizens in Texas and they no longer wanted to submit to Mexican authority.

In 1836, Texas declared its independence, a status that was never recognized by Mexico. Texas then petitioned the United States for statehood, which was granted in 1845. Because Mexico still claimed the territory encompassed by Texas as part of its nation, war between Mexico and the United States was inevitable.

The Mexican-American War lasted from 1846 to 1848, when the Treaty of Guadalupe Hidalgo was signed. This treaty added more than a million square miles to the United States. Residents of this land included about 80,000 Mexicans, who were given the choice of moving south to remain in Mexico or accepting U.S. sovereignty and being allowed to keep their land holdings. Most stayed in the United States.

The final piece of land acquired from Mexico (about 45,000 square miles in Arizona and New Mexico) came through the Gadsden Purchase in 1853.

1850s–1920s

The Mexicans who stayed in the United States after the war were treated as a colonized people. The United States began its pattern of breaking guarantees with these Mexicans, guarantees that had been a part of the treaty. Using various means, among them fraud, violence, and systematic market competition, the United States displaced most of the landed Mexicans so that by 1920 they had become landless, dependent wage laborers.

Back in Mexico the *Porfiriato* regime, which was in control from 1876 to 1911, came to an end, a victim of the Mexican Revolution (1910–1917). The revolution caused many Mexicans, rich and poor, to flee to the United States to escape the violence.

If we think in terms of the traditional push-pull model of immigration, in which populations are "pushed" from their homeland for a variety of reasons (e.g., economic, political, war, family issues) and "pulled" to a new land, also for a variety of reasons (e.g., freedom, exile, economic opportunities, family reunification), then the revolution provided the push. Besides the ease of crossing the border into the United States, because Mexican settlements already existed in the United States this country was attractive as a resettlement choice. However, the major pull was economic. The U.S. Southwest presented new economic opportunities because it was expanding in areas of railroad construction, commercial agriculture, and the development of manufacturing and service industries. In addition to the opportunities provided by this expansion, many jobs were opening up for cheap labor as a result of World War I. The United States had already curtailed Asian immigration, and the war had put an end to the flow of European immigrant labor, so new sources of labor were required. Also, the war caused an increased demand for manufacturing goods (especially arms) as well as food production. U.S. indigenous farmers in the Southwest were decreasing in number while the demand for workers was increasing, so the United States was more than happy to absorb the incoming Mexican laborers.

During the nearly eighty years encompassing this phase of Mexican immigration, the U.S. Mexican population exhibited a number of characteristics. First, the population had grown tremendously, to 478,000 by 1920, and continued to grow during the 1920s. Second, social networks were established, which not only supported more immigration but also steered new immigrants to particular areas in the United States.

A third characteristic was that throughout this period Mexicans were regarded as "inferior beings and inherently unassimilable and foreign" (Estrada et al. 1981, 112). They received seasonal and unstable work, faced a dual-wage system that gave them much lower "'Mexican wages' for Mexican work" (Bean and Tienda 1987, 18), and were barred from supervisory positions. The only middle class that emerged was in the Southwest, and it tended to be confined to servicing the Mexican community only.

Finally, the 1920s saw Mexicans dispersing from the Southwest to take advantage of manufacturing opportunities—"meat-packing plants and steel mills in the Chicago area; automobile assembly lines in Detroit; the steel industry in Ohio and Pennsylvania; and Kansas City's meat-packing plants" (Estrada et al. 1981, 113). Chicago became the most important midwestern city for Mexican migrants, and it developed its own social network with towns in Mexico (Massey 1986). Urbanization of Mexicans was taking place in both the Midwest and Southwest. By 1930, for the first time, "over half the Mexican population in the United States [was classified] as urban" (Gann and Duignan 1986, 41).

Throughout this period, Mexican immigrants thought of themselves as temporary sojourners in the United States. They expected to return to Mexico in time. We mentioned the reluctance of Mexicans to be naturalized—their rate of naturalization was lower than that of any other immigrant group (Gann and Duignan 1986, 44)—and this sojourner attitude was one of the reasons for that reluctance. Another reason was that Mexicans were bitter, distrustful, and suspicious of the Anglo dominant population because of the broken guarantees, exploitation, and manipulation of Mexicans by the United States.

The Depression

The Depression years of 1929–1935 were difficult for everyone. U.S. workers were out of jobs. Poverty was widespread and included large numbers of families who had always relied on work for their income (a group referred to as the "deserving poor"). Social programs were begun to help many, but resentment was growing toward "foreigners," who were using up scarce resources. The U.S. government responded by working out a deal with Mexico to repatriate indigent Mexicans. "In all, the number of people repatriated between 1929 and 1935 must have exceeded 415,000 persons, by far the largest number of aliens of any nationality ever forced to leave the United States" (Gann and Duignan 1986, 51).

Besides breaking up family units and whole communities, these repatriation efforts also trampled the rights of U.S. citizens. Many of those sent back to Mexico had U.S.-born children who were U.S. citizens by birth but were forced to leave with their parents. Estrada et al. (1981) reported that about half of those who were repatriated were actually born in the United States. Indigence was more important than immigrant-citizenship status in determining who would be sent back.

The injustice and dehumanization involved in repatriation have caused lasting scars among Mexican Americans. These scars have increased Mexican insecurity and distrust of the United States, which had already been simmering from the earlier treaty violations and labor exploitation.

World War II

World War II changed the economic situation in the United States. The war once again created an increased demand for U.S. food and manufacturing products, including arms. It also resulted in a shortage of workers because many U.S. workers had enlisted in the military. With product demand increasing and labor supply decreasing, the United States had to quickly find and develop a large pool of cheap labor. Once again, they turned to Mexico. The two countries worked out a deal, called the *bracero* program, whereby the United States would pay transportation costs for Mexicans to come to the United States on labor contracts. The United States also agreed to ensure minimum wages and just and equitable treatment for the Mexican workers. The Mexican government agreed to this because it perceived three benefits for its country: (1) Mexicans who worked in the United States would send money home to help their families; (2) the sting of unemployment in Mexico would be alleviated; and (3) farm migrants would be exposed to the latest agricultural technology, which they could then bring back home with them.

Two major problems evolved from the *bracero* program. First, the news of available jobs brought not only the contracted workers to the United States but also large numbers of undocumented workers. Second, once again the United States reneged on its promises because it could not enforce the just and equitable treatment guarantee, so Mexican workers continued to be exploited.

The war also had some positive effects for Mexicans in the United States. First, because of the number of new jobs available, both blacks and Mexicans had the chance to take positions that had always been closed to them. Second, many Mexican Americans fought in the war and were eligible for benefits under the GI Bill. This bill provided both housing benefits, which led to Mexicans being able to move outside the *barrios* for the first time, and educational benefits, which allowed them to train for technical employment and professional positions.

After the war, the United States continued to need laborers and extended the *bracero* program to 1964, but the United States was becoming more upset with illegal immigrants. In 1954, again through an agreement with the Mexican government, the United States initiated Operation Wetback to deport large numbers of Mexicans, and once again, U.S.-born children were forced to leave with their parents. Also, legal, and not just undocumented, immigrants were caught in the sweep. " 'Looking Mexican' was often sufficient reason for official scrutiny" (Estrada et al. 1981, 120). For those who remembered the repatriation days, it was *déjà vu*. "[Both programs] emphasized the foreignness of the Mexican Americans. Both programs were massive in their impact, removing not isolated individuals but large groups. Both involved Mexican as well as U.S. authorities. Both were grim reminders that for low-status members of the groups a claim to citizenship is always subject to question" (Grebler, Moore, and Guzman 1970, 525).

1965–Present

The *bracero* program officially ended in 1964, but the stream of both legal and illegal immigrants has continued. We typically expect high immigration rates when economic indicators are better in the United States than in Mexico. In the 1970s the United States was facing rising unemployment and falling real wages while Mexico was experiencing a boom in the oil extraction industry. If we view immigration as motivated purely by economics, we would have thought Mexican immigration would slow down and maybe even reverse (with more Mexicans returning to Mexico than coming to the United States) during those years. However, immigration actually rose. Once social networks of immigration were established between areas in the United States and areas in Mexico, these networks became strong enough to promote a "self-perpetuating social phenomenon" (Massey 1986, 103); in other words, people were no longer making choices based solely on economics—social (including familial) motivations had become important. This change is significant because one result is that immigration has continued at high levels regardless of how the U.S. economy has been able to incorporate the new arrivals.

Not only has Mexican immigration (legal and illegal) continued at high levels, but also the Mexican population in the United States has had a high birthrate. These two factors together have contributed to a high growth rate for Mexicans in the United States (54.4 percent growth between 1980 and 1990).

The Present

We have seen that the majority of Mexicans in the past chose to live in the Southwest, with some migration patterns leading to manufacturing centers in the Northeast and Midwest (especially Chicago). The question now is whether this settlement pattern has continued or whether it is changing. How has urbanization affected this group?

Some patterns of dispersion have been evidenced with Mexicans; however, they are still strongly entrenched in the Southwest. In 1990, Texas and California together contain 74.1 percent of all Mexicans in

Table 2-1

Top Ten U.S. Metropolitan Areas with Mexican Populations (in thousands)

Metropolitan Areas	1990	2000
Los Angeles/Long Beach, CA	2527	3042
Riverside/San Bernardino, CA	592	996
Houston, TX	580	908
San Antonio, TX	567	572
Chicago, IL	495	1062
Anaheim/Santa Ana, CA	475	
San Diego, CA	439	628
El Paso, TX	392	447
Dallas, TX	316	643
McAllen/Edinburgh/Mission, TX	311	
Orange County, CA		712
Phoenix, AZ		668

Source: U.S. Census, 1990 STF 1C; U.S. Bureau of the Census 2001b.

the United States. If we look at the top ten metropolitan areas with Mexican populations in 1990, except for Chicago, they are all in Texas or California (see Table 2–1).

By 2000 Phoenix has been added to the list, and the Mexican American population in Chicago has increased dramatically. Despite the Chicago figures, even with dispersion the Mexican population has remained extremely concentrated in the original settlement areas, a pattern that does not seem to be changing substantially. However, year 2000 preliminary figures reveal continued, and at times surprising, dispersion. The percentage share of California and Texas combined dropped to 65.5 percent despite huge increases in Mexican population (2,337,000 and 1,181,000, respectively). The surprising increases came in the South—Georgia, North Carolina, and Florida each gained more than 200,000 Mexicans. In terms of percentage increases, North Carolina had an incredible 655 percent increase between 1990 and 2000. Georgia, Tennessee, Arkansas, South Carolina, Alabama, and Delaware all increased by more than 300 percent.

We noted earlier that Mexicans were becoming urbanized, so that by 1930 more than half were classified as urban. By 1990 that percentage had increased to 89.4 percent. This is the lowest percentage of any of the Hispanic groups, but we definitely can no longer think of Mexicans in the United States as primarily being migrant farm laborers.

The Cuban Journey

Cubans make up the third largest national Hispanic group in the United States. Although some migration occurred in the early nineteenth century, most literature on Cuban migration starts with what happened after Castro's takeover of Cuba in 1959. The earlier migration, though relatively small numerically, is important in terms of establishing a tradition of moving to the United States in response to political or economic conditions on the island. We begin our survey with those early years and then follow the Cuban journey through the Spanish-American War and on to the responses of various groups to Castro's coup.

Pre-1898 Migration

Spain ruled Cuba as a colony from 1511 to 1898. The first Cuban immigrants to the United States arrived in the 1820s and settled primarily in New York, Philadelphia, and New Orleans. These early settlers were motivated by three forces: (1) political dissidence resulting in exile communities; (2) the development of commercial relationships with the United States, especially in the cigar industry; and (3) a desire for their children to acquire an education in the United States. Unlike the Mexican workers described earlier, "Prior to the 1860s most Cuban émigrés were presumably and predominantly white professionals, merchants, lawyers and students" (Poyo 1984, 46).

After the U.S. Civil War, a general tariff increase made it cheaper for Cuban entrepreneurs to import unprocessed tobacco from Cuba and make cigars in the United States than to import finished cigars, so that is when workers began migrating. The workers were not filling in gaps in the regular U.S. labor pool, however, but were primarily involved in working in the Cuban-owned cigar industry in New York, Key West, and New Orleans.

Cuba's Ten Years War, starting in late 1868, caused political refugees of all classes and races to come to U.S. cities. This war caused devastating effects on the Cuban economy throughout the 1880s, which resulted in labor emigration. Many of the affected Cubans ended up in the United States. After the war, many of the professionals making up New York's Cuban community returned to the island, and more working-class immigrants replaced them.

Florida's Cuban community developed much later than did New York's. The first Cuban community, and the only important émigré community in Florida during the 1870s, was in Key West. Although it included some political exiles, its growth was primarily the result of the cigar industry. In 1886 the Tampa Bay Cuban community of Ybor City was begun, centered around the cigar industry which was fleeing a strong labor union movement in Key West.

Key West, Tampa, and New York City became important centers for Cuban political exiles who were planning an overthrow of their Spanish rulers and who were financially supporting the separatist movement on the island. Maximo Gomez, Antonio Maceo, and José Martí were three of the Cuban exile leaders. In 1895 they assessed that the time was right to attempt the revolution, and they returned to lead it. Maceo and Martí were both killed, but Spain was losing ground. As Spain was weakening, the United States entered the war against Spain because of the questionable sinking of the *Maine* in Havana harbor in 1898. Spain surrendered to the United States four months later, and the Cubans were ignored in the armistice proceedings.

1898–1959 Migration

For a brief time after the Spanish-American War (1898–1902), the U.S. military governed Cuba. In 1902 Cuba was granted its independence but with strings attached, including the use of Guantanamo as a U.S. military base and the right of the United States to intervene in the affairs of Cuba. The first half of the twentieth century also saw the development of Cuban economic dependence on the United States.

Miami became a Cuban center in the 1930s when exiles fled from the revolution against Gerardo Machado. From 1953 to 1959, another surge of exiles arrived, this time made up of would-be revolutionaries against the Fulgencio Batista regime. The discontent in Cuba during that period was not so much caused by poverty but, at least in part, by an uneven rate of development. The revolution initially looked for leadership and motivation from dissident middle-class people and then received support from other social classes, especially the most poverty-stricken peasants. By 1958 all classes were disgusted with the Batista regime, and the revolution took on a truly "popular character" (Gann and Duignan 1986, 98).

By the time the revolution had run its course, Cubans "had established a considerable legacy of settlement in the United States" (Boswell and Curtis 1983, 39). The experiences of Cubans who settled in New York and Florida during this time became crucial in assisting the future waves of Cuban refugees in their adjustment to life in the United States.

1959–1965 Migration

Fidel Castro arrived in Havana in January 1959. His coup changed the character not only of Cuba itself but also of the Cuban American population. Before this time, New York City had been the capital of Cuban activity in the United States. After the revolution, however, South Florida became the undeniable center of Cuban American life. No one was surprised that Batista supporters would flee Cuba, nor were many surprised that they would turn to the United States for exile because Cuban political dissidents already had a history of seeking refuge here. However, nobody thought the exodus would be so large. By 1969 approximately 10 percent of Cuba's population emigrated, mostly to the United States. This was, "considering Cuba's population, the greatest population shift in Latin America" (Gann and Duignan 1986, 101). "Except for Puerto Rico, no other island in the Caribbean has experienced a comparable outpouring in such a short period of time" (Boswell and Curtis 1983, 41).

Beginning with the *Batistianos*, Batista's closest supporters, the stream of émigrés increased dramatically after Cuba's October 1960 nationalization of industries. Castro had hidden his communistic convictions during the revolution by leading under a banner of social justice. When the revolution was over and Castro was in power, he quickly broke relations with former allies and moved Cuba into a communistic state. "The middle class was excluded from political participation and its economic power was shattered. Dissident intellectuals suffered brutal persecution. There was a mass exodus of specialists, technicians, and academic people" (Gann and Duignan 1986, 98).

This group of exiles was dubbed the "Golden Exiles" because of the perception that it comprised Cuba's elite. Although a disproportionate number of elite were in this group, including former businessmen, entrepreneurs, and professionals, they still made up less than 40 percent of the total movement. The rest represented much more of a cross section of the Cuban population. Many businessmen sent their wives and children but stayed behind themselves, hoping to salvage their investments and property. This decision cost many of them all their holdings and a great deal of personal trouble and danger before they finally made it out of Cuba themselves.

For the first two years, it was relatively easy for refugees to take advantage of the daily flights between Havana and the United States. Before the Bay of Pigs fiasco in April 1961, refugees were allowed to take their assets out with them. This allowed the elite to enter the United States with their resources and social connections fairly well intact, which, in turn, enabled them to reestablish themselves relatively quickly. After the Bay of Pigs invasion, resources could not be taken but the people were still free to leave. Emigration to the United States continued until October 1962, when the Cuban Missile Crisis caused the United States to break diplomatic relations with Cuba and end the daily flights to the United States. Cubans then had to either escape, usually by small boat, or go through a third country, which meant losing their refugee status and entering as part of that country's regular immigrant quota. Children aged six to sixteen, however, received special assistance to protect them from communist indoctrination (Azieri 1981–82, 56–57).

As with many of the Mexican American agreements previously described, this initial wave of refugees represented perceived benefits for both countries. For Cuba, even though the mass migration caused a serious "brain drain" and embarrassment because many of those who fled were the very ones the revolution was supposed to help, having so many dissidents leave was a means of "purification," allowing Castro's regime to make changes into communism more swiftly. For the United States, the refugees provided a great source of propaganda against communism. Pérez went so far as to say that "promoting migration from Cuba was a ploy on the part of the United States to weaken the revolution" (L. Pérez 1984, 14). The United States used this opportunity to slander Cuba and to become the "good guys" by putting together the most generous assistance package ever accorded an immigrant group.

1965–1978 Migration

The next wave of refugees began in September 1965, when Castro opened the Camarioca port for emigration. Two months later, because of the chaos and tragedy on the seas caused by U.S. Cubans grabbing anything they thought could float to go to Camarioca and pick up family and friends, the port was closed and the United States and Cuba negotiated the "Memorandum of Understanding" that led to the Freedom Flights to Miami. These flights began in December 1968 and were ended by Cuba in 1973. They were designed to reunify families, but military-aged men and highly skilled people were not allowed to leave, at least not until a replacement could be trained. The elderly and the sick represented a drain on the state, so Cuba let them go. This acted as a safety valve and allowed Cuba to develop under the new regime without a large drain on its economy.

This second major wave of refugees contained fewer professionals and more skilled workers. Immigrants in this wave looked much more like the turn-of-the-century European immigrant, with one major exception—they were entering an immigrant community that was already established by the earlier middle- and upper-class immigrants. About half the Cubans in this wave entered the labor force of Cuban-owned businesses and received better earnings than their counterparts entering the nonenclave labor force.

Many of these refugees were small entrepreneurs and their employees who had been victimized by the final nationalization moves of Castro. Once they applied for their exit visas, they lost their jobs and had to work for up to two or three years, often in the cane fields, before they were allowed to leave. If they refused to work in the cane fields, they were imprisoned.

For the five years following this second wave, there was virtually no Cuban migration flow. The few who did come to the United States once again had to go through a third country.

1978–Present Migration

In November 1978, Castro and representatives of the U.S. Cuban exiles met and worked out what has been called "The Dialogue." Basically, Cuba agreed to release some political prisoners, allow for reunification of families, and allow Cubans in the United States to return to Cuba to visit family members. Cuba had hoped that allowing the family visits would (1) bring United States money into Cuba from the visitors, which would help the economy; (2) demonstrate that Castro's government was in complete control and thus discourage future revolutionary attempts; and (3) improve Cuba's image in other countries in terms of human rights. However, the plan backfired. U.S. Cubans told exaggerated tales of luxury in the United States at the same time that the Cuban government was frustrated in trying to motivate proper production and consumption limits within the island. The end result was a great deal of discontent among the Cuban people. Castro stopped the visits in March 1980, but the next month the Peruvian Embassy was suddenly opened for Cubans who wanted to leave the island. Castro did not realize how many would want to take advantage of this opportunity. The large-scale exodus of almost 11,000 people to Latin American countries became an embarrassment to the Cuban government. Therefore, the port of Mariel was opened for direct access to the United States, thus diverting émigrés from Central and South America.

Once again there was a disorderly flotilla of boats going back and forth between Cuba and the United States. This time, however, no agreement had been reached between Cuba and the United States, and the United States was not happy to receive this new wave of émigrés. This group was not afforded refugee status but was allowed to enter the United States through a special "entrants" status. Also, the emigrants' motivation seemed to be based more on consumerism than a distaste for communism, thus they seemed more like economic than political refugees. Another problem was that Castro, especially at the end of this period, would not let boats return unless they took criminals, mental patients, and other "undesirables" with them. Many of these "criminals" were not what we would consider criminals. Their crimes were political or they refused to work in the cane fields. Some were involved in the black market, but only a relatively small proportion (about 16 percent of individuals fourteen years or older) had participated in acts that the United States considered criminal (Bach 1987, 117). Unfortunately, just as the first wave was stereotyped and sensationalized as the "Golden Exiles," this group was stereotyped and sensationalized as antisocial and as criminals. Even Castro referred to these émigrés as belonging to a nonperson, noncitizen category of *escoria* ("scum") (Levine 1987, 6).

The *Marielitos*, although similar to the 1970 emigrants in terms of education and occupational backgrounds, were darker (approximately 40 percent were mulattos or black), were younger, and included more single males. Also, their experiences had been shaped by Castro's communism, rather than the capitalism that had shaped the earlier groups' experiences. This experiential conditioning probably hindered these refugees in their ability to anticipate and cope with the process of seeking employment in a capitalistic country that was facing high unemployment and inflation rates.

For Cuba, this boat lift relieved the housing shortage and unemployment, got rid of supposed dissidents, provided Castro with scapegoats on whom to blame Cuba's economic woes, and was a way to taint the image of the Cuban American community. When Cuba finally closed the Port of Mariel, "There was a deep sense of relief not only in Washington but in the Cuban-American community as well, particularly in Miami" (Azieri 1981–82, 57).

Since the 1980 Mariel boat lift there have been no major waves of Cuban entrants.

Internal Migration

The special refugee assistance package put together by the United States to welcome the initial wave of Cuban refugees was termed "the largest in the history of the country" (Boswell and Curtis 1983, 3). It included cheap airfare, permission to enter the United States without a visa, special entrants classification, and enormous resettlement assistance including job training, professional recertification, assistance in securing employment, reimbursement to public schools for instituting bilingual education programs, and funds for special research and teaching opportunities for Cuban scholars (Bean and Tienda 1987). It also included a policy of dispersal with extensive relocation aid to lessen the load on Miami. By 1967, 60 percent of those registered with the government's refugee program had relocated away from Miami. Since that time, however, Cubans have been returning to South Florida in large numbers. By the 1990 census, 64.6 percent of all U.S. Cubans lived in Florida, and by 2000 that figure grew to 67.1 percent. The

Table 2-2

Top Ten U.S. Metropolitan Areas with Cuban Populations (in thousands)

Metropolitan Areas	1990	2000
Miami/Hialeah, FL	564	651
New York, NY	62	47
Los Angeles/Long Beach, CA	46	39
Jersey City, NJ	44	34
Tampa/St. Petersburg/Clearwater, FL	32	42
Ft. Lauderdale/Hollywood/		
Pompano Beach, FL	24	51
Newark, NJ	21	18
West Palm/Boca Raton/Delray, FL	16	25
Chicago, IL	16	17
Orlando, FL	10	19

Source: U.S. Census, 1990 STF 1C; U.S. Bureau of the Census 2001b.

trend toward centralization is obviously continuing. Another way to view the overwhelming significance of South Florida, especially the Miami area, is to look at the size of the Cuban population in the top ten Cuban metropolitan areas in 1990 (see Table 2–2). Although there was some switching of rank between 1990 and 2000, the same ten areas are still at the top of the list. Although these metropolitan areas represent all four regions of the United States (Northeast, South, Midwest, and West), Miami has more than twice as many Cubans as the other nine areas combined.

Cubans are the most urbanized of the three major Hispanic subgroups, with 97.1 percent living in "urban" areas. However, when considering those living in census-designated metropolitan areas, we find that Cubans in all regions of the United States are highly suburbanized.

Comparison Between the Mexican and Cuban Journeys

The Cuban and Mexican Hispanic groups have vastly different histories that cannot help but affect their life chances in the United States. Both were colonized by Spain and both represent a mixture of races, but their relationships with the United States took vastly different turns.

Both groups trace their initial U.S. populations to the 1800s. However, Mexicans did not immigrate to the United States, they were losers in their war with the United States. Cubans, on the other hand, were still struggling with Spain and had political, educational, and entrepreneurial reasons for wanting to establish communities in the United States.

Mexican migration began with the U.S. annexation of Mexican land. Although there have been periods of ups and downs (mostly manipulated by the United States during repatriation and Operation Wetback), Mexican migration has never ceased—it continues today, and there is no reason to believe it will lessen. Therefore, Mexican communities include numerous generations. However, Cuban immigration, apart from those early small communities, began in force in 1959 with Castro's takeover and ended, for all extents and purposes, in 1980 after the close of the Mariel boat lift. Although most Cubans are first, second, or third generation, the end of their immigration has allowed the Cuban community to stabilize and adapt much better than the Mexican community, which continuously faces the challenges of absorbing newcomers.

Although the original Mexicans were middle-class, landed people, they quickly lost their land, and almost all of Mexican immigration can be categorized as comprising laborers. On the other hand, from the earliest days, we find Cuban professionals and businessmen laying the groundwork for absorbing their own working class, from the cigar workers of the late 1800s to the second and third waves of post-Castro émigrés who entered the Miami enclave.

Mexicans have traditionally entered and settled in the Southwest as farm laborers or industrial workers, with some dispersion into Midwest and Northeast industrial centers. Cubans, however, entered South Florida at a time when it was developing as a tourist center. Through their business acumen and usage of the Spanish language, Cubans have been responsible for transforming Miami into a banking and international business center with Latin American countries.

Because Mexicans need to go where the jobs are, we are finding the community in a slow but definite pattern of decentralization. The Cuban community, on the other hand, is doing just the opposite as it centralizes even more in South Florida.

Both Mexicans and Cubans initially thought of themselves as sojourners. Mexicans wanted to earn enough money to return to Mexico and care for their families, while Cubans thought Castro could not stay in power for too long. Both groups have had to face the disappointment of not realizing their dreams, but Mexicans can and do go back and forth to Mexico with relative ease, whereas Cubans have had to accept huge limitations on returning to Cuba.

Mexicans faced a U.S. Anglo majority that has looked on them with contempt and exploited them in every way possible. With the exception of the mixed reaction to the Mariel entrants, Cubans faced a U.S. government that offered open arms and hands filled with assistance.

The purpose of drawing these comparisons is to point out that the histories of the different Hispanic groups have a great deal to do with their eventual well-being in this country. Cubans, with their initial advantages of both position and U.S. acceptance, could not help but thrive. Conversely, poor Mexican laborers, with a history of being lied to, cheated, exploited, and manipulated by U.S. government and business interests, have had a much more difficult time achieving socioeconomic mobility in this country.

Next we examine how these histories compare with the history of the Puerto Rican people. Where are the similarities? Where are the differences? What is responsible for the differences? The next chapter lays out Puerto Rican-U.S. migration factors, including developing internal migration patterns.

3

The Puerto Rican Journey

uerto Rico, like Mexico and Cuba, was a Spanish colony. Because it is situated so close to Cuba, one would think Puerto Rico would have developed along similar lines. Up to a certain point in its history, this was true, but then the United States entered the picture.

This chapter sketches out the history of Puerto Rico's involvement with the United States and culminates in its current status, the factors affecting people movements between the island and the mainland, and Puerto Rican movements within the mainland. We also draw relevant comparisons with the experiences of Mexicans and Cubans related in Chapter 2. At the end of this chapter, we should be convinced that we cannot seek to understand the Hispanic people by lumping them all together. Instead, we must look at each group from the perspective of its own history, especially its history in relationship to the United States.

Pre–Spanish-American War Migration

Puerto Rican immigration to the United States dates back to the early nineteenth century. Its early pioneers chose to settle in New York City and consisted of three groups: (1) well-to-do merchants and students, (2) adventurers and distinguished political activists, and (3) field and factory workers.

During this period, there was a great deal of intermixing with Cubans at all levels.

By 1830 Cubans and Puerto Ricans in New York had built up enough trade with the two islands to establish the *Sociedad Benéfica Cubana y Puertorriqueña*, a benevolent society made up of merchants from the two islands. This commercial relationship grew to the point where more trade was taking place between Puerto Rico and the United States than between Puerto Rico and Spain.

Puerto Rican political exiles, such as Ramón E. Betances and Luis Muñoz (father of Luis Muñoz Marín, later to be the first Puerto Rican elected governor of the island), joined with Cuban patriots in their revolutionary movement. Even many of the skilled and unskilled Puerto Rican workers who came to New York were involved with Cubans because they were *tabaquereos* (skilled tobacco workers) coming to work in Cuban cigar factories.

During this time in their histories, Cubans and Puerto Ricans in the United States shared the same interests and goals and worked in cooperation with each other. The importance of this period for Puerto Ricans was that it established a pattern for them to look to New York as a primary migration target.

1898–World War II Migration

The United States "won" Puerto Rico at the close of the Spanish-American War, just as it had won Cuba. Again, the treaty agreement worked out between Spain and the United States ignored the indigenous people. Both Cubans and Puerto Ricans were upset that they were treated as "spoils of war" rather than as equal parties in the treaty negotiations. However, this is where Cuban history and Puerto Rican history take a sharp turn from each other. The United States granted Cuba its independence while it kept Puerto Rico as a U.S. possession, an act that sorely disappointed Puerto Rican political activists from New York and firmly established Puerto Rico as a U.S. colony.

The island remained under military rule until 1900, at which time the Foraker Act outlined the official relationship between Puerto Rico and the United States. This act immediately set the tone of U.S. disrespect for Puerto Rico and its residents because its first peacetime military governor "ordered that the name of the island be changed to 'Porto' Rico, an Americanized corruption of Spanish that remained the official spelling until 1932" (Dietz 1986, 85). Also, this act offered "Spaniards or nationals of other countries residing in Puerto Rico the right to choose United States citizenship. This right was not extended to the people of Puerto Rico. They were defined as just that—the People of Puerto Rico—but since Puerto Rico had no legal existence other than as a possession of the United States, its people had no genuine legal existence or representation among the nations of the world" (Williams 1972, 131).

Just before the Spanish-American War, Puerto Ricans were developing a strong "sense of national identity and political articulation" (Rodriguez 1989, 10). The Autonomous Charter granted by Spain in 1897 had actually given Puerto Ricans a fair amount of political and economic autonomy. Now they were back to being a colony totally controlled by an outside country—the United States. The United States established a civil government in Puerto Rico headed by a governor and an Executive Committee (eleven members, no more than five of whom were to be Puerto Rican), all of whom were appointed by the U.S. president. Congress and/or the president had the right to overrule unconditionally anything decided on by this island government.

Puerto Ricans lost whatever degree of political autonomy they had attained from Spain, but they also lost their economic base. Before the U.S. takeover, Puerto Rico's economy was diversified with four basic export crops—tobacco, cattle, coffee and sugar (Rodriguez 1989, 11). U.S. business interests quickly changed this to a sugar-crop economy controlled primarily by U.S. absentee owners. Fitzpatrick points out the significance of this change.

> The preeminence of sugar had two important consequences. First, it was a cash crop, and the cash income was used to purchase the staple foods that residents of the island had to import. Puerto Rico still does not have a subsistence economy, which has left the island dependent on economic fluctuations in international markets. Second, a sugar economy requires large amounts of labor for five or six months of the year, leaving the labor force with little or no employment for the other six months. (1987, 33)

Having a single cash crop leaves a nation tremendously vulnerable to the world economy. A decline in cane sugar in the 1920s, combined with no reinvestment and a high rate of population growth, resulted in high unemployment, poverty, and overall desperation on the island. The decreased world demand for cane sugar, two hurricanes, and the Depression of the 1930s, left the Puerto Rican economy in shambles, with little hope for its workers.

Under Spanish rule, the sugar plantations were relatively small *hacendados* run by Spanish owners who paternalistically took care of their laborers year-round. Laborers lived on the *hacendados* and had small plots in which to plant gardens for their families' food. None of this continued with U.S. control. "With North American rule Spanish paternalism was swept away and the cold cash relationships of capitalism were imposed. There was no relief from *el tiempo muerto* ['dead' time when cane was not being harvested]" (Peoples Press 1977, 42).

Coffee, which had been Puerto Rico's number one crop during the late 1890s, fell victim to unfavorable tariff rates, a hurricane, and U.S. intervention to thwart efforts for coffee plantation mortgage extensions. This led to the migration of mountainside coffee farmers to urban slums and sugar plantations. It has also led to the abandonment of many plantations, leading to erosion and wasted land because the mountains are not suitable for other crops. González expresses the sadness of this loss: "The Puerto Rican mountaineer lost not only skills, but even the capacity and desire for continuous effort. And skills and values lost by one generation seemed to be irretrievably lost" (1964, 99). Besides losing mountainside land for cultivation, Puerto Rico lost a great deal of property when it was appropriated for U.S. Navy and Army use.

Many rural workers went to the cities of the island, but conditions were not much better there: "The colonial relationship between Puerto Rico and the United States discouraged the formation of native industry or internal markets which might have provided an anchor for urban workers" (Korrol 1983, 25).

Mills, Senior, and Goldsen (1950) point out that the sugar industry depended on the tariff for its well-being. The United States, not Puerto Rico, set the tariff rates as well as the quotas for how much sugar was to be raised and refined. Although Puerto Rico was a rural society, it had to import its food. U.S. capital, through market competition, was responsible for virtually destroying Puerto Rican individual land ownership on the island. U.S. business consolidated land holdings into large corporations. The result of all these limitations was economic dependency on the United States, structural unemployment, and an increase in the marginal workforce. In other words, early U.S. policies in Puerto Rico hurt the workers tremendously.

Before continuing this discussion, two other provisions of the Foraker Act and their ramifications should be mentioned. First, the act made Puerto Rico part of the U.S. monetary system by converting pesos at 60 cents each. This "constituted a de facto devaluation from the peso's value of 66 2/3 cents at the time" (Dietz 1986, 89), which meant higher prices on the island. For example, an item that cost $US6.66 used to cost 10 pesos. After enactment of the Foraker Act, the same item cost more than 11 pesos. Prices were further increased by another provision, which stipulated that all goods moving between Puerto Rico and the United States had to travel via U.S. shipping. Most countries ship along routes where items are exchanged at ports. Therefore, their ships would want to drop off goods at Puerto Rico, pick up Puerto Rican goods to go to the United States and continue from there. Because this could no longer be done, conducting business with countries other than the United States became difficult: "Prior to passage of the Foraker Act, less than 16 percent of Puerto Rico's exports and 22 percent of imports had been carried on U.S. ships, even though more than 80 percent of its trade was conducted with the United States. Following its passage, the prices of imported goods rose, because the U.S. merchant fleet was more expensive than that of other countries" (Dietz 1986, 89–90).

In 1917 the Jones Act replaced the Foraker Act. It reorganized the government but kept all U.S. controls on government in place. The one major change was that the Jones Act extended U.S. citizenship to all Puerto Ricans. Economic trends begun under the Foraker Act continued under the Jones Act, and we begin to see a discrepancy in how the Puerto Rican economic situation was explained. Although in 1916 "three-fourths of the population was starving for lack of work" (González 1964, 118), "inflation and price increases in land and foodstuff gave an impression of a deceiving prosperity which was not the result of the effort of the weakened Puerto Rican economic forces but of the invasion of foreign capital" (González 1964, 128). This deception led many to believe that Puerto Rico was a model of prosperity, but it did not take into consideration the absentee foreign owners of a few sugar corporations and most other productive enterprises, which reversed the order of finances. "By 1922, forty-four native corporations had a capital of $124,791, while foreign corporations had a capital of $15,657,981, and 90 per cent of the trade was with the United States" (González 1964, 138).

With declining opportunities on the island, Puerto Ricans began to migrate to the mainland, where employment opportunities were increasing. Between 1914 and 1930, this outmigration involved 3.4 percent of the 1930 population and became a kind of safety valve for unemployment. Much of this outmigration was in response to contract labor recruitment.

The idea of labor recruitment, and specifically the use of contract labor, is familiar in immigrant studies. We noted in Chapter 2 how contract labor was used as a vehicle for bringing Mexican labor to the United States. Contract labor was also a means used by U.S. business to entice Puerto Rican workers to the mainland, but there was one big difference: Puerto Ricans were U.S. citizens. This fact made the whole process much easier for U.S. companies, because they no longer needed to go through the red tape of having to get visas and alien registrations for their workers. On the other side, Puerto Ricans did not have to, and often did not, return home after the term of the contract was over. As with other contract workers before them, Puerto Rican workers communicated with family and friends on the island and started social networks for later migrants.

Recruitment of Puerto Rican labor by U.S. concerns actually started right after the Spanish-American War when Hawaiian sugar cane growers recruited field labor. Not only was this recruitment the beginning of the Hawaiian Puerto Rican community (Hawaii actually had close to 26,000 Puerto Rican residents in 1990), but it was responsible for the start of a number of California settlements as well. Because there was no air travel at the time, Puerto Ricans had to travel by boat from the island to the mainland, cross the whole United States by train, and then take another long boat trip from California to Hawaii. Not surprisingly, many of these weary travelers got to California, looked at the ocean, said, "Enough is enough," and stayed where they were (Korrol 1983). California was the second largest state for Puerto Rican settlement from 1910 to 1950 (E. Maldonado 1979, 115).

Recruitment of both agricultural and industrial workers continued.

Arizona recruited cotton pickers in 1926. Most of the New England set-tlements started with recruited agricultural seasonal workers, who later moved on to neighboring cities to fill low-skill manufacturing jobs. Other communities also began in this same way.

Then the Depression struck. As devastating as the Depression was for the United States, it was worse for Puerto Rico. At the beginning of the Depression, things were not too bad on the island because sugar was one of the few industries that was actually growing. But then, in 1934, the U.S. Congress set quotas on sugar production, supposedly to stabi-lize the price of sugar on the mainland. This meant sugar production had to be cut drastically. Although the owners (primarily from the United States) were reimbursed for their nonproduction, no allowance was made for the increased unemployment caused because plantations needed fewer workers. Unemployment rose to unbelievable levels—as high as 40 percent (Peoples Press 1977, 41). In 1936 "roughly 80 per cent of the people were on federal relief rolls" (González 1964, 210).

During World War II, German submarine attacks in the Caribbean effectively cut off Puerto Rico, which had two effects on the people of the island. First, it led to the threat of starvation, because the island was dependent on shipping for food imports and for its exports. Second, it almost stopped migration from Puerto Rico. Employment eventually picked up on the island, especially as a result of military projects (be-cause soldiers were drafted and military installations on the island needed workers).

Meanwhile, on the mainland, the United States established the War Manpower Commission to recruit labor from other countries. It brought Caribbean workers to the United States in military transports, but not Puerto Ricans. Finally, after being pressured, it established a branch of the United States Employment Service in Puerto Rico and started bringing workers over in military transports. E. Maldonado (1979) points out that one reason the War Manpower Commission was so slow to recruit Puerto Rican workers was that people in the United States were afraid that Puerto Ricans might stay in this country, whereas other Caribbean peoples could be deported: "Fears in this regard mounted to something of a political issue as early as 1943. . . . New legislation was actually enacted in 1945, banning the appropriation of public monies for 'the importation of citizens' " (Portes and Borocz 1989, 610).

This legislation effectively ended the importation of Puerto Ricans until after the war. "After forty years of colonialization, Puerto Ricans were still considered second-class citizens and, as the deportation issue shows, citizenship did not mean free access to mainland jobs during the war" (E. Maldonado 1979, 110). Bean and Tienda echo this sentiment: "Of the 400,000 foreign contract workers brought to the United States during World War II, few were Puerto Ricans, despite a 100 percent increase in unemployment on the island and despite the fact that Puerto Ricans were legal U.S. citizens who were serving in the military. This unfortunate fact concurs with the view that Puerto Ricans were incorporated into the mainland society as a second-class citizenry" (1987, 25).

After World War II

The largest influx of Puerto Ricans to the mainland began right after the war. Business in the United States was doing well, and many airlines were competing for Puerto Rican business with frequent, cheap flights from the island to the mainland. This caused a 1946–1947 boom in Puerto Rican migration, beginning what has been referred to as the Puerto Rican Diaspora. From 1947 to 1973, about 700,000 Puerto Ricans migrated to the United States and primarily to New York, New Jersey, Connecticut, and Chicago, Illinois (R. Maldonado 1976, 7). Ultimately, this migration has led to the shift of fully one-third of the island's population to the mainland since World War II (Nelson and Tienda 1985). "It is doubtful that a single Puerto Rican family was left unaffected by this massive exodus" (U.S. Commission on Civil Rights 1976, 18–19).

All the governors appointed by the president for Puerto Rico were Anglos until 1946, when President Harry Truman appointed Jesús T. Piñero as governor. This was the "first time in Puerto Rico's history a Puerto Rican occupied the highest government post in the island" (Williams 1972, 168). Then, in 1948, "the people of Puerto Rico for the first time in the island's post-Columbian history elected their own governor" (Williams 1972, 168), Luis Muñoz Marín. Marín favored a form of government that would create a sense of autonomy on the island while still being part of the United States, rather than seeking independence for the island. Because of this stance and U.S. government sensitivity to accusations of maintaining a colonial relationship with Puerto Rico, the island was granted commonwealth status in 1950.

While the political status of the island was changing, economic development was also an issue, and Operation Bootstrap was initiated. This was the beginning of a two-stage industrialization-development program in which "(1) Puerto Rico would provide social capital and infrastructure, financed primarily through the sale of bonds in mainland capital markets and local taxes; and (2) American firms would be induced to locate in industrial sites through an elaborate incentive program" (Holbik and Swan 1975, 16).

Beginning in 1947, Operation Bootstrap "was sold to the Puerto Rican people on the grounds it would help them to help themselves" (Peoples Press 1977, 68). This program had mixed results. "Between 1940 and 1964, the GNP increased nearly ninefold and the manufacturing output went up eighteen times" (Gann and Duignan 1986, 73). Theoretically, this growth should have provided jobs and curbed emigration; however, just the opposite happened: rather than unemployment being reduced, it increased, and instead of providing for more local ownership of capital, it provided huge incentives for more U.S. capital investment on the island.

Dietz (1986) points out a paradox. The same people who recognized the dangers and disadvantages of having absentee sugar plantation owners were now doing everything they could to entice absentee industrial ownership. Rather than curbing emigration, this stance caused the dislocation of large numbers of rural workers at a time when the industrial sector was increasingly capital intensive. The result was a "growing surplus population that could not be accommodated in Puerto Rico's new industrial order" (Rodriguez 1989, 12).

From 1947 to 1970 (a span of only 23 years) the number of U.S. owned factories increased from 13 to 2,000. "No colonial country in history was industrialized so quickly and completely as Puerto Rico" (Peoples Press 1977, 68). Unfortunately, the large Puerto Rican working class base was particularly vulnerable to "double exploitation," meaning that as consumers of U.S. goods, they paid 25 percent more than North Americans but as workers producing manufactured goods, they were paid 1/3 to 1/2 the wages of North American workers (Peoples

Press 1977, 101). Puerto Rico's minimum wage was not raised to the level of that of the United States until January 1, 1981.

Unemployment and poverty remained high on the island, causing a dependency on welfare and other federally funded programs. "Some 15 percent of the entire U.S. supply of food stamps finds its way to Puerto Rico. In 1984, approximately 60 percent of Puerto Rico's population qualified for food stamps" (Morales 1986, 35–36).

At the same time that unemployment and underemployment on the island were increasing, mainland businesses and politicians were busy recruiting Puerto Ricans to fill the large number of job openings after the war, especially in New York City. A 1954 article in the *New York Times* talks about these migrants: "If two-thirds of them [Puerto Ricans] continue to enter operative and service occupations . . . then it would seem as though the Puerto Rican migration would be doing no more than filling the vacancies created by death and retirement in these two major occupations" (Kihss 1954, L-1, L-8).

New York City Mayor Wagner visited Puerto Rico in the early 1940s to tell the people about job opportunities in his city. In 1949, Mayor William O'Dwyer established the Mayor's Committee on Puerto Rican Affairs to work with the government of Puerto Rico and to establish offices in New York to aid the new migrants in their job searches.

European immigrants at the turn of the twentieth century accepted menial jobs but were able to take advantage of built-in ladders to higher-level positions. This in turn led to economic mobility and eventual assimilation into the social and economic mainstream. After World War II, jobs were available in New York for the new Puerto Rican migrants, but the paths to mobility were limited at best. Although receiving higher wages than they would have had on the island, more than a third of the migrants had to take jobs that represented downward mobility. Once they had a job, moving upward was not easy. By the end of the 1940s, it was already being reported that Puerto Ricans "are most likely to remain at the skill level at which they enter the New York labor market. Those who do move upward occupationally meet a ceiling at the handwork level. They may rise from unskilled to semiskilled or even to skilled levels, but white-collar work or small business, to which, in the classic pattern they should aspire, is largely closed to them" (Mills, Senior, and Goldsen 1950, 76). An important result of these early mobility barriers is that Puerto Ricans did not develop patterns that would help them survive the move into a postindustrial economy.

A third of the early postwar Puerto Rican migrants were black. Mobility was even more difficult for them: "In their first jobs in New York, the white [Puerto Rican] men's advantage tends to disappear, but after they have been here a while their chances for more skilled occupations may rise, while Negroes [*sic*] are likely to remain in semiskilled jobs" (Mills, Senior, and Goldsen 1950, 71).

Puerto Rican blacks soon learned that non–English-speaking blacks had a better chance in the labor market than did American blacks, so they had little reason to take steps toward assimilating. In fact, in 1950 researchers found that they had "less incentive and less opportunity to follow the pattern of Americanization than any other immigrants America has known" (Mills, Senior, and Goldsen 1950, 86). Gann and Duignan (1986) also noted that darker-skinned Puerto Ricans continued to use Spanish as their major language to differentiate themselves from black Americans.

Although the major postwar recruitment efforts came from New York City, other cities were also involved: In 1946 Chicago recruited Puerto Ricans for domestic and foundry work. The National Tube Company, a subsidiary of U.S. Steel, in 1947 contracted for several hundred Puerto Ricans to work in Lorain, Ohio; this settlement remained stable for many years. In 1948 U.S. Steel recruited workers to Gary, Indiana. Philadelphia drew workers that had been recruited by the Campbell Soup Company in Camden, New Jersey.

The early postwar migration was impressive, but it decreased almost as dramatically during the 1960s. U.S. labor opportunities were declining by the 1970s and presented a bleak picture for mainland Puerto Ricans. There had always been some return migration, but the 1970s produced a net outmigration to the island. An interesting and important side note to this return migration is that skilled workers found more mobility on the island, and unskilled laborers found more mobility on the mainland. Therefore, skilled people were more apt to return to the island, leaving the U.S. Puerto Rican community with a lower aggregate skill level (Gann and Duignan 1986). The 1980s showed yet a different trend in that more skilled and professional people were leaving the is-

land. Because the flow of skilled workers was moving in both direc-
tions, however, Puerto Rico did not suffer from a brain drain.

U.S.–Puerto Rico Relationship

From the very beginning of its control over Puerto Rico, the United
States made decisions for the island based on mainland business and
economic concerns and showed little consideration for the Puerto Rican
people. The U.S. attitude toward Puerto Rico has been one of disrespect and exploitation, leading to a relationship of Puerto Rican dependency on the United States.

Some people may assume Puerto Rico's situation is no different from
that of other third-world nations. However, there is a big difference. In
essence, Puerto Rico is still a colony. "Commonwealth status" sounds
better than "colony," but Latin American censors say that commonwealth designation "changed the form but not the substance of colonial
rule" (Gann and Duignan 1986, 69). The island's status has "obliterated
economic boundaries and protective mechanisms that Third World nations are beginning to develop in order to defend local interests" (Nelson and Tienda 1985, 57). Puerto Rico cannot determine its own foreign policy, nor can it determine separate tariffs to protect itself against
American products. In fact, it has been said that "Puerto Rico by the
early 1980s had become one of the worst instances of a colonial welfare
economy, with few of its virtues and most of its vices" (Gann and Duignan 1986, 77).

In its desire to "modernize" the island, the United States destroyed
the native economy and developed a dependent people. On the island,
"the economy is kept alive by the transfer of payments from the federal government. . . . It is estimated that 70 percent of the . . . residents
of Puerto Rico receive some form of assistance from the federal government" (Fitzpatrick 1987, 34–35).

On the mainland, Puerto Ricans took jobs in the lowest level of the
industrial sector and became the most vulnerable to the changes inherent in entering a postindustrial economy. They are still faced with exploitation and discrimination and are "locked in an unbreakable vise of
poverty" (Gann and Duignan 1986, 69). Foreign appearing, and yet

American citizens, Puerto Ricans have been marginalized on both the island and the mainland.

Puerto Ricans did not aspire to dependency on welfare. A simple rationalization of the welfare problem is to blame the victim and say that Puerto Ricans would rather take welfare than have to work. This description is contrary to what researchers have found, however. Rodriguez determined that Puerto Ricans "do *not* migrate to secure greater welfare benefits" (1989, 7, emphasis in original). Gann and Duignan contend that "most Puerto Ricans . . . had little desire to go on welfare when they arrived on the mainland. All knowledgeable witnesses agreed that the newcomers preferred work to drawing relief. They placed high value on dignity, independence and self-respect" (1986, 88).

A 1953 *New York Times* article stated, "Puerto Ricans who come here want to work. . . . Those who do go on relief for a while, perhaps one out of fourteen, tend to get off faster than non–Puerto Ricans" (Kihss 1953, L-18).

With this kind of evidence, how do we account for the current high numbers of Puerto Rican welfare recipients both on and off the island? Ortiz looks to U.S. colonialism for an answer: "The U.S. has dominated, historically and presently, the political and economic systems in Puerto Rico . . . the combination of industrial development and migration have generated a new Puerto Rican social structure . . . in which conditions for Puerto Ricans, both in Puerto Rico and the U.S., have deteriorated rather than improved" (1986, 626).

Bonilla and Campos, in reviewing U.S. corporate and governmental control over the island's decisions and programs, have determined that these forces have caused "what is essentially a unitary labor market" (1981, 152) in which Puerto Ricans are assigned the role of surplus labor. With these thoughts in mind, we can understand that "it is in the dilution of alternatives that the system forces Puerto Ricans into welfare" (History Task Force 1979, 217). In essence, there's no place left for them to turn.

Current U.S. Puerto Rican Settlement Patterns

As we have seen, the original Puerto Rican immigrants settled in New York, and though other areas recruited Puerto Ricans, most continued to choose New York and the surrounding areas as their settlement site.

Puerto Ricans are still concentrated in the Northeast, with 39.8 percent of them living in New York State and 11.7 percent residing in New Jersey in 1990. Together, these two states accounted for over half the Puerto Rican population on the mainland at the time of the 1990 census (U.S. Bureau of the Census 1991).

Puerto Ricans are extremely urban, as are the other Hispanic groups. Of all Puerto Ricans residing in the mainland in 1990, 96.8 percent lived in metropolitan areas. However, metropolitan areas are composed of central cities and their suburbs. Almost three-fourths of Puerto Ricans living in metropolitan areas are found in the central cities as compared with only about half of the Mexicans, Cubans, and those in the Other Hispanic category.

Interestingly, this pattern is not the same in all areas of the country. In the Northeast and Midwest—the old industrialized areas often referred to as the Rust Belt—Puerto Ricans are definitely stuck in central cities, with well over 80 percent living there. However, in the South 65.6 percent and in the West 58.8 percent are suburbanites. This is our first indication that Puerto Rican experiences vary depending on where they live in the United States.

Puerto Ricans are dispersing rapidly. In 1950, 81.3 percent of U.S. mainland Puerto Ricans lived in New York City. In 1960, this figure decreased to 69.0 percent. It dipped lower, to 61.8 percent, in 1970 and to 42.7 percent in 1980. In 1990 this percentage decreased even more to only 32.9 percent. In just forty years, New York City lost more than half of its percentage share of mainland Puerto Ricans. This does not mean, however, that New York has lost its significance for Puerto Ricans. Table 3–1 shows that New York City still has, by far, the largest Puerto Rican population in the United States.

Dispersion continued between 1990 and 2000. New York State actually lost 36,000 Puerto Ricans and was the only state to report a decrease. The New York City metropolitan area lost nearly 100,000 Puerto Ricans. With so many Puerto Ricans locating in places other than New York, where are they going? It is interesting to note that of the top ten Puerto Rican metropolitan areas in 1990, two are in Florida and by 2000 three are in Florida. Orlando's Puerto Rican population almost tripled. Is this a clue we can use to discover new settlement preferences for Puerto Ricans? The answer is yes.

Table 3-1

Top Ten U.S. Metropolitan Areas with Puerto Rican Populations (in thousands)

Metropolitan Area	1990	2000
New York, NY	933	837
Chicago, IL	131	152
Philadelphia, PA	120	160
Newark, NJ	77	N/A
Miami/Hialeah, FL	73	80
Nassau/Suffolk, NY	62	75
Jersey City, NJ	59	58*
Bergen/Passaic, NJ	55	
Orlando, FL	52	140
Boston, MA	4x	
Hartford, CT	N/A	83
Tampa-St. Petersburg-Clearwater, FL	N/A	76
Springfield, MA	N/A	61

*Jersey City and Boston are tied for tenth place.

Source: U.S. Census, 1990 STF 1C; U.S. Bureau of the Census 2001b.

The U.S. Census provides individual sample data on computer tape for researchers to use to find answers to just this kind of query (U.S. Bureau of the Census 1992). One of the questions the census asks is where a person lived five years earlier. In other words, for the 1990 census people were asked where they lived in 1985. By looking at Puerto Ricans who lived in one state in 1985 and in another state in 1990, we can determine the numbers who moved during those five years and where they went. We can do the same thing in tracking movements between the island and different states on the mainland. The results are really interesting.

Let's begin unraveling these migration patterns by looking at the back-and-forth flow to the island. We found that 187,000 people moved from Puerto Rico to the mainland and that 129,000 returned to the island. Of those coming to the mainland, New York received 19.1 percent, but Florida received even more—21.1 percent. Four other states—Massachusetts, New Jersey, Connecticut, and Pennsylvania—also received large shares. Obviously, the Northeast is still a major pull, but the number one state was Florida.

Conversely, the Northeast contributed almost three-fourths of the returnees to the island. New York alone was responsible for 44.6 percent of those moving back, while Florida contributed only 5.6 percent. To make better sense of this, let's look at the actual numbers of movers. New York had a net loss to the island of close to 22,000 people, while Florida showed a net gain of over 32,000. This indicates that Florida is increasing its significance as a settlement choice for those from the island.

Now let's look at the flow between New York and other states. Close to 76,000 Puerto Ricans moved from New York to other states. Of these, more than a third went to Florida; New Jersey attracted 15.5 percent; and Massachusetts, Connecticut, Pennsylvania, and California each attracted a good share. From these data we can determine that (1) Florida has become an important pull for Puerto Rican internal migration, (2) other northeastern states have maintained their importance, and (3) we're beginning to see California as an attractive alternative.

If we look at movers from states other than New York, we find that just over 17,000 moved to New York. However, the number one choice for relocation was again Florida, which received 19.6 percent of the total or just over 27,500. Comparing just the interstate movements of Puerto Ricans, we find that New York lost almost 58,500 people.

The trend of Puerto Ricans migrating to Florida has been noticed before. Using the 1980 census, Bean and Tienda, in collaboration with Douglas Massey, documented a southern and western internal migration pattern for Puerto Ricans and found that "the most significant part of this migration . . . [was] to and from Florida" (1987, 162).

How did all the paths of movement affect the Puerto Rican populations in Florida and New York? Along with a natural increase from births, net migration contributed to a growth in Florida's Puerto Rican population from 94,775 in 1980 to 247,010 in 1990, a 160.6 percent increase. New York's total Puerto Rican population also grew between 1980 and 1990, by 100,000, but it had a five-year net migration loss of almost 70,000. This indicates that the natural increase from births, not migration, is responsible for New York's continued growth in real numbers.

Although detailed data from the 2000 census are not yet available, we do know that Florida gained 235,000 Puerto Ricans to take over second place, with more Puerto Ricans than New Jersey. The state of New York now has 30.8 percent of the Puerto Rican population, followed by Florida with 14.2 percent and New Jersey with 10.8 percent.

In Chapter 6 we will try to determine exactly who is moving, but, for now, we can speculate that all this relocation and decentralization is in response to the increasingly difficult economic conditions found in New York and other northeastern states.

Comparisons with Mexican and Cuban Journeys

Throughout this chapter we have spent a great deal of time discussing the situation on the island, much more so than we spent discussing the homeland situations facing Mexicans or Cubans. This is because for Puerto Ricans the events on the island and the events on the mainland are two parts of a single whole. These two parts are politically and economically orchestrated by U.S. political and business interests. It is impossible to grasp the tensions involved in Puerto Rican migration or understand their poverty and dependency without digging deeply into the historical relationship between the island and the U.S. mainland.

In Chapter 2 and in this one, we have described journeys. These journeys have had some similarities, but they have had even more differences. We found that in the nineteenth century the Puerto Rican and Cuban communities in the United States were developing in a similar way. The situations on the two islands were also similar. This changed when Cuba gained its independence and Puerto Rico did not.

Cubans entered the United States in large numbers because of political rather than economic concerns. They were cordially greeted and received generous government assistance. From their favored starting position, Cubans advanced in a way more reminiscent of earlier white European immigrants' experiences than of those of Puerto Ricans or Mexicans. Cubans were "never restricted to a position of second-class workers in an ethnically split labor market" (Bean and Tienda 1987, 31).

Both Mexican and Puerto Rican migration primarily entailed the movements of low- or no-skilled wage laborers, and both groups faced severe discrimination. There were also differences, however, not the least of which was that Mexican immigrants include large numbers who are undocumented, whereas Puerto Ricans are citizens.

Before moving on, we should reemphasize that Puerto Rican citizenship has not been treated as equal to that of other U.S. citizens. Contreras, in a recent *Philadelphia Inquirer* article, explains this: "Puerto

Ricans are as American as apple pie. Congress said so in 1917, when Puerto Ricans were made citizens—except they are 'statutory citizens,' not constitutional citizens" (1998, A-13). Puerto Ricans on the island cannot vote for president. Although they elect their own governor now, they are still controlled in federal matters by the U.S. Congress, in which they have no voting representative, only one nonvoting member who is currently Carlos Romero-Barcelo. When Congress recently voted on making English the official language of the United States and allowing Puerto Rico to vote on its status, Romero-Barcelo was quoted as saying, "I am the sole representative to this House for 3.8 million U.S. citizens, and I cannot vote. . . . This legislation [allowing Puerto Rico to vote on its status] would end 100 years of Puerto Rico's colonial relationship with the nation, yet I cannot vote" (Contreras 1998, A-13).

Our survey of the Puerto Rican journey indicates that from the time they were granted citizenship, Puerto Ricans have been politically and economically treated as second-class with minimum representation in matters concerning their fate.

Besides legal status, other differences exist between Mexicans and Puerto Ricans in the United States. The major migration of Puerto Ricans to the mainland happened quite quickly after World War II and concentrated primarily in New York City. However, Mexican immigration has been going on for more than 100 years, is much less concentrated, and is found mainly in the Southwest.

Fitzpatrick further lays out the uniqueness of the Puerto Rican experience:

1. Puerto Ricans have come in the first great airborne migration of people from abroad; they are decidedly newcomers of the aviation age.
2. They are the first group to come in large numbers from a different language and cultural background who are, nevertheless, citizens of the United States.
3. They are the first group of newcomers who bring a cultural practice of widespread intermingling and intermarriage of peoples of many different colors.
4. Furthermore, they come to New York City at a time when aspects of the city make their experience different from that of former newcomers. (1987, 2–3)

Mexicans were lied to, cheated, and forcibly pushed around by the United States; Cubans were embraced; and Puerto Ricans had their citizenship treated as second-class. Each of the three groups settled in a different region of the United States. Since their arrival Mexicans have been slowly dispersing, Cubans were initially forced to disperse but are now becoming more centralized, and Puerto Ricans are showing significant dispersal patterns. Mexicans and Puerto Ricans are still very much ensconced in the surplus labor pool, whereas Cubans have exhibited economic mobility and are found at all economic and labor levels.

The journeys of these three Hispanic groups leave no doubt that we must study each group separately if we want to find answers to the pressing issues each one faces.

4

How the Journeys End

n Chapters 2 and 3, we traced the journeys of Mexicans, Cubans, and Puerto Ricans as they left their homelands to become part of the United States. We found major differences in these journeys that lead us to believe there should also be major differences in how well each group has been able to adapt to U.S. economic and occupational structures. In short, some groups should quite understandably be doing better than others as we compare their well-being in 1990. Before looking into their present status, however, let's review what we discovered in their journeys.

Hispanic Journeys Recap

The first difference we found had to do with timing—when the major influx of each group occurred and how long it lasted. Mexicans began immigrating after the Mexican-American War and developed patterns and networks that are still at work today despite two major setbacks—the U.S. repatriation efforts of the 1930s and Operation Wetback in the 1950s. Although Cuban settlements date back to the late nineteenth century, the major influx started in 1959 after Castro's takeover of Cuba and ended after the 1980 Mariel boat lift. Even during those years, the flow was not constant but came in waves. Puerto Ricans also had small settlements dating to the late nineteenth century, but their major influx began after World War II. Because their citizenship status makes it easy to return to Puerto Rico, a cyclical pattern began emerging in the 1960s. Since then net migration for any given period could be in either direction (to the island or to the mainland) depending on the comparative economic advantages of the two areas. However, new arrivals are still coming to the United States in large numbers.

Timing of immigration is important for a number of reasons. First, because the U.S. economic system changes, when new arrivals come determines the opportunities available to them. Second, when a group's major influx ends relatively quickly (as with the Cubans and the white European immigrants before them), its members can concentrate on settling into their new environment and establishing stability in their lives. However, groups with an essentially unending flow of new entrants must constantly be adapting. They also continuously face their homeland's culture, which slows the group's acculturation process. Third, Mexicans have had much longer to adapt and their group includes many more generations than the other two groups. If timing were the only immigration difference, this third point would lead us to expect that Mexicans would be much better off than the others—but there are other issues.

A second major difference between the journeys of the three groups is where they settled in the United States. Mexicans primarily went to the Southwest with a secondary pattern of going to midwestern industrial cities, primarily Chicago. Cubans landed in Miami, where they stayed. Even those who were forced to relocate as part of the U.S. refugee program have been returning to South Florida. Puerto Ricans chose* the Northeast, primarily New York City, and have been decentralizing rapidly. The major importance of where each group settled is that the mix of agriculture, service, manufacturing, and other businesses has been different in each region. In addition, the economic transition taking place in the United States as it moves into the postindustrial era has affected different regions to varying degrees. Regions that rely on manufacturing as

---

*To say that Puerto Ricans *chose* to locate in a particular region may not be totally accurate. Because of the colonial nature of U.S.–Puerto Rican relations, it may be closer to the truth to say that Puerto Ricans were *manipulated* into locating where they were needed to fill vital but temporary positions in the midst of an economy in transition, especially in New York.

their base have been affected much more drastically than those with a more diversified economic base. All of these factors, of course, affect labor opportunities available to the various populations in those regions.

A third area of difference we found is that Cubans were political refugees, and the initial wave of immigrants included large numbers of professional and well-off people, whereas the early Mexicans and Puerto Ricans were primarily low-skill laborers coming to the United States to seek economic opportunities. This difference allowed Cubans to quickly adapt and begin over. They built an enclave economy where they own a wide variety of enterprises, including banks and other international businesses. These concerns could then incorporate the later waves of laborers. Mexicans and Puerto Ricans, however, had no base of their own and had to find their way in mainstream labor markets.

The final difference we found had to do with how the United States accepted each group. Cubans, except for the last wave, were embraced with open arms. They were used for anticommunist propaganda and were helped by an extremely generous U.S. refugee aid program. Both Mexicans and Puerto Ricans were marginalized, exploited, and suffered discrimination. U.S. citizenship of Mexican children meant nothing when forcing the return of families to Mexico, and Puerto Rican citizenship has always been treated as second class. Obviously, Cubans were at an advantage when it comes to how they were received by the United States.

With all these points in mind, let's now draw a profile of how each group has developed in the past couple of decades and where each one stands now. We will do this in three parts. First, we will compare socioeconomic indicators, including the incidence of female-headed families. Second, we will review characteristics usually included as human capital—nativity, language, and education. Finally, we will look at the labor force structure of each group. Most detailed data from the 2000 census are not yet available. However, the U.S. Census Bureau did publish a special Current Population Report on Hispanics in March 2000 (U.S. Bureau of the Census 2001a). We will use these figures to get an idea of continuing trends, but we need to be aware that because of different sampling procedures these figures are not as precise as the census itself. Therefore, analysis based on this data should be considered tentative.

Socioeconomic Status

In determining the economic standing of a group at any particular time, a number of statistics can be used, such as household mean or median income, household per capita income, or family mean or median income. These categories allow us to examine the income of households, families, or individuals. When we talk about poverty issues, we further refine our focus by looking at types of families (particularly female-headed families) and different age groups (particularly children under the age of eighteen). Therefore, our first task is to decide exactly what information we want to explore to bring maximum understanding to how these groups compare.

When using census data, the term *household* "includes all the persons who occupy a housing unit" (U.S. Bureau of the Census 1993a, 30), regardless of whether they are related. A household can include a single person, or roommates, or any of a variety of family types. A *family* is defined as "a householder and one or more other persons living in the same household who are related to the householder by birth, marriage, or adoption" (U.S. Bureau of the Census 1993a, 32). A family can be a husband and wife with no children, a single mother or father with children, a grandmother with grandchildren, or another combination of relatives.

Although the concept of family has been stretched a great deal and no longer can be assumed to mean a traditional nuclear unit of husband, wife, and their children, the family is still the basic social unit in this country. Therefore, throughout this book we concentrate primarily on family economic standing as opposed to that of households. Let's begin our analysis.

Female-Headed Families

Over the last few decades, a great deal of dialogue has taken place regarding the deterioration of the family in the United States. Single parents, and particularly single mothers, have become more and more common. The numbers or percentages of female-headed families directly affect the economic well-being of a group, because these families represent much lower incomes than married-couple families. Therefore, even before we begin looking at income or poverty figures, we need to compare the family structure of these Hispanic subgroups.

Our first question is whether the problem of female-headed families found throughout the U.S. has plagued the Hispanic groups. The answer is yes, but to varying degrees as can be seen in Table 4–1.

We can see one very encouraging trend from this table, and that is that very little relative growth in the female-headed population took place between 1980 and 2000 for any of the groups. In fact, the percentage of Puerto Rican female–headed families has decreased slightly. However, the discouraging news for our purposes is that the incidence of female-headed families among Puerto Ricans is still much higher than that of Mexicans and Cubans. Indeed, single females head more than one-third of all Puerto Rican families. Because the phenomenon of female-headed families has frequently been associated with economic hardship, the overall economic well-being of the Puerto Rican population must be affected.

To determine just how Puerto Ricans are doing economically and how they fare relative to Mexicans and Cubans, we now want to turn our attention to two economic measurements—median family income and poverty levels.

Median Family Incomes

In discussing income trends, we must take into account the cost of living increases over time. To get a truer picture of how the groups have progressed economically, we will look at median family income from 1969, 1979, and 1989, but the 1969 and 1979 amounts have been adjusted to reflect what their value would be in 1989 dollars using the Consumer Price Index (U.S. Bureau of the Census 1993c). This will let us know if a group

Table 4–1
Percentage Distribution of Female-Headed Families for Selected U.S. Hispanic Origin Groups, 1980–2000

	1980	1990	2000
Mexican	18.9	18.2	21.2
Cuban	16.0	16.3	18.3
Puerto Rican	36.5	36.6	35.8

Sources: Bean and Tienda 1987, 192; U.S. Bureau of the Census 1993d, table 2; U.S. Bureau of the Census 2001a, table 4.1.

is improving from one period to the next. These numbers are shown in Figure 4–1.

From this figure, we can see a number of interesting trends. First, as was to be expected, Cubans were better off than Mexicans and Puerto Ricans were in all three time periods. In addition, of the three groups only the Cubans did not have a period of decline. Cuban median family income did not increase much between 1979 and 1989, but it did increase.

Puerto Ricans had the lowest median income in all three time periods. They hit hard times earlier than the other two groups, declining during the 1970s instead of the 1980s. When they did recover during the 1980s, they were not able to catch up to the other groups. This resulted in only an 11.0 percent increase in income over the twenty-year period as compared to 16.1 percent for Mexicans and 17.8 percent for Cubans. Comparatively speaking, Puerto Ricans have not only had the lowest median family income of the three major Hispanic subgroups

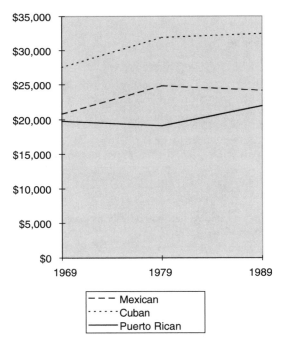

Figure 4-1: Median Family Income of Selected Hispanic Subgroups (in constant 1989 dollars)

but have also had the least growth, leaving them in an even worse comparative position at the end of the twenty years than at the beginning. To see this more clearly, look at the figures in Table 4–2, which show Puerto Rican income in each of the three time periods as a percent of Mexican and Cuban incomes.

We can see how during the 1970s (between 1969 and 1979) the comparative well-being of Puerto Ricans dipped tremendously (see Table 4–2). Whereas Puerto Rican median family income was 95.1 percent of Mexican median family income in 1969, it was only 77.0 percent of Mexican median family income in 1979. Although it rose during the 1980s to 91.0 percent of Mexican median family income in 1989, this did not make up for the huge dip in the 1970s. The same pattern can be seen when comparing Puerto Rican incomes to Cuban incomes. Even after their "recovery," the Puerto Rican median family income was only about two-thirds that of the Cubans'.

Poverty Levels

The federal government establishes official poverty levels. Originally laid out in the 1960s, the basis for determining the levels was the lowest cost of feeding families of varying sizes. A mathematical formula then determines which families are living in poverty based on their size and income. Any individual in those families, whether related by blood or not, is considered a person in poverty. With this generalized explanation of the poverty level, we need to stress that it is almost impossible for a family to live at that level, let alone below it. Therefore, the percentage of families and people in poverty is very important to know

Table 4–2
Puerto Rican Income as a Percent of Mexican and Cuban Income, 1969–1989

Puerto Rican Median Family Income	1969	1979	1989
As a percent of Mexican median family income	95.1%	77.0%	91.0%
As a percent of Cuban median family income	71.8%	59.9%	67.7%

Sources: Bean and Tienda 1987, 350; U.S. Bureau of the Census 1993d, table 5.

in determining the overall well-being of a group. Statistics to help us understand the ramifications of poverty on the three groups are found in Table 4–3.

Let's look at the figures in this table a few at a time. To begin, look at the percentage of families in poverty for each of the three groups in each year. We find the same general pattern that we found when looking at median family income. Puerto Ricans in 1970 were already suffering from higher poverty levels than the other two Hispanic groups. Poverty levels for both Mexican and Cuban families decreased from 1970 to 1980, while they increased for Puerto Ricans, and a full one-third

Table 4–3
Percent in Poverty Distribution of Selected U.S. Hispanic Origin Families, 1970–2000, and Types of Families and Persons, 1990 and 2000

Families/Persons in Poverty	Mexican	Cuban	Puerto Rican
% Families in poverty			
1970	26.8	13.1	28.2
1980	21.4	11.2	33.4
1990	23.4	11.4	29.6
2000	21.2	15.0	23.0
% Married-couple families in poverty			
1990	18.1	8.2	12.2
2000	16.7	8.1	10.3
% Female-headed families in poverty			
1990	45.4	25.3	57.3
2000	38.4	33.8	47.4
% Persons in poverty			
1990	26.3	14.6	31.7
2000	24.1	17.3	25.8
% Children, under age 18, in poverty			
1990	32.0	17.0	41.7
2000	31.5	20.2	37.2

Sources: Bean and Tienda 1987, 356; U.S. Bureau of the Census 1993d, table 5; U.S. Bureau of the Census 2001a, tables 14.1 and 15.1.

of all Puerto Rican families were in poverty in 1980. Between 1980 and 1990, poverty levels increased some for Mexicans and Cubans while they decreased for Puerto Ricans. As with median family income, however, the recovery for Puerto Ricans did not even bring them back to their 1970 level, so at the end of the twenty-year period, the gap between Puerto Ricans and the other two groups was wider than it had been to begin with. By 2000 we begin to see an improvement in Puerto Rican poverty levels. They still have the highest rate in poverty, but they are not very far from Mexicans and the Cuban percentage is actually increasing.

Looking at the difference in poverty levels between married-couple families and female-headed families for each group, we get an even better idea of why Puerto Ricans suffer from so much poverty. Mexicans had the highest percentage of married-couple families in poverty, with 18.1 percent in 1990 and 16.7 percent in 2000, but the big numbers fall under the category of female-headed families. Not only do Puerto Ricans have a much higher percentage of families headed by single females, but also a huge percentage (57.3 percent) of those families were in poverty in 1990. There was improvement in 2000, but it is still a large problem. This feminization of Puerto Rican poverty is so important that we have included a separate chapter in this book solely to cover the plight of Puerto Rican women.

The pattern found in the final section of Table 4–3 regarding poverty holds no surprises. Cubans have the lowest percentage of people in poverty, and Puerto Ricans have the highest. The most difficult figure to deal with is that, in 1990, 41.7 percent of Puerto Rican children under the age of 18 were growing up in poverty, and this percentage improved only slightly, to 37.2 percent, in 2000. This figure paints a rather pessimistic picture of the future of Puerto Ricans in the United States.

We have looked only at families and individuals living below the poverty level, but we would be remiss if we did not mention that many people earning enough income to be considered above poverty level are still very poor. The government-established levels of poverty are so extreme that even government relief efforts often use 150 percent of the poverty level as a cutoff point for services. For example, in colder climates, heat is essential in the winter months and some assistance programs are available to deal with the large heating bills. If a family falls into a bracket with $10,000 as the poverty level, the 150 percent of poverty low-income classification would allow them to receive assistance if they had incomes up to $15,000. Therefore, families whose income lies between poverty levels and 150 percent of poverty levels are not reflected in Table 4–3 but are recognized, even by government agencies, as being very needy and at risk.

General Population Characteristics

Having established that of the three largest Hispanic national groups Puerto Ricans are indeed in the worst position economically, we want to try to unravel the dynamics affecting economic status to begin discovering the roots of the problem. We begin by reviewing three factors generally associated with a group's human capital, but first we need to know what we mean when we use the term *human capital*. Sakamoto describes it as follows: "The main idea of the human capital model is that the productivity of labor is essentially lodged within individual workers, and that individual workers can augment their productivity by increasing their educational training and labor market experience" (1988, 87). Basically the idea is that the better equipped a group is to deal with the labor market, the better off it will be.

The level of education is considered the most important measurement of human capital. However, two other measurements are also pertinent. First is the issue of nativity. Foreign-born and -speaking persons quite naturally tend to be less capable of functioning in English or adapting to a labor market that is not only new to them but that often is structured differently from that in their homelands. An added problem for them is that the education they received in their homeland may not fit the needs of the U.S. labor market, so their educational attainment may not translate into the same wage levels of those born and schooled in the United States A final problem is that they are more easily perceived by businesses as being "foreign."

The other measurement of human capital used in this chapter is proficiency in English. Although some areas, such as Miami and some southwestern metropolitan areas, approach being bilingual, the major language one encounters throughout the United States, and particularly in the labor market (apart from enclave economies), is English. Therefore, a group's proficiency in English is an important characteristic for economic success. This factor interacts with our nativity argument in that the first generation is more reluctant to learn English, and English is definitely a second language. On the other hand, second-generation immigrants typically are bilingual because they speak the language of their parents at home (in our case Spanish), but they go to U.S. English-speaking schools and are much more a product of the U.S. location in which they are growing up. Regardless of nativity, those who speak English well will adapt to the U.S. labor market much better and have more opportunities to advance than those who do not.

We begin our discussion by reviewing the nativity status of each of our Hispanic subgroups. Then we will determine how proficient each group is in English. Finally, we will focus on educational attainment.

Nativity

In looking at nativity for Puerto Ricans, we run into a problem. Most U.S. Census special studies on Hispanics recognize Puerto Ricans born in Puerto Rico as native born, which is unfortunate because first-generation Puerto Ricans face the same adaptive struggles as true immigrants. Conversely, primarily because of the back-and-forth flow between Puerto Rico and the U.S. mainland, which tends to reinforce both cultures in both locales, some researchers say that being island born does not hinder a Puerto Rican as much as being foreign born hinders other immigrants (Borjas 1983, Bean and Tienda 1987). Regardless of this argument, we will treat U.S. Puerto Ricans born on the island as foreign born.

Table 4–4 shows the distribution of the Hispanic-origin populations by nativity for 1970 to 1990. These figures are very interesting, because if we used only the nativity figures to determine the comparative well-being of our three groups, we would make a huge mistake.

We begin by looking at the Cubans. The percentage of Cubans who were foreign born in each of the periods was overwhelmingly higher than that of either of the other two groups. This would seem to indicate that Cubans were, at the very least, suffering from a large handicap. However, if we remember the Cuban journey from Chapter 2, we know three things:

1. Many of the Cuban refugees, especially from the initial refugee wave, were highly educated professionals who, with time, were bound to do better than poorly educated laborers.
2. The U.S. refugee package assisted Cubans in upgrading their credentials in a relatively short period of time.
3. The Cuban economic enclave in Miami minimizes the effects of being foreign born. In fact, even second- and third-generation Cubans find it necessary to maintain the Spanish language and to some degree Cuban customs if they want to participate in the enclave economy.

Neither Mexicans nor Puerto Ricans are privy to the advantages of an enclave. On the one hand, even though Puerto Ricans have a higher percentage of foreign born individuals than Mexicans do, each year their percentage is steadily declining. On the other hand, the Mexican percentage of foreign born is steadily increasing. Aponte points out that "whereas rapid inmigration by Puerto Ricans has long ceased, Mexican immigration continues at a rapid pace" (1993, 529). If we look at the figures for any one year, we would assume that Puerto Ricans are more hindered by nativity than Mexicans. If we look at the pattern over the years, however, we realize that nativity is becoming less of a hindrance for Puerto Ricans and more of a hindrance for Mexicans, who must embrace an ever-increasing number of new arrivals. In fact, if the trends have continued, the 2000 census may show the percentage of foreign-born individuals for the two groups to be close to identical.

Table 4-4
Percentage Foreign Born of Selected U.S. Hispanic Origin Populations, 1970–1990

	1970	1980	1990
Mexican	17.9	26.0	33.3
Cuban	73.4	77.4	71.7
Puerto Rican	54.2	50.6	45.4

Sources: Bean and Tienda 1987, 10; U.S. Bureau of the Census 1993d, table 1; U.S. Census 1990 PUMS, 1-Percent Sample.

English Proficiency

In our effort to understand how well a group has become proficient in English, we will look at two different measurements. The traditional measure is the percentage of persons aged five years and older who do not speak English "very well." A newer measure, called linguistic isolation, was established by the census in 1990 and will also be reviewed.

By way of clarification, the census determines linguistic isolation by how well any member of a household fourteen years or older speaks English:

> A household in which no person age 14 years or over speaks only English and no person age 14 years or over who speaks a language other than English speaks English "very well" is classified as "linguistically isolated." All the members of a linguistically isolated household are tabulated as linguistically isolated, including members under age 14 years who may speak only English. (U.S. Bureau of the Census 1993a, 42)

We begin by reviewing the pattern of the traditional measurement of English proficiency—the percentage of each group that does not speak English "very well." All three groups made large gains in English proficiency between 1980 and 1990. Cubans, as could be expected from their nativity, lag behind the other two groups in English ability, but less than half the Cubans aged five and over were still hampered by language in 1990. The trend we noticed with Mexican and Puerto Rican nativity is also seen here. Although both groups improved, Puerto Ricans had more problems with English in 1980. Mexicans did not improve as much during the 1980s, so by 1990 Mexicans had a higher percentage in this category. One-third of all Puerto Ricans and close to 40 percent of Mexicans were still hampered by poor English in 1990.

Our second measure of English proficiency, available only for 1990, showed the same general pattern of English ability. The U.S. Census (1993d, table 3) determined that 23.2 percent of Mexicans, 27.9 percent of Cubans, and 17.3 percent of Puerto Ricans aged five and older were linguistically isolated. Not only do we see that the Cuban disadvantage is greatly reduced by using this measurement, but we also see that Puerto Ricans have a clear advantage. The importance of this measure is that it adds dimension to our understanding of the potential severity of hindrances as families with limited ability in English try to function in an English-speaking society. Persons with poor English ability but who live with teenagers or other adults who are proficient in English have better access to opportunities than those who have no one else in the family to assist them.

Education

Educational attainment is probably the human capital characteristic that affects economic mobility the most. The census determines the highest grade level attained by those aged twenty-five and over. By using these figures, we can compare the percentages of each population that have less than a high school diploma, that have a high school diploma but not a college degree, and that have a college degree. The greater the levels of high school and college completion, the better are the chances in the labor market. Table 4–5 shows the distribution of these educational attainment levels for each of our Hispanic groups for the years 1970, 1980, 1990, and 2000.

We see some very interesting patterns in this table. First, Cubans have lower percentages of dropouts, those who never finished high school, than the other two groups in all four time periods and higher percentages of college graduates. Between 1980 and 1990, the Cuban situation worsened. The figures for those years are a reflection of the lower educational attainment levels of the Cubans entering the United States during the 1980 Mariel boat lift, which took place just after the 1980 census was taken. However, by 2000 the Cubans seem to have gotten back on track.

Another interesting pattern is that Puerto Ricans in 1970 had a higher dropout incidence than Mexicans did, with a correspondingly lower level of both high school graduates and college graduates. But by 1980 the pattern was reversed, with Mexicans having slightly higher levels of dropouts and lower levels of high school and college completions. By 1990 the gap between Puerto Ricans and Mexicans was widening, a pattern that continued into 2000. Mexican comparative educational attainment levels were getting progressively worse (even though real levels were improving slightly) while Puerto Rican levels were progressively improving.

The ultimate effect of dropping out is apparent by noting the percentage who have not attained a high school diploma. It would be help-

Table 4–5
Percentage Distribution of Selected Adults Aged 25 and over by Highest Level of
School Completed for Selected U.S. Hispanic Origin Groups, 1970–2000

Educational Level	Mexican	Cuban	Puerto Rican
1970			
Less than H.S. diploma	66.6	51.8	74.2
H.S. diploma	29.1	35.6	22.3
College degree or more	4.3	12.6	3.4
1980			
Less than H.S. diploma	60.6	43.0	57.7
H.S. diploma	33.7	39.5	35.9
College degree or more	5.7	17.5	6.3
1990			
Less than H.S. diploma	55.8	43.4	46.6
H.S. diploma	37.9	40.1	43.9
College degree or more	6.3	16.5	9.5
2000			
Less than H.S. diploma	49.0	27.0	35.7
H.S. diploma	44.1	50.0	51.4
College degree or more	6.9	23.0	13.0

Sources: Bean and Tienda 1987, 238; U.S. Bureau of the Census 1993d, table 3; U.S. Bureau
of the Census 2001a, table 7.1.

ful if more studies specifically focusing on dropouts included figures for
each of our Hispanic groups. One such study, the High School and Beyond study, was done in 1980 on sophomores with a 1982 follow-up.
This study determined that the "dropout rate for Puerto Ricans aged 14
to 30 was over 2.5 times that for their Cuban counterparts (31% versus
12%). Mexican American youth showed a 27% dropout rate" (Fernandez, Paulsen, and Hirano-Nakanishi 1989, 22). Their results appear to
present a different picture from our other educational data. The U.S.
Census Bureau data indicated that the Mexican dropout rate was not
decreasing as quickly as that of Puerto Ricans and had surpassed the
Puerto Rican dropout rate by 1980. This study, however, indicates that
Puerto Ricans have a higher dropout rate. However, the High School
and Beyond study included U.S. students only. Mexicans continue to
immigrate in large numbers, and the lower educational levels of the

Mexican foreign born more than offset the slightly higher percentage of U.S.-educated Puerto Rican dropouts.

None of the figures compiled regarding human capital variables—nativity, English proficiency, or educational attainment—explain why Puerto Ricans have the lowest median family income and the highest rate of poverty of the three Hispanic groups. In fact, nativity and English proficiency point to Cuban hindrances. The Mexican foreign-born percentage is quickly overtaking that of Puerto Ricans, and Puerto Rican English proficiency is already ahead of that of Mexicans. With education, Cubans do come out on top, but again, from 1970 to 2000 Puerto Ricans surpassed Mexicans in their educational levels. There is no doubt that poor educational attainment by Puerto Ricans (regardless of Mexican low levels) is a factor in their economic problems, but something else must also be taking place. Certainly this analysis indicates that the answers to Puerto Rican poverty are *not* primarily to be found in the characteristics of the individuals. Therefore, it is time to look at yet another framework to help us understand what is happening, and that is the labor force structure of the three groups.

Labor Force Structure

The major focus of this discussion is employment status—employed, unemployed, or not in the labor force. Each of these figures is important. However, we will also look at the sources of income for each group as well as the number of workers per family in each group to help us better disentangle all the factors involved in determining a group's economic status.

Employment Status

When we talk about unemployment rates, we often don't realize how that figure is calculated. The base figure for this calculation is the total of all people age sixteen and over (because in most states children under the age of sixteen either cannot work or have severe legal restrictions placed on their right to work). This group is then broken down into three categories: those working for the military, the civilian labor force, and those civilians who are not in the labor force. The civilian labor force is then subdivided between employed and unemployed. The unemployment rate is calculated as the percent of the civilian labor force that is unemployed. There are two major problems with this. First, the calculation does not take into consideration the underemployed, or those who work part time or work only seasonally. With the transition from a manufacturing to a service-based economy, underemployment has become a major issue. The other problem with the unemployment calculation is that more and more people are becoming "discouraged workers." These are people who have been out of work for a long time and have become so discouraged that they left the labor force and are no longer counted in the base civilian labor force figures. Normally the "not in labor force" figures have included young people still in school, women who either do not have to work because their husband supports the family or who choose not to work to care for children, older people who have retired, disabled people who cannot work, and so forth. With the inclusion of discouraged workers who really would like to work but cannot find a job, however, the "not in labor force" figures actually act to hide the true unemployment rates.

Regardless of the above objections, the unemployment rates are still important in our overall comparisons. In looking at 1970 through 2000, Puerto Ricans have had the highest unemployment rate of all three groups in every decennial census. Their unemployment rate in 2000 was 8.1 percent, compared with 7.0 percent for Mexicans and 5.9 percent for Cubans.

Along with the highest unemployment rates, Puerto Ricans in 1990 also had the highest "not in labor force" rates. This was true whether we look at the population as a whole or just at women. However, this seems to be changing, which is a hopeful sign for Puerto Ricans.

Cubans had a higher not-in-labor-force percent in 2000 as a whole, with Puerto Ricans in second place, but the percent of women not in the labor force for Puerto Ricans was actually the lowest of the three groups. Conversely, the Puerto Rican male not-in-labor-force percent was the highest of the three groups by quite a bit, so this problem may not be improving as much as it is changing in nature.

Income Sources

A trend has been found that "Puerto Ricans who work do quite well, but an increasing share have no job at all. This suggests a pattern of social and economic bifurcation" (Gill, Glazer, and Thernstrom 1992, 378). Public assistance and other types of government programs generally do not provide as high a level of income as wage earnings. Table 4–6 allows us to see how our three groups compare concerning various types of income.

First we should mention that within each group the figures do not total 100 percent. That is because many households have more than one type of income. Still, we see that Puerto Ricans have the lowest percentage of households with earnings income (meaning that at least one person in the household has a job). However, those who do have workers average more money than Mexican households with workers. Puerto Ricans also have, by far, the highest percentage of households with public assistance income. This high number is not to be misconstrued as meaning that Puerto Ricans want to be on welfare. Remember our discussion about that issue in Chapter 3: the dependency of the Puerto Rican people, both here and on the island, is an outgrowth of the colonial nature of U.S.–Puerto Rican relations. The mean public assistance income for Puerto Ricans is higher than that of the other two groups, which reflects the relatively higher benefits allotted in the Northeast (Aponte 1991), where Puerto Ricans have settled. However, it is still extremely low—only $4,843—and more than one-quarter of Puerto Rican households rely on public assistance to some degree. The significance of this phenomenon lies in the fact that "increased welfare dependency is accompanied by equally striking rates of income poverty exhibited by Puerto Rican families with single heads" (Tienda and Jensen 1988, 43).

Why do so many Puerto Ricans rely on such low welfare payments,

Table 4–6
Percent Distribution by Income Source for Selected U.S. Hispanic Origin Groups, 1990

Households	Mexicans	Cubans	Puerto Ricans
% with earnings income	88.8	82.1	75.5
Mean earnings income	$29,722	$39,455	$30,973
% with social security income	13.9	23.8	14.7
Mean social security income	$ 6,146	$ 6,651	$ 5,715
% with public assistance income	12.5	15.2	26.9
Mean public assistance income	$ 4,376	$ 4,286	$ 4,843
% with retirement income	7.5	9.7	7.2
Mean retirement income	$ 6,782	$ 5,825	$ 6,814

Source: U.S. Bureau of the Census 1993d, table 5.

when those who work tend to do fairly well? This is difficult to explain apart from the possibility that there are just not enough jobs to service Puerto Ricans. The lower percentages of Puerto Rican households with earnings income and the higher percentages of Puerto Rican households with public assistance income is another indication that employment access issues exist.

We also wonder at the level of poverty among Mexican families, yet relatively few Mexican households have public assistance income. "Many more Mexican families in poverty have members in the work force than do poor Puerto Rican families, while a substantially higher proportion of the latter group receive government assistance" (Aponte 1991, 521). This phenomenon indicates that there may be a difference in the kind of poverty in the two groups, with Mexicans having more "working poor" and Puerto Ricans having more "dependent poor."

Number of Workers

Along with reviewing earnings income for each group, we want to look at how many people are involved in earning that money. The census provides figures for families with no workers, one worker, two workers, or three or more workers. Puerto Ricans have twice the percentage of families with no workers at all than Cubans do, and even more than twice the figure for Mexicans. Puerto Ricans also have a far lower percentage of families with two, or three, or more workers.

Our earlier figures for earnings income were for households with workers and now we're looking at families with workers, yet we can still combine what we've learned—Puerto Rican households with workers do better than Mexicans, and Puerto Rican families have fewer workers than Mexicans—and we are once again struck by the fact that Puerto Ricans who work do relatively well. Each Puerto Rican worker would have to earn more than each Mexican worker by quite a bit to achieve the higher mean household earnings income exhibited in Table 4–6.

Conclusion to Part I

Part I addressed the issue of how Puerto Ricans fare in relationship to the other two major Hispanic national groups in the U.S.—Mexicans and Cubans. We traced the histories of each group as well as discerning when, where, and why each group settled in the United States. We noted how different the journeys of each group were and speculated that these experiences would lead to different outcomes for each group.

This chapter then documented the economic outcomes and began the process of trying to understand exactly what was happening to cause the differences. We did not find human capital factors to be particularly helpful in explaining why the economic outcomes of each group varied the way they did. We found more assistance in this effort by looking at labor force structure.

We next shift the focus of our comparisons. We have completed our discussion of Mexicans and Cubans and will look only at Puerto Ricans for the remaining two parts of this book. In Part II we will compare Puerto Ricans from different areas in the country to determine how much the settlement area affects Puerto Rican chances of succeeding in this country.

Viewing Puerto Ricans Across the United States

5

How Puerto Ricans Fare from Place to Place

As we saw in Part I of this book, Puerto Ricans have a different history from that of other Hispanic groups in the United States, which has led to a difference in how they have fared socioecomonically in this country. What does that mean exactly? Are Puerto Ricans in the United States doomed to remain "low man on the totem pole"? Are all Puerto Ricans facing the same problems? Have Puerto Ricans been taking steps to improve their situation? These are all important questions to ask if we want to understand why Puerto Ricans are having so much difficulty advancing in this country.

Suppose we could show that Puerto Ricans who live in some parts of the country do much better than those who live in other parts of the country. Might this indicate that factors outside of the people themselves influence their ability to succeed and that we should probe deeper to understand what's going on?

This chapter compares various socioeconomic indicators of Puerto Ricans at both the regional and metropolitan levels to document that, indeed, Puerto Rican well-being does vary from place to place. Next we will begin our probe to try to understand what outside factors are at play. Chapter 6 will further explore the internal migration patterns discussed in Chapter 3. We want to learn whether migration is being used as a means of upgrading socioeconomic position or whether it represents a "skimming" of those already doing better. Chapter 7 will explore how residential segregation interacts with socioeconomic indicators to affect overall well-being. The final chapter of Part II, Chapter 8, will take a special look at the role of Puerto Rican women culturally and economically to see how historical changes in their roles have interacted with other dynamics to produce the feminization of poverty in this group.

How We Made Comparisons

The 1990 U.S. census identified forty-two Metropolitan Statistical Areas (MSAs) with a Puerto Rican population of at least 10,000. Of these, forty met the criteria to be included in the One Percent Public Use Microdata Sample (PUMS), meaning that of 10,000 people approximately 100 were chosen for the sample (U.S. Bureau of the Census 1992). The listing of these MSAs is included as Appendix 1. Because this sample includes children, we actually had as few as forty-nine adults (those age 18 or older) selected for one MSA, and the samples for eighteen of the MSAs included less than one hundred adults. These small sample sizes pose some problems when we analyze the data, but we will let you know where those problems occur.

When we make regional comparisons, we will use the totals, percentages, or averages of the selected MSAs in those regions. It will also be important at times to be aware of the differences between the MSAs within each region. Also, we should keep in mind that the Rust Belt (made up of the Northeast and Midwest regions) has suffered much more from the overall U.S. economic transition from a manufacturing to a service-oriented economy than the Sun Belt (the South and the West). Now, with the technical explanations out of the way, let's begin trying to make sense out of what is going on in U.S. Puerto Rican communities.

Socioeconomic Comparisons

When addressing Puerto Rican income level, we will again use median family income as our measure. We will also average the median family incomes from the selected MSAs of each region and then compare those averages.

The cost of living varies significantly from region to region, so we want to find a way to take this into account and make our comparisons more meaningful. Because we generally judge how well an ethnic group does by how it stacks up against the white majority, we will develop an indicator that looks at Puerto Rican income as a percentage of non-Hispanic white (called simply "white" from here on) income in each MSA. For example, if the white median family income for a particular place is $30,000 and the Puerto Rican median family income is $15,000, our income indicator would be 50 percent, meaning that Puerto Rican median income is only half of the white median income in that area. Santiago and Galster (1995) also used this method of controlling for regional differences.

Another important economic indicator is poverty, and we will examine poverty levels of our Puerto Rican populations to determine the depth of the economic problems they face across the nation. Finally, we will look at the instances of female-headed families. We found in Chapter 4 that Puerto Ricans in the United States have a much higher rate of female-headed families than do Mexicans or Cubans. Does this hold true in all Puerto Rican communities, or is it primarily confined to communities suffering from other socioeconomic woes?

Median Family Income

As we look at the median family incomes of the regions, we notice something unusual (see Figure 5–1). The average median family incomes for Puerto Ricans in the Northeast and Midwest (Rust Belt) are much lower than those in the South and West (Sun Belt). The Northeast's average Puerto Rican median family income was only $18,708 and the Midwest's was $19,740. However, the South's was more than $23,000 and the West's was above $26,500.

Our immediate response is that Puerto Ricans seem to do much better in the South and the West. However, one of the features of the overall U.S. economic transformation is that it affects MSAs unevenly, depending on how dependent an area was on manufacturing. This means that median family income might vary quite a bit between MSAs within any one region.

Let's take another look at the Northeast. Puerto Rican median family incomes vary from $7,842 in Buffalo to $35,000 in Orange County.

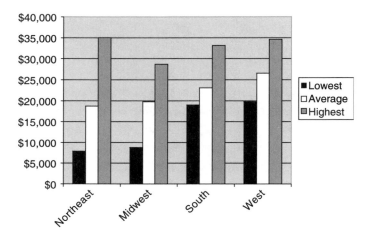

Figure 5-1: Puerto Rican Median Family Income of Selected Metropolitan Areas in the U.S. by Region, 1989

Even though the average Puerto Rican median family income in the Northeast is the lowest of that in all regions, Orange County had the highest median family income of any of the forty MSAs we selected. This shows us that there is a huge range of possibilities within the Northeast. Again looking at Figure 5–1, we can see the lowest and highest figures for each region. We can also see that the ranges (between the MSA within the region that has the lowest median family income and the one with the highest median family income) in these figures for the Rust Belt regions are much larger than the ranges for the two Sun Belt regions. This agrees with what we stated earlier about the economic transformation unevenly affecting the Rust Belt regions.

We already noted that comparisons between median family incomes can be deceptive because of the cost of living differences between areas. For example, the high cost of housing in New York City pushes its cost of living way up, whereas housing in Philadelphia, just two hours away, is relatively inexpensive. Both these major cities are in the Northeast, so perhaps our range is more a matter of cost-of-living differences than of incomes. To see whether this is the case, let's look at the indicator we mentioned earlier that compares Puerto Rican median income to white median income (see Figure 5–2).

When we compare our two graphs, we notice some differences be-

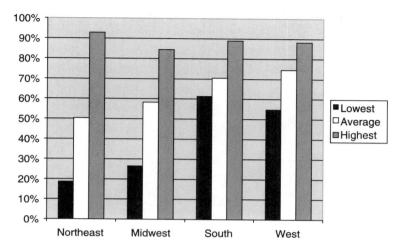

Figure 5-2: Puerto Rican Median Family Income as a Percent of White Median Family Income of Selected Metropolitan Areas in the U.S. by Region, 1989

tween our two indicators, but we find the same overall pattern. The average figures are significantly lower for regions in the Rust Belt than they are for those in the Sun Belt, and the ranges are more extreme in the Rust Belt regions.

What could be causing these differences? One response might be that because the majority (twenty-four) of our MSAs are in the Northeast, we should expect more variation there. This may be true, but the Midwest has only five MSAs and exhibits the same large range of incomes.

Another explanation may be found in the fact that two MSAs in the Northeast have no central city (in other words, they are considered 100 percent suburban). One of these is Orange County, which is the MSA with both the highest median family income and the highest control percentage. That might make us think the range is skewed because of the inclusion of these areas. However, the MSA with the second highest control percentage (78.6 percent) is Atlantic City, New Jersey, an economically specialized city that also has the fourth highest Puerto Rican median family income. Trenton, New Jersey, the state capital, has the third highest actual median family income. Taking all this information into consideration, we have to conclude that skewing from the suburban-only MSAs is too simple an explanation.

The Midwest also shows a large range of incomes and control percentages, and none of the Midwest MSAs are suburban only. Surprisingly, all five Midwest MSAs—Chicago, Cleveland, Detroit, Lorain (Ohio), and Milwaukee—have been highly dependent on heavy industry. Therefore, the economic transformation alone does not seem to be the entire answer to our question of why such large ranges in economic well-being exist in the Rust Belt.

We seem to be raising more questions than we are finding answers. By the end of our investigation, however, we hope to have a better handle on what all this information means.

Poverty

No query into economic well-being is complete without looking at poverty figures. Massey and Eggers (1990), in their study on income inequality, separated families into "poor" (at or below poverty level), "lower-middle class" (101–199 percent of the poverty level), "upper-middle class" (200–399 percent of the poverty level), and "affluent" (400 percent or more of the poverty level).

We use the same percentage breakdowns but will apply slightly different labels. We call the lowest category "poverty." We do not agree with the designation of "lower-middle class" because 101–199 percent of the poverty level is still barely enough to live on. Remember our discussion in Chapter 4, which showed that even some government programs (e.g., LIHEAP, a program that offers assistance for heating bills during the winter months) use 150 percent of the poverty level as the cutoff line for providing assistance. Therefore, for our purposes we use the term "low-income" for the category of 101–199 percent of the poverty level.

Another difference we make is that because there are relatively so few "affluent" Puerto Rican families, we combine all those with 200 percent or greater of the poverty level and call them "middle-income." Therefore, we have divided our families into "poverty," "low-income," and "middle-income." These are the categories used in Table 5–1.

Labels can be a bit confusing, so let's try to understand what we are attempting to show in Table 5–1. First, there are higher levels of poverty in the two Rust Belt regions, with the Northeast being the highest. The difference between these percentages is quite large—the percentage in

Table 5-1
Percent of Puerto Rican Families by Income Levels in Selected U.S. Metropolitan
Areas by Region, 1989

Income Level	Northeast	Midwest	South	West
Poverty	37.8	33.3	21.7	20.8
Low-income	20.0	22.5	22.9	23.1
Middle-income	42.2	44.2	55.5	56.1
Highest percent in poverty in an MSA	63.2	47.3	34.8	30.3
Lowest percent in poverty in an MSA	6.8	30.2	8.1	11.2
Range of MSA percents in poverty	56.4	17.1	26.7	19.1

Source: U.S. Census 1990 PUMS, 1-Percent Sample.

the Northeast (37.8 percent) is 17 points above that of the West (20.8 percent). When we look at the middle category of "low-income," we find very little variation, but the "middle-income" category again varies considerably.

When we look at the MSAs within regions, we find that the Northeast contains both the MSA with the lowest percentage of poverty (6.8 percent in Atlantic City) and the one with the highest percentage 63.2 percent in Springfield, Massachusetts). The variation occurs between MSAs both within and between states. In Connecticut, for example, half of Waterbury's Puerto Rican population is in poverty, whereas Hartford and New Haven have relatively low poverty percentages of 26.6 and 28.5, respectively. Once again we realize that the local setting is the place where we will find the best explanations.

Female-Headed Families

In the literature, the incidence of female-headed families is often connected to economic difficulties (Tienda 1985, 66). Looking at our own sample of Puerto Ricans, we found that the correlation (Pearson's R correlation, significant at the .001 level) between female-headed families and percentage of persons in poverty is .7989, a very high correlation indeed. Therefore, we want to take a brief look at this phenomenon before leaving the socioeconomic indicator section.

Generally speaking, the patterns we have found with income and poverty levels also hold true for female-headed families. The Northeast stands out because it has the highest overall percent and the highest variations between MSAs. Although the suburban-only MSAs, as expected, have lower percentages of Puerto Rican female-headed families than most, the MSA with the lowest rate is Trenton, New Jersey (15.1 percent), although this may be one of those places where the small number of adults sampled (58) may not have been truly representative of the total population. Five of the six MSAs with the highest percentages of female-headed families (all higher than 50 percent) are in Connecticut and Massachusetts. New York City, as we would expect, was not far behind, with 47.9 percent of its Puerto Rican families headed by females.

If we compare just the four regions in our analysis to this point, we have not found any surprises. However, it has become increasingly clear that Puerto Ricans fare quite differently from metropolitan area to metropolitan area within the same region and even within the same state. Now, let's continue our exploration.

General Population Characteristics

As we mentioned in Chapter 4, it is always important to look at human capital factors when analyzing a group's socioeconomic standing. Therefore, we now turn to the issues of nativity, English proficiency, and education to see how Puerto Rican communities vary across the United States. Because we will be looking at a number of different breakdowns, be aware that that our small samples may mislead us. Therefore, we will make regional comparisons but not MSA comparisons.

Nativity

First we need to understand the idea behind "native born" versus "foreign born." Remember that Puerto Rico is part of the United States so almost all Puerto Ricans are considered "native born" in the U.S. census. This means we have to be a little more creative in how we determine nativity. One question on the census asks where you were born. We will take the answers to that question and calculate the percentages of those born on the mainland, those born in Puerto Rico, and those born elsewhere (although this small category is used only so the totals equal 100 percent).

Figure 5–3 provides some unexpected and interesting findings. Presumably the areas that have the highest level of mainland-born Puerto Ricans should be those with the highest socioeconomic standings. This holds true in the West. With almost 70 percent of its Puerto Rican population born on the mainland, it does indeed do comparatively well economically. However, the South also does quite well, and it has a much smaller percentage of mainland-born Puerto Ricans than any other area. We have to conclude that nativity may be important, but obviously other, more important factors are at work. Because most of the southern MSAs included in our study are found in Florida, we could speculate that the Cuban enclave provides a relatively friendly setting for those coming straight from Puerto Rico. We'll talk about this more in Chapter 6.

A second aspect in understanding how nativity works is the timing of the major migration flows. This is important for two reasons. First, if the migration flow from Puerto Rico is more recent, they have had relatively less time to establish a second- or third-generation mainland-born population. Second, the more recent the migration flow, the less time the migrants have had to successfully confront the labor force structure. Table 5–2 shows us the decade of arrival from Puerto Rico of first-generation Puerto Ricans currently living in each of the regions.

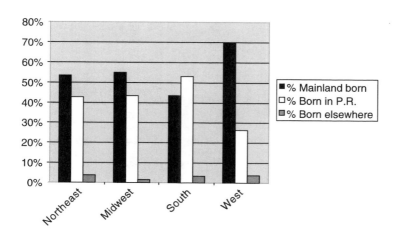

Figure 5-3: U. S. Regional Distribution of Puerto Rican Nativity by Percent, 1990

Once again we notice the relative newness of southern Puerto Ricans, with 45.8 percent of the first generation arriving in the 1980s. Be careful here: we are talking only about first-generation Puerto Ricans. When we look at the entire Puerto Rican population, including those born in the United States, we still find that more than 25 percent of southern Puerto Ricans are new immigrants from Puerto Rico, having arrived in the 1980s. Populations with such a high percentage of newcomers are not expected to do as well as those that are more settled and stable; yet we are finding that just the opposite is true. What can be happening? Let's continue our search.

English Proficiency

Speaking English fluently is closely associated with nativity because those Puerto Ricans who were born and educated on the mainland would undoubtedly be better at speaking English than those coming straight from the island. With the large percentage of island-born Puerto Ricans in the South, we would expect that region to lag behind the others in terms of English proficiency. However, this is not the case.

To get a good profile of each region's English-speaking ability, we will look at three different indicators: the percent of persons over the age of five who speak English "very well," the percent of households that speak Spanish at home, and the percent of households that are linguistically isolated. (This third indicator was explained in chapter 4.) Table 5–3 shows us the percentages.

All three of our indicators show that the South and the West are fa-

Table 5-2

U.S. Regional Percentages of First-Generation Puerto Ricans as of 1990 by Decade of Arrival

Decade of Arrival	Northeast	Midwest	South	West
1980s	29.0	32.5	45.8	26.5
1970s	17.4	21.0	19.0	19.9
1960s	22.3	20.4	12.4	18.6
1950s	21.1	22.1	13.4	20.3
pre-1950s	10.3	4.1	9.4	14.7

Source: U.S. Census 1990 PUMS, 1-Percent Sample.

Table 5-3
U.S. Puerto Rican English Proficiency Indicators by Region, 1990

Language Indicator	Northeast	Midwest	South	West
% Persons age 5 or over who speak English "very well"	57.8	56.1	63.1	62.8
% Households that speak Spanish at home	91.8	91.5	89.3	71.9
% Households that are linguistically isolated	26.4	22.8	16.5	15.5

Source: U.S. Census 1990 PUMS, 1-Percent Sample.

vored over the Northeast and Midwest in terms of English proficiency. The South and the West have higher percentages of Puerto Ricans who speak English "very well," lower percentages of households that speak Spanish in the home, and lower percentages of linguistically isolated households. When we realize how many Puerto Ricans in the South were born in Puerto Rico and how recent their migration is, we are surprised at how well they speak English. We do find a high percentage of households that speak Spanish at home, but this has not hurt their ability to speak English elsewhere, nor has it resulted in a large percentage of linguistically isolated households. At this point we can only wonder why these newcomers are so proficient in English, but in Chapter 6 we will add some more insight to the issue.

Education

Traditionally, first-generation (or foreign-born) populations have lower educational levels than do native-born groups. The new immigration laws detailed in Chapter 1 have changed this to some extent. Because the United States now favors professionals rather than laborers, new immigrants may actually have higher educational levels than those who have been in the United States for a number of decades. (See Goode and Schneider [1994] for an example of the tensions caused among established immigrants when new, more highly educated professional immigrants join their communities.) However, remember that the immigration laws do not affect Puerto Ricans. We would still anticipate areas with high percentages of newer groups to have lower educational levels. We would also anticipate lower educational levels to translate into lower socioeconomic levels. Let's take a look at regional levels of educational attainment of Puerto Ricans in Table 5–4.

We are not surprised that the Northeast and Midwest have high percentages of dropouts and low percentages of those with higher education degrees. This does indeed correspond with the lower income levels found in these regions. The South and the West do much better both educationally and economically—gain, no surprises. But what about all the newcomer Puerto Ricans in the South? We already saw that their English proficiency is much higher than we would normally expect for newcomers. Now we see that their educational levels are also higher. In fact, the South is the region with the highest percentage of those with college degrees or higher—13.6 percent.

Bean and Tienda note, "Completing high school is the most important transition in the formal schooling process" (1987, 270). Therefore, the dropout figures are extremely important. We notice that more than half the Puerto Ricans (age 25 and older) in both the Northeast and Midwest have dropped out of school before graduating. Only about a third of those in the South and the West have dropped out. This certainly goes along with our economic findings but still leaves us confused regarding the newness of southern Puerto Ricans. It seems that, for Puerto Ricans, educational attainment is much more important in determining economic well-being than nativity is.

Educational attainment is a characteristic, like English proficiency, that requires at least some degree of motivation. In general, the moti-

Table 5–4
U.S. Regional Distribution of Puerto Rican Educational Attainment
(Age 25 and over), 1990

Percent by Highest Level of Education Attained	Northeast	Midwest	South	West
% "Dropout"	53.5	55.6	34.3	31.2
% High school diploma	40.0	38.2	52.1	59.0
% Bachelor's degree	3.8	3.9	10.4	6.6
% Graduate/prof. degree	2.7	2.3	3.2	3.3

Source: U.S. Census 1990 PUMS, 1-Percent Sample.

vation is economic. People go further in school because they want to get better-paying jobs. But is this always true? Do people always find better-paying jobs when they get more education? We may be quick to say this is true of Puerto Ricans, because we showed that, on the regional level, education and income levels seem to be related, but then why are some of the oldest Puerto Rican settlements still lagging behind in terms of education?

A number of hypotheses suggest why Puerto Ricans are not pursuing education. One of these deals with the ethnocentricity of schools, particularly institutions of higher learning. "[There is] a strong need among many Puerto Rican youth to maintain their cultural and linguistic identity. . . . They want desperately to develop skills that will enable them to live useful, rewarding lives, but they want to do so without having their values and heritage ridiculed and denied" (U.S. Commission on Civil Rights 1976, 129).

Bean and Tienda also express concern for developing "a culturally sensitive educational environment" (1987, 277). The lack of such an environment can act as a disincentive, even if payoffs are reasonably high.

Another hypothesis is that Puerto Ricans do not stay in school longer because they do not perceive significant payoffs for the additional time in school. In short, they do not see a big enough difference in their paychecks to warrant all the time and expense of furthering their education. If they can't do better with more education, why not just go to work and at least start earning money sooner? Rodriguez (1989) expresses concern about the earning gaps by educational level between whites and Hispanics. She notes that these gaps get even larger at the higher levels of schooling. In addition, Neidert and Tienda found that "Puerto Rican men received rather high returns to college education" (1984, 317). Both these findings need to be substantiated. Reviewing this information by region will also be helpful.

Table 5–5 looks very complicated at first glance, but let's go through it section by section and try to understand what is happening. The first section of the table simply is the average amount of wages (not total income) Puerto Ricans age 25 and older can make at different educational levels across the country. Not surprisingly, wages increase as education increases for all four regions. Puerto Ricans in the West do better than those in the other regions at all four levels of education, which may have

Table 5-5

U.S. Puerto Rican Mean Wage Statistics by Educational Attainment
(Age 25 and over) and Region, 1990

Mean Wage Statistic	Northeast	Midwest	South	West
P.R. Mean Wage in Dollars				
"Dropout"	$15,673	$15,653	$12,156	$17,908
High school diploma	$20,806	$18,882	$17,567	$21,357
Bachelor's degree	$27,811	$23,195	$25,901	$32,169
Graduate/prof. degree	$35,877	$28,177	$40,239	$46,464
Puerto Rican Mean Wage				
as %of White Mean Wage				
"Dropout"	78.1	78.7	71.9	86.0
High school diploma	80.6	76.7	74.2	78.8
Bachelor's degree	72.5	64.2	73.6	84.9
Graduate/prof. degree	71.0	57.8	81.4	93.1
% Increase in P.R. Mean				
Wage Between Educational				
Levels				
"Dropout" to H.S.	32.8	20.6	44.5	19.3
H.S. to Bachelor's	33.7	22.8	47.4	50.6
Bach. to Grad./prof.	29.0	21.5	55.4	44.4

Source: U.S. Census 1990 PUMS, 1-Percent Sample.

something to do with cost of living. But the South is the interesting region. For Puerto Rican workers with less than a bachelor's degree, wages in the South are the lowest of all regions; wages start going up for college graduates, however, and increase a great deal more for those with graduate and professional degrees. This trend is interesting in part because of the large percentage of Puerto Ricans in the South who have higher levels of education. We will try to sort this out a little more in Chapter 6.

The second section of this table tries to take the cost of living into consideration. The average wages of Puerto Ricans are displayed as a percentage of the average wages of whites. When compared, and not surprisingly, Puerto Ricans with the same level of education as whites make significantly lower wages. However, the patterns are somewhat different from looking at just the wages themselves. First, the West has by far the best comparative wages of the four regions. At both ends of the spectrum—the dropouts and those with college degrees or more—

the percentages are much higher than in any other region. However, getting a high school diploma does not seem to help very much in the West—Puerto Ricans must get through college to again compare relatively well with their white counterparts. Again we see that the South does not compare well in wages at the lower levels of education but picks up with college and graduate/professional degrees. In the Midwest we find that those with college degrees or more are in a much worse comparative position than in any of the other regions (which can also be seen in the comparisons of average wages). The Northeast has the greatest advantage for those with a high school diploma but no college degree, but then loses its edge.

The third section of this table may be the hardest to understand. It looks at the increase in wages between two educational levels as a percentage of the lower level. The basic idea here is that the higher the percentage, the greater will be the motivation to get more education. For example, in the West there is only a 19.3 percent increase in wages between dropouts and high school graduates with no further education. In the South there is a 44.5 percent increase between those two educational levels. If this were the only factor in motivating people to continue in school, those in the South would be more than twice as motivated as those in the West. However, look at the 50.6 percent increase in the West between high school graduates and those with a college degree (but no postgraduate degree). Again, if this were the only factor involved, we would probably see a large number of people completing high school and then continuing until they receive their bachelor's degree.

Apart from the low increase in the West between dropout and high school graduate, the South and the West offer much better "returns" for education. The Midwest has low returns at all levels, which presumably means that there is very low motivation in the Midwest MSAs for Puerto Ricans to continue with their education.

Overall, we find two patterns emerging. In the South, Puerto Ricans can recognize large gains in their wages by increasing their educational level. Remember that the major internal migration of Puerto Ricans is to the South, primarily Florida. One reason for this movement may be the ability to advance economically. The West does not offer as good an opportunity to advance economically based on education, but it does have the highest wages when compared to the white population. Internal migration to the West may be based on the desire to be better off relative to others in the area. We will discuss this factor more in Chapter 6.

Labor Force Structure

When we compared our three major Hispanic groups in terms of employment, we found large differences. Our contention is that these differences should also be seen in regional comparisons of Puerto Ricans, and they are, as shown in Table 5–6.

Both the unemployment rate and the percent of Puerto Ricans age 16 and over who are not in the labor force are significantly higher in the Rust Belt. If we combine the unemployment and nonparticipation rates in the Northeast, we find that 57.5 percent of all Puerto Ricans age 16 and older were not working. The Midwest also had more than 50 percent not working, whereas in the South and the West less than 40 percent of Puerto Ricans were not working.

Conclusion

Throughout this chapter we have reiterated two basic observations. First, there are very distinct differences in the status of Puerto Ricans depending on their region of residence. Puerto Ricans in the Northeast and Midwest are in much worse shape economically as well as in terms of both human capital and labor market structure characteristics. The only finding that poses some perplexity in this chapter is the nativity distribution found in the South, a fact that needs further investigation.

Table 5–6
U.S. Regional Puerto Rican Employment Statistics (Age 16 and over), 1990

	Northeast	Midwest	South	West
% Civilian labor force unemployed	14.1	15.5	8.6	10.0
% Not in the labor force	43.4	36.2	29.0	29.1

Source: U.S. Census 1990 PUMS, 1-Percent Sample.

Our second basic observation is that the Sun Belt regions seem to be fairly uniform in terms of comparing characteristics across the individual MSAs. However, the Rust Belt regions exhibit much more variation. This confirms our supposition that the economic transformation that has hurt the Rust Belt in general has had an uneven effect on Puerto Ricans depending on their MSA of residence. Part III of this book will present MSA case studies in the hope of shedding some light on why this occurs.

Internal Migration: A Response?

hapter 5 documented differences in Puerto Rican experiences depending on place of residence. These differences were seen at both regional and metropolitan levels. We must now ask ourselves some new questions. Why are we seeing such differences? Can Puerto Ricans in depressed areas do better if they move? What are the characteristics of Puerto Ricans who choose to relocate? Do these characteristics differ from those of Puerto Ricans who do not move? Does higher economic attainment in some regions represent better opportunities, or merely the fact that Puerto Rican inmigrants to those areas are better off to begin with? All these questions beg us to explore the concept of selectivity—who moves and why.

We can only begin to address some of these questions. If we think of the fifty states in the United States as well as Puerto Rico, we have fifty-one possible areas to and from which Puerto Ricans can choose to move. We have a way of monitoring such movement by using the U.S. Census.

One question on the census form asked for place of residence in 1985, five years earlier. For our purposes, we decided that Puerto Ricans who remained in the same state from 1985 to 1990 (even if they lived in a different home or different city during that time period) would be called "stayers," meaning they stayed put. If their place of residence in 1985 was in Puerto Rico or a different state from their 1990 residence, we designated them "movers." The matrix of fifty-one by fifty-one yields 2,550 combinations for movers. This large number would not only make analyzing the data a horrendous task but would also result in many empty or meaningless cells. For example, how many Puerto Ricans do you think moved from South Dakota to Hawaii during that five-year period, and if there was only one, what are the chances that that particular Puerto Rican was selected for the one percent sample? Therefore, we needed to have a different approach.

We decided to select only two places from which Puerto Ricans were moving. There were almost 187,000 movers from Puerto Rico to the fifty states, and there were almost 76,000 movers from New York State to other states, representing 34.9 percent of the total number of Puerto Rican interstate movers. New Jersey, with 12.5 percent of the movers, was the only other state that commanded more than 10 percent of all movers. Puerto Rico and New York State are both intuitively and empirically the logical choices for our sending locations. We also decided to divide the data on movers by region according to destination state. This enabled us to determine regional differences in both the outcomes and the human capital characteristics.

We can only cursorily examine selectivity, for a number of reasons. First, we could not use the one percent sample to find the island's stayers because Puerto Rico is not included in it, so we used the printed *1990 Census of Population, Social and Economic Characteristics for Puerto Rico* (U.S. Bureau of Census 1993b). However, using this document meant that we had to look at all 1990 residents regardless of where they lived in 1985.

Second, we maximized our sample size by selecting Puerto Ricans from all U.S. MSAs, rather than just the 40 we have used in previous analyses. We are still concerned about sample size, however, because we selected movers from New York State and Puerto Rico only.

Third, again dealing with sample size, some analyses have inherent selection restrictions (e.g., only age 25 and older for educational attainment analysis). This, too, limits the sample size. In some cases we have had to divide the data into numerous cells (e.g., three educational attainment levels by four regions by two sending locales, for a total of 24 cells). Obviously the potential for small sample numbers for some cells is very much an issue. Therefore, throughout this section all percentages or figures representing a weighted number (n) of less than 500 (roughly equivalent to a sample n of 5 from a one percent sample) will be noted. We are particularly suspicious of our findings regarding New York movers to the Midwest because relatively few took this route. However, even though these sample size issues may hinder our analyses, we believe it will be beneficial in pointing toward an area of worthwhile future research. These technical explanations can be tedious but are important for understanding just how reliable our information is.

We now begin our analysis of movers and stayers by again reviewing socioeconomic status indicators, followed by a description of selected general population characteristics, and finally a look at labor force structure.

Socioeconomic Status Indicators

By this time you are familiar with the indicators we consider to determine socioeconomic status. We will look at three different indicators: median family income, persons in poverty, and female-headed families. For all our analyses, we will compare movers and stayers. We begin by looking at the sending areas and then move on to characteristics found in regional destinations for the two mover groups.

Median Family Income

New York stayers had a median family income of $17,000, whereas the same indicator for residents of Puerto Rico was only $9,988. Table 6–1 shows income levels for our movers.

As can be seen, New York movers seem to have done better than New York stayers if they moved elsewhere in the Northeast or to the Midwest. However, the movers did worse in both the South and West. Movers from Puerto Rico did worse in the Midwest than those staying in Puerto Rico, but they did a little better in the Northeast and made greater gains in the South and West.

Taken by themselves, these data seem difficult to analyze. Taken in conjunction with the data on poverty to be reviewed next, though, a pattern begins to take shape.

Poverty

Both sending locales had extremely high percentages of persons in poverty: New York's rate was 36.0 percent, and Puerto Rico's an as-

Table 6-1

U.S. Regional Median Family Income of Puerto Rican Stayers and Movers from
New York State and Puerto Rico, 1989

	Stayers	Movers to			
		Northeast	Midwest	South	West
New York	$17,000	$19,500	$22,000	$12,000	$11,000
Puerto Rico	$ 9,988	$10,320	$ 7,000	$11,400	$14,000

Sources: U.S. Census 1990 PUMS, 1 Percent Sample; U.S. Bureau of the Census 1993b, table 3.

tounding 58.9 percent. In both situations, movers have lower percentages in poverty regardless of regional destination. New York movers to other states in the Northeast have only a slightly smaller percent in poverty than New York stayers, and New York movers to the Midwest suffer from low sample size. However, New York movers to the South and West, and particularly the West, fare much better. Movers from Puerto Rico, again, do only slightly better in the Northeast, but their largest gain seems to be in the South.

We seem to have two different dynamics going on in Table 6–2. First, even though New York movers take a loss in median family income by going South or West, they seem to make up for this by having a much better chance to escape extreme poverty. Wages are generally lower in the Sun Belt, which can account for some of the decline in income, but apparently the low incomes that movers report are not as difficult to deal with, as is the high poverty level their counterparts face in New York. Movers do not immediately fit into the higher overall Puerto Rican income levels of the South and West that we noted in Chapter 5. However, in comparison to the general Puerto Rican poverty figures in the South and West reported earlier, movers do quite well.

The second dynamic is found with Puerto Rico movers. Neither group of movers seems to do much better by moving elsewhere in the Rust Belt. However, the above analysis seems to indicate that New York movers do the best in the West. Now we will see that the South seems to provide the best scenario for Puerto Rico movers. Again, the key seems to be found in the poverty figures rather than in median family income. Although the income level for Puerto Rico movers is highest in

Table 6-2
U.S. Regional Distribution of Percent of Persons in Poverty for Stayers
and Movers from New York State and Puerto Rico, 1990

| | | **Movers to** | | | |
	Stayers	Northeast	Midwest	South	West
New York	36.0%	35.2%	15.4%	28.4%	18.8%
Puerto Rico	59.9%	50.8%	40.1%	22.5%	39.4%

Sources: U.S. Census 1990 PUMS, 1-Percent Sample; U.S. Bureau of the Census 1993b, table 3.

the West (and higher than that of New York movers), their poverty level in the West is almost 40 percent. In the South, with a slightly lower income level than that of New York movers, the island movers report a much lower poverty level.

One hypothesis is that the labor market structure in the South, and especially in Florida, does not penalize as much for being first generation. This could also account for the place of birth and migration data we noted in Chapter 5, which showed a large percentage of recent migrants from Puerto Rico to the South.

Female-Headed Families

New York stayers reported that single females headed 45.7 percent of their families. Puerto Rico had a much lower percentage of female-headed families at 22.9 percent. As seen in Table 6–3, again we seem to have different patterns depending on the sending community.

New York movers to other parts of the Northeast are similar in family makeup as the stayers. The percentage of female-headed families moving to all other regions, however, is much lower. This, of course, makes some sense in that it would be financially more difficult for single-female heads of families to relocate, especially to distant regions. The issue of support systems is probably also a factor, because single-female heads may need the support of extended family members more than do married-couple families, who have each other. Regardless of the reason, the selectivity is clear.

Movers from Puerto Rico, however, present a curious pattern. A much higher number of female-headed families are moving to the Northeast

Table 6-3

U.S. Regional Distribution of Percent of Families Headed by Females for Stayers and Movers from New York State and Puerto Rico, 1990

| | | Movers to | | | |
	Stayers	Northeast	Midwest	South	West
New York	45.7%	46.1%	24.9%	22.3%	29.8%
Puerto Rico	22.9%	48.7%	39.9%	11.5%	18.7%

Sources: U.S. Census 1990 PUMS, 1-Percent Sample; U.S. Bureau of the Census 1993b, table 9.

and Midwest than are in the island population in general. In addition, the percentage of female-headed families going to the South is only equal to half the percentage of female-headed families on the island. The rationale here most likely lies in the relatively more generous welfare benefits of the Rust Belt. Female-headed families are among the poorest families, and life on the island can be extremely difficult for them. Even though they may remain in poverty, they may perceive that the welfare levels provided in the Rust Belt will still be better than what the island has to offer them.

General Population Characteristics

We have seen that outcome levels, especially for persons in poverty, seem to favor movers from both sending locales. However, the gains are not evenly reported across regions: the West is most favorable for movers from New York, and the South is most favorable for movers from Puerto Rico.

By looking at differences in nativity, English proficiency, and education of stayers and movers, we hope to start sorting out any selectivity characteristics of the migrants.

Nativity

Our primary concern with reviewing nativity is to determine the percentage of the various populations that were born in the United States. More than half (52.4 percent) of our New York stayers were born in the United States. The census reports that 6.5 percent (more than 230,000) residents of Puerto Rico were born in the U.S. Some of these are American businessmen and their families who moved to Puerto Rico, but most of these reflect the return (or back and forth) migration detailed in Part I. Table 6–4 shows the nativity of our movers.

If we first look at New York movers, we see an interesting pattern. There is very little difference in nativity makeup between New York stayers and New York movers to other areas in the Northeast. New York movers to the Midwest actually have a lower percentage of U.S.-born; however, when looking at the South and the West, New York movers definitely include an overrepresentation of U.S.-born. This makes sense if we understand the risks involved in moving great distances to regions that afford different labor market opportunities. Those born in the U.S. are less intimidated by these risks because they are more familiar with the United States in general. Also, they are not as dependent on established communities to maintain strong ethnic ties because they are generally more "Americanized."

Although most of our movers from Puerto Rico were not born in this country, movers to all four regions contain significantly more U.S.-born individuals than the general island population—almost four times higher than in the West. It is not our intention to deal at great length with migration issues per se, but we ought to at least point out the curiously high percentage of U.S.-born movers who went to the Midwest. Without doing a detailed analysis, we venture to say that the South (particularly Florida) and the Northeast are more "natural" migration routes for Puerto Rican movers born on the island. Therefore, the Midwest

Table 6–4
U.S. Regional Distribution of U.S.-Born Puerto Rican Stayers and Movers from New York State and Puerto Rico, 1990

| | | **Movers to** | | |
	Stayers	Northeast	Midwest	South	West
New York	52.4%	54.7%	48.9%	59.2%	64.4%
Puerto Rico	6.5%	11.3%	21.1%	12.2%	25.3%

Sources: U.S. Census 1990 PUMS, 1-Percent Sample; U.S. Bureau of the Census 1993b, table 4.

and West attract higher percentages of those who have at least some level of comfort in U.S. society: those who were born here.

English Language Proficiency

English is still a second language for most Puerto Ricans, regardless of where they live or settle. However, 60.6 percent of New York stayers responded to the census that they spoke English "very well." We would expect English to be used less in Puerto Rico, and indeed it is, but still almost a quarter (23.6 percent) of island residents age five or older speak English "very well." With these percentages as our base, we can review the English abilities of our two mover groups as laid out in Table 6–5.

Although all New York mover groups report better English proficiency than New York stayers, the group moving to the Midwest is only slightly more fluent, and mover groups to the other three regions seem to be evenly advantaged in this characteristic. However, the same is not true of movers from Puerto Rico. Again, mover groups to all four regions have a language advantage over the residents of Puerto Rico, but the groups going to the South and West are decidedly better off linguistically than those going to the Northeast and Midwest.

We see two types of selectivity taking place here. The first is a general upgrading of English proficiency when comparing movers to stayers. The second is selectivity within Puerto Rico movers based on destination region, with the South and West commanding higher levels of proficiency.

Table 6–5

U.S. Regional Distribution of Percent of Stayers and Movers from New York State and Puerto Rico Who Speak English "Very Well," 1990

	Stayers	Movers to			
		Northeast	Midwest	South	West
New York	60.0%	68.0%	61.8%	68.9%	70.9%
Puerto Rico	23.6%	29.3%	28.5%	42.4%	40.7%

Sources: U.S. Census 1990 PUMS, 1-Percent Sample; U.S. Bureau of the Census 1993b, table 5.

Educational Attainment

In reviewing educational attainment, we need to keep in mind the over-all low numbers of college graduates. Therefore, to maximize the number of cells with significant figures, we do not distinguish between those with a bachelor's degree and those with a graduate or professional degree. We will instead use only three levels of attainment—dropout, high school diploma, and college degree or more.

Of our New York stayers, 53.0 percent are dropouts, 40.9 percent attained a high school diploma but no college degree, and only 6.1 percent have a college degree or more. Amazingly, this is a worse distribution than on the island itself, where 50.3 percent are dropouts (slightly less than the percentage among New York stayers), 35.4 percent attained a high school diploma but no college degree, and 14.3 percent have at least a college degree (more than twice the percentage of New York stayers). One explanation for the higher education level difference on the island stems from the return migration dynamic. Dominguez (1975) explains how lower-class migrants from the island make gains in the United States and return to the island as part of the middle class.

Table 6–6 shows the educational attainment levels for our two mover groups. So few of the New York movers to the Midwest met our selection criteria that we will concentrate on the other three areas only.

New York movers obviously have a much lower percentage of dropouts and a much higher percentage of those with a high school diploma but no college degree than New York stayers. This seems to be where the selectivity occurs, with a slightly better distribution in the South. When it comes to those with a college degree or more, however, the main area of selectivity seems to be closer to home, namely, other states in the Northeast. Morales (1986) describes how professionals moved from New York to New England to service Puerto Rican communities there. Although the small numbers of college graduates picked up for the West may dictate caution in relying on this distribution, it is obvious that the most educated New York movers did not elect to go South or West in disproportionate numbers. High school diploma movers more disproportionately going South than West could be related to the higher rate of wage returns to education between the dropout and high school levels of attainment found in the South (see Chapter 5).

Table 6-6

U.S. Regional Distribution of Educational Attainment Levels for Stayers and Movers from New York State and Puerto Rico, 1990

Educational Attainment	Stayers	Movers to			
		Northeast	Midwest	South	West
New York					
Dropout	53.0%	35.8%	46.6%*	36.2%	43.6%
H.S. Dipl.	40.9%	51.3%	36.4%*	57.7%	50.6%
College+	6.1%	12.9%	17.0%*	6.1%	5.8%
Puerto Rico					
Dropout	50.3%	56.1%	62.5%	24.8%	19.9%
H.S. Dipl.	35.4%	33.4%	24.7%	53.8%	62.9%
College+	14.3%	10.6%	12.8%	21.5%	17.1%

*Cell had weighted n less than 500.

Sources: U.S. Census 1990 PUMS, 1-Percent Sample; U.S. Bureau of the Census 1993b, table 1.

Puerto Rico movers present an interesting situation. Dropouts seem to be overrepresented among movers to the Northeast and Midwest, whereas among movers to the South and West a large underrepresentation is apparent in dropouts, with high percentages at the high school level and comparatively high percentages at the college or more level. This disparity seems to represent both negative selection to the Rust Belt and positive selection to the Sun Belt, making the overall differences between these mover groups quite large indeed.

All these numbers can be mind-boggling. We will try to summarize our findings in the conclusion to this chapter.

Labor Force Structure

We have reviewed regional differences in economic outcomes as well as some dynamics of selective migration to advantageous areas. However, regardless of human capital level or more advantageous economic conditions, if the movers cannot find a place within the labor force structure, they will find no gain in moving. Therefore, before we leave this chapter, we want to study unemployment and labor participation rates.

New York stayers had an unemployment rate of 13.1 percent, with 46.0 percent not in the labor force. In Puerto Rico, the situation was even worse: an unemployment rate of 20.4 percent and a very large 52.7 percent not even in the labor force. Table 6–7 shows these figures for our movers.

New York movers to other areas in the Northeast had a slightly better employment situation than stayers but still had the highest percent not in the labor force of all the New York mover groups. Those going to the South had the same rate of unemployment but a much lower percentage not in the labor force than the stayers. Although our analysis of the Midwest and West suffers from small cell sizes, we believe that two different dynamics are occurring. First, the Midwest has too few movers included from which to select, but the questionable conclusion is that unemployment is a serious issue for them. However, the migration size to the West is not as much a problem to our analysis as there being so few who were unemployed or not in the labor force. Even though we cannot rely on the low figures for the West, the indication is that the West holds out the best employment scenario for New York movers, a fact that agrees with our previous analyses.

Table 6–7
U.S. Regional Labor Statistics for Puerto Rican Stayers and Movers from New York State and Puerto Rico, 1990

Employment Statistics	Stayers	Movers to			
		Northeast	Midwest	South	West
New York					
Unemployed	13.1%	10.6%	30.8%*	13.1%	0.0%*
Not in labor force	46.0%	35.4%	8.7%*	27.4%	18.6%*
Puerto Rico					
Unemployed	20.4%	17.3%	13.2%	9.6%	6.2%*
Not in labor force	52.7%	50.9%	45.6%	32.6%	23.3%

*Cell had weighted n less than 500.

Sources: U.S. Census 1990 PUMS, 1-Percent Sample; U.S. Bureau of the Census 1993b, table 2.

Movers from Puerto Rico do better in the United States, no matter what the region. However, their gains in the Northeast are minimal. Employment and labor force participation prospects seem much better in both the South and the West, and participation in the West is the best. The unemployment figure in the West is unreliable as a result of our sample size constraints.

We've been looking at employment figures for all movers. However, Rivera-Batiz and Santiago have noted, "Unskilled migrants [from Puerto Rico] moving to smaller cities in the Northeast face unemployment rates of between 20 and 30 percent" (1996, 159). This indicates that employment experience is not uniform but can and does change depending on the skill level of those entering the labor force of any particular community.

Conclusion

We began this section by reviewing economic conditions for Puerto Rican movers in each region. Although the median family income analysis is somewhat confounded with general regional wage differences, the percent of persons in poverty showed advantages for Puerto Rican movers from New York to the West as well as an advantage for movers going from the island to the South. We began to realize that there may be different patterns for movers depending on where they originated. When we reviewed the patterns for female-headed families, we again found different patterns for movers from New York and those from Puerto Rico. Movers from both sending areas showed declines in percentages of female-headed families in the South and West. However, New York female-headed family movers did not move far from home (they stayed in the same region, not even going to the Midwest), but Puerto Rico female-headed family movers did not seem to be affected by distance. Instead, they seemed more affected by conditions in the receiving region, which, because of the welfare structure, are more favorable for this type of family in the Rust Belt.

In an attempt to discern any selectivity of movers, we looked at nativity, language, and education issues. New York movers to the Sun Belt included decidedly more second-generation individuals, especially those going to the West. However, there was a mixed pattern for island movers that, we speculated, may be the result of ease of migration issues for the island born. Mover groups from both New York and Puerto Rico had better English skills than stayers and definite selectivity advantages for those going South and West. There was some educational selectivity for New York movers, but the pattern showed higher education selectivity primarily to the Northeast and high school selectivity for the Sun Belt (the Midwest was questionable because of sample size constraints). Island movers displayed negative selectivity when they went to the Rust Belt and positive selectivity at both high school and higher education levels when metropolitan areas in the Sun Belt were their destinations.

In reviewing labor force statistics, we also found advantages in the South and West in terms of both lower unemployment rates and lower rates of labor force nonparticipation.

This analysis leaves many questions unanswered in terms of both understanding the nature of Puerto Rican migration selectivity and determining how many of the Sun Belt economic advantages are the result of this selectivity, rather than the dynamics found within the regions. We believe, nevertheless, that we can safely conclude that (1) selectivity is taking place, (2) the selectivity operates differently depending on whether the movers come from New York or Puerto Rico, and (3) the South and West are the regions attracting individuals with higher levels of human capital and rewarding them with higher returns on that capital.

1

How Segregation Fits In

esidential segregation is a phenomenon that many of us would like to think was obliterated with the civil rights legislation of the 1960s. It is still with us, however, and is linked very closely to issues of poverty. It makes sense, therefore, to take a look at how segregation affects people groups. This chapter begins by describing segregation and the arguments surrounding the connections between segregation and poverty. We then look at how Hispanic, and more particularly Puerto Rican, segregation has been treated in the past. The next section explains how we measure segregation, and we will look at our own figures for Puerto Rican, black, and non–Puerto Rican Hispanic segregation in our selected metropolitan areas. We conclude with our argument against current explanations of Puerto Rican segregation.

Segregation and Poverty

In its simplest form, *segregation* means the setting apart of a group from the main mass of people. Although used in other contexts (e.g., genetic research), we usually think of this word in terms of separating populations by race-ethnicity. Certainly we are most used to hearing this word as it is applied to the African American experience in this country. We recall memories of the Jim Crow laws in the South, which made it legal to separate blacks from whites in every aspect of life. If there is any doubt that segregation still exists, just go to New York City, Chicago, Los Angeles, or any one of a number of other major cities across the country.

But why does segregation still exist, and what does it have to do with poverty? Let's first take a look at what is called "self-segregation." This typically occurs among new immigrant or migrant groups, who band together to ease the transition into a new and unfamiliar cultural and, often, linguistic setting. Immigrant groups in the past tended to be poor, so when they segregated themselves, they were not only ethnically separated but that separation was also economic. As groups adapted to their new surroundings, began to climb the ladder economically, and acculturated themselves to the U.S. majority culture, they usually moved out of their enclaves and began assimilating. Part of this movement involved residential dispersion, so that eventually the original enclaves were dissipated and left for the next new group of immigrants.

In the case of blacks, there was an added dimension. White discrimination constructed barriers hindering black economic gains, and white flight all but ensured that once a community was "invaded" by a few black families it would quickly "tip" and become all black. Therefore, instead of economic gains for blacks translating into assimilation, they often merely enlarged the ghetto. Even with black suburbanization efforts of the last twenty years, we find that some suburbs have become "black suburbs" (e.g., see Fazlollah 1993).

After World War I, when southern black migration to urban cities really took off, like other new groups blacks tended to self-segregate. White discrimination against blacks, however, made the experience of blacks quite different from that of other newcomer groups. Massey and Denton explain it this way:

> Black segregation is not comparable to the limited and transient segregation experienced by other racial and ethnic groups, now or in the past. No group in the history of the United States has ever experienced the sustained high level of residential segregation that has been imposed on blacks in large American cities for the past fifty years. . . . Not only is the depth of black segregation unprecedented and utterly unique compared with that of other groups, but it also shows little sign of change with the passage of time or improvements in socioeconomic status. (1993, 2)

Okay, segregation still exists, but what does that have to do with poverty? One problem we face when we try to understand social dynamics is the old "chicken and egg" question: Which comes first—does poverty cause segregation, or does segregation cause poverty? The answer, as with our chicken and egg, is that causation can go both ways. A chicken lays an egg, the egg becomes a chicken, that chicken then lays an egg, and so forth. Poverty does feed into segregation because poverty in and of itself limits residential choices. Financial considerations result in housing that is most likely found in the oldest areas and characterized by disrepair and general overcrowding. As long as poverty is high, a certain amount of segregation will always be based on class, but many areas house low-income families as well as families of different economic levels. In other words, poverty in groups who do not face strong discrimination is not nearly as concentrated. Poverty does contribute to segregation but cannot explain the degree of segregation currently found in U.S. urban centers.

Still, how can segregation be said to cause poverty? Massey and Eggers argue that "housing segregation is a key factor behind the unusual and growing concentration of poverty among blacks and some Hispanics [Puerto Ricans] and that the persistence of residential segregation is essential to understanding the plight of the underclass" (1990, 1155–56). Massey and Denton further note that segregation exacerbates poverty because it "concentrates poverty to build a set of mutually reinforcing and self-feeding spirals of decline into black neighborhoods. . . . The damaging social consequences that follow from increased poverty are spatially concentrated as well, creating uniquely disadvantaged environments that become progressively isolated—geographically, socially, and economically—from the rest of society" (1993, 2).

Let's try to think this through. One way to keep a group down economically is to discriminate in educational opportunities. Despite forced busing, most major cities still primarily operate on the basis of neighborhood schools, especially for the early grades. If a neighborhood is mixed, the only way discrimination can take place in the schools is on an individual basis in a classroom. We don't deny that this takes place, but it is more visible and more apt to be confronted. If a neighborhood is segregated, however, systemic discrimination can take place: good teachers request assignments in other schools, facilities are maintained better in other areas, and even curriculum options can be altered. It is not unusual for a large high school (2000–4000 students) in a predominantly black community to have one honors or college preparatory class per grade for a total of 60 students, and all the other thousands of students may not even be offered the courses that could potentially allow them to compete at the college level. This facet of systemic discrimination is extremely important to understand. "Prejudice alone cannot account for high levels of black segregation . . .[this] requires the erection of systematic barriers to black residential mobility" (Massey and Denton 1993, 11).

As another example, we might be tempted to say that segregation provides some political advantages to the affected group. Segregated communities have a better chance to elect a member of their own group to city government positions. This is true as far as it goes, but what is missing is a complete understanding of how politics work. To influence votes on measures that allocate funds to a particular community, politicians need partners. Integrated communities allow for benefits to be dispersed among a number of interest groups. However, segregated communities allow those monies to benefit blacks only and thus make it difficult for black representatives to build the coalitions necessary to affect voting. "Although segregation paradoxically makes it easier for blacks to elect representatives, it limits their political influence and marginalizes them within the American polity" (Massey and Denton 1993, 14).

Not to belabor this point, but by concentrating poverty, segregation also causes the withdrawal of commercial institutions, concentration of welfare recipients, and a corresponding absence of role models for those who are able to advance economically and has many other deleterious effects. This knowledge allows us to begin to understand what has been termed "the underclass."

Hispanic Segregation

We have addressed black segregation in some depth, but what about Hispanic segregation? Sánchez understands Puerto Rican segregation and its interaction with poverty. He found that, as with blacks, "Puerto Rican housing needs were affected by class processes that were more complex and general than those consisting of income-imposed limits on individual purchasing power" (1986, 215). He found the same reciprocal roles of economic and residential mobility in his study of Puerto Ricans that we have outlined for blacks: "Although surplus-labor status and idleness have taken their toll on the Puerto Rican housing situation, these housing conditions themselves have had an important reciprocal effect on the employment and class condition of Puerto Ricans" (Sánchez 1986, 203). He goes on to explain how this works: "The ultimate impact of their housing distress has been to help make Puerto Rican workers more available to capital: It perpetuates the role of Puerto Ricans as a cheap labor reserve poised, at demand for either idleness or work" (Sánchez 1986, 203). Santiago and Galster (1995) also found this bidirectional relationship between poverty and residential segregation.

But we're getting ahead of ourselves. How has Hispanic segregation been studied in the past? Segregation research has primarily been an outgrowth of the ecological research program. In other words, most researchers are, at least to some degree, tied in to the idea of how European immigrants entered this country, then self-segregated, became more mobile, and, finally, assimilated. Blacks have always been an exception, and their experience has been explained by including white discrimination in the process. Therefore, the major focus of Hispanic segregation research has been on discerning whether Hispanics followed the ecological model of ethnic assimilation or the invasion-succession model documented for blacks.

Massey was the first to do a national study of Hispanic residential segregation. He concluded that "patterns of Spanish American segregation resemble those of European ethnics more than they do those of blacks" (1979, 560). One of the problems with this type of research is that all Hispanic national groups were combined. As we have already determined, it is not helpful to combine the groups, because of their different histories and experiences.

As Massey continued his research on Hispanic segregation, he realized that a study had never been done to compare the patterns of segregation among the different Spanish ethnicities "using a national sample of urban areas" (1981, 311–12), so he proceeded to do just that. Using 1970 data he compared Mexican, Cuban, and Puerto Rican segregation patterns and reached two conclusions. First, he found different patterns between Puerto Ricans and the other two Hispanic groups: "The vast majority of Puerto Ricans are quite highly segregated from whites, and less segregated from blacks, compared to other Hispanic groups" (Massey 1981, 315). Second, he looked at central city concentrations and again found that Puerto Ricans did not follow the same pattern as other Hispanic groups. In fact, Puerto Ricans in New York and Chicago were "more highly concentrated than any other group [including blacks] in any other city" (Massey 1981, 315).

Massey and Denton (1989a) repeated this comparative study of Mexican, Puerto Rican, and Cuban residential segregation using 1980 data. They again found that Puerto Rican segregation patterns differed significantly from those of Mexicans and Cubans. Their conclusion was that "Puerto Ricans began the decade of the 1970s being spatially isolated from the rest of American society; by the end of the decade, they were well on the way to being socially and economically isolated as well" (Massey and Denton 1989a, 79).

Massey and his colleagues were not the first to discover that Puerto Ricans were not following the same pattern of residential assimilation as European ethnics did. Kantrowitz, in studying New York, found that Puerto Rican segregation levels were much higher than those ever reached by European ethnic groups and "about equal to that of black-European ethnic segregation" (1973, 26). Rosenberg and Lake questioned whether the ecological model of assimilation could be applied to Puerto Ricans. They found that the New York Puerto Rican settlement patterns "coincide neither with models of ethnic assimilation nor with models of black segregation and succession" (1976, 1143). Jackson (1981) also notes the same phenomenon in his article entitled "Paradoxes of Puerto Rican Segregation in New York."

With all these findings the next logical question is: what is going on? Massey and Bitterman attempted to find an answer to this query by using 1960 and 1970 data for Puerto Ricans in New York and all Hispanics (78 percent Mexican) in Los Angeles. They concluded that "Puerto Ricans differ in two ways that have powerful effects on their spatial situation: they are poorer and they are blacker" (1985, 326). We have major concerns with these findings, which are addressed in the last section of this chapter. For now, let's just say that the way turn-of-the-century European immigrants and U.S. blacks were incorporated into U.S. cities was a product of their history, and these histories were taken into account when developing theories. We believe that the same thing should hold true for Puerto Ricans—their history, which is different from that of either the Europeans or U.S. blacks, should be considered, rather than trying to force them into one of the two preset molds. Santiago and Galster support this theory as well. They found "evidence to suggest that the relationships between residential location and economic status for Puerto Ricans differ in important ways from those observed for Blacks and other Latino groups" (1995, 361).

Puerto Rican Segregation, 1990

Numerous researchers have addressed the issue of determining a quantitative measure for residential segregation (Jahn, Schmid, and Schrag 1947; Duncan and Duncan 1955; Taeuber and Taeuber 1965; Taeuber and Taeuber 1976; Cortese, Falk, and Cohen 1976; Winship 1977; Massey and Denton 1988a). We will not review all the technical discussion but only look at the two basic requirements that result in a satisfactory segregation index:

> First, "no segregation" exists if the proportion of Negroes [*sic*] to the number of persons in any given census tract is equal to the proportion of Negroes in the total population of the city. The "segregation score" for any tract, area (combination of census tracts), or city which fulfills this specification should be zero. Second, "complete segregation" exists if the Negroes reside only in census tracts in which there are no non-Negroes. Any tract, area (combination of tracts), or city which fulfills this specification should have a "segregation score" of 100. Hence, the range of possible scores should be 0 to 100. (Jahn, Schmid, and Schrag 1947)

The most common measure of segregation is the index of dissimilarity (D), which is interpreted as "the proportion of nonwhites who would have to change their tract of residence" (Duncan and Duncan 1955, 211) to result in an even distribution of nonwhites across all tracts. Massey and Denton (1988a) stated that the dissimilarity index had been used as the standard segregation measure for more than twenty years (and now it has been for more than thirty years). Although a number of objections have been raised concerning the use of this index, according to Massey every alternative index actually "does a worse job of measuring segregation empirically" (1978, 587). Therefore, we will use the dissimilarity index for the following analysis.

The one problem that should be noted is the possibility that the dissimilarity index can be affected by random factors when the minority population size is too small. Massey and Denton tried to minimize this possibility by imposing "an arbitrary lower limit of 5,000 persons in reporting intergroup scores" (1989a, 74). We will follow their lead in our own analysis. The next logical question for us is: How can we interpret these indexes? What index levels have to be reached to state that segregation is a problem? Obviously, no place is completely integrated. Kantrowitz offers this as a rule of thumb: "Indexes upward of 70 [should be considered] as high, indexes of 30 or less as low, and variations in level of less than five points as unimportant, unless they are otherwise correlated" (1973, 15). Massey and Denton alter this formula slightly and use a less conservative level of 60 as the cutoff for "high" segregation (Massey and Denton 1988b; Massey and Denton 1989b). For easy reference, Table 7–1 summarizes these levels.

The usual expectations of ecological theory assume that new groups will segregate but that they will be less segregated from whites (with whom they presumably will eventually want to assimilate) and more segregated from blacks. Again, for easy referral we have summarized this as follows: *The expected ecological results for new groups are that there will be lower segregation from whites and higher segregation from blacks.*

Although the existence of a Puerto Rican paradox or possible anomaly (see above discussion) has been amply documented, and the work of Massey and his colleagues has looked at segregation levels of the various subgroups across fifty-eight metropolitan areas, the research dissecting Puerto Rican segregation differences has concentrated primarily on the New York metropolitan area. (For an exception, see Santi-

Table 7–1
Levels of Segregation

Level	Dissimilarity Index
High	70.0 and over
Less Conservative High (LC High)	60.0–69.9
Moderate	30.0–59.9
Low	Below 30.0

Sources: Katrowitz 1973; Massey and Denton 1988b.

ago and Galster 1995, although their selection criterion was all areas with 4,000 or more Puerto Ricans—a figure smaller than the limit we choose to use.)

Massey and Bitterman (1985) tried to explain this paradox by taking into account that many Hispanics are black racially. Therefore, the basic premise is that when a Hispanic group includes a large composition of blacks, that group is more likely to have contact with blacks and less contact with whites. In other words, rather than expecting the normal ecological pattern we would expect just the opposite.

In keeping with the general premise of this book—that Puerto Rican experiences in the United States vary depending on metropolitan area—we believe a need exists to review patterns of Puerto Rican segregation across the United States. Therefore, a number of dissimilarity indexes have been calculated for the forty-two MSAs identified for our research (see Appendix 2). We have a number of goals in using this approach. First, we want to establish the presence of continued high levels of Puerto Rican segregation from whites and establish whether this is uniform across the country or unique to certain areas. Second, we want to review levels of segregation between Puerto Ricans and blacks and determine whether Puerto Rican segregation patterns fit the ecological model or Massey and Bitterman's expectation of the reversal of that model. Third, we review Puerto Rican segregation from All Other Hispanics (meaning all non–Puerto Rican Hispanics) to determine how well these groups intermingle. We realize that the All Other Hispanic group includes a great deal of variation because of its heterogeneity, but we chose to use the combined category for a number of reasons: (1) our primary focus is on Puerto Ricans, rather than seeking an in-depth understanding of any or all of the other Hispanic groups; (2) the All Other Hispanic mix from one metropolitan area to another varies greatly; and (3) the literature points to the fact that Puerto Rican segregation is unique, so we believe the variation within the All Other Hispanic grouping will not be as great as it is between it and Puerto Ricans. Next, we will review the segregation patterns of All Other Hispanics to see whether they continue to be different from those of Puerto Ricans. Last, we will look at the ten MSAs with the largest numbers of Puerto Ricans to see if segregation levels have been changing significantly.

When we look at Table 7–2, we are struck by the fact that there is a great deal of difference between regions as well as from MSA to MSA in all measures of segregation.

Overall, twelve MSAs have indexes that fall into the "high" category of 70 and above. If we use the less conservative (L.C.) level of 60 for high segregation, we add another twelve MSAs for a total of twenty-four. All of these are located in either the Northeast or the Midwest. No MSAs in the South or West have scores higher than 43.9, easily in the middle "moderate" range. Regional averages reflect this difference as well, with quite high indexes for the Northeast and Midwest (64.4 and 69.3, respectively) and quite low average indexes for the South and West (36.9 and 39.6, respectively). Therefore, we conclude that the un-expected high levels of segregation between Puerto Ricans and whites is continuing but is not uniform and is confined to the Rust Belt regions.

A different pattern emerges when looking at Puerto Rican/black dis-similarity indexes (see Table 7–3).

Whereas no Puerto Rican/white index was in the "low" category of under 30, five MSAs have low Puerto Rican/black indexes. Also, only five MSAs have Puerto Rican/black "high" indexes (greater than 70); seven more are included if we lower the "high" level to 60. Therefore, a superficial overall look documents the noted anomaly of higher seg-regation from whites than from blacks.

Let's take a closer look at this paradox. We want to establish whether Puerto Rican segregation patterns conform to the regular ecological pat-tern or not. Table 7–4 notes how many MSAs in each region conform or

Table 7-2
Puerto Rican Segregation from Whites in Selected MSAs by Region, 1990

	Northeast	Midwest	South	West	Total
# MSAs by level					
of segregation					
High	10	2	0	0	12
L.C. High	9	3	0	0	12
Moderate	7	0	6	5	18
Low	0	0	0	0	0
Average dissim. index	64.4	69.3	36.9	39.6	

Source: U.S. Census 1990 STF 1A.

Table 7-3
Puerto Rican Segregation from Blacks in Selected MSAs by Region, 1990

	Northeast	Midwest	South	West	Total
# MSAs by level of segregation					
High	1	4	0	0	5
L.C. High	4	0	2	1	7
Moderate	16	1	4	3	24
Low	4	0	0	1	5
Average dissim. index	46.7*	75.3	60.1	46.2	

*One MSA (Lawrence, Mass.) did not have 5000 blacks and was not included.
Source: U.S. Census 1990 STF 1A.

do not conform to this regular pattern. Additionally, we've separated those that are too close to call but tend to conform or not conform.

Table 7–4 again clearly shows the regional differences. Outside the Northeast, only Lorain, Ohio, does not follow the expected ecological pattern. Within the Northeast itself, nineteen MSAs do not follow the pattern, and two more are too close to be sure about but tend not to follow the pattern, and one MSA isn't counted because too few blacks reside there for a reliable Puerto Rican/black index. Later we will refer more to the racial composition of Puerto Ricans, but neither the data nor the literature indicates that darker Puerto Ricans (those who are more racially black) are concentrated in one region more than in the others. This leads us to believe that considering Puerto Ricans as "blacker" (Massey and Bitterman 1985) is far too simplistic a rationale.

Table 7-4
Number of MSAs by Region That Conform to Ecological Expectations, 1990

	Northeast	Midwest	South	West
Conform to ecological model	2	3	6	3
Conform, but too close to be significant	2	1	0	0
Do not conform	19	1	0	0
Do not conform, but too close to be significant	2	0	0	2

Source: U.S. Census 1990 STF 1A.

Although not a necessary factor in our ecological testing, it is interesting to note how segregated Puerto Ricans are from the All Other Hispanics group (see Table 7–5). The Northeast and Midwest regional averages tend to be higher than those in the South and West, indicating more separation, but even these indexes are well within the moderate range. No MSA had a high level of Puerto Rican segregation from All Other Hispanics, even when the less conservative level was used. Therefore, we find a significant mixing among the Hispanic subgroups, even though some of these groups are fairly new arrivals in the United States.

As mentioned earlier, Puerto Rican segregation patterns have been shown to be different from those of other Hispanic groups. Even though the other groups were combined, we should determine whether previous research results still hold true—and indeed they do. Only Lawrence, Massachusetts, has an All Other Hispanic/white index higher than 70, but six of the All Other Hispanic/black indexes are in that "high" category. Only four MSAs show the unexpected lower black indexes, and none of the regional totals fall into this category. Therefore, we can conclude that the situation among Puerto Ricans is still unique, but that uniqueness seems to be regionally concentrated.

Finally, before leaving this part of the discussion, it would be help-

Table 7–5
Puerto Rican Segregation from All Other Hispanics in Selected MSAs by Region, 1990

	Northeast	Midwest	South	West	Total
# MSAs by level of segregation:					
High	0	0	0	0	0
L.C. High	0	0	0	0	0
Moderate	16	3	3	2	24
Low	5	1	3	3	12
Average dissim. index	35.8*	42.1*	26.5	27.1	

*Five MSAs in the Northeast and one in the Midwest did not have 5000 Other Hispanics and were not included.

Source: U.S. Census 1990 STF 1A.

ful to discern how Puerto Rican segregation levels are changing over time. Massey and Denton (1989a) calculated Puerto Rican/white and Puerto Rican/black dissimilarity indexes for the ten MSAs with the largest Puerto Rican populations. Although the boundaries of some of the MSAs changed between 1980 and 1990, we will still compare Massey and Denton's indexes for 1980 with our own for 1990 (see Table 7–6).

All the white and black dissimilarity indexes in the MSAs decreased during that time period, with the exception of a slight increase in the Paterson black index (and the Paterson MSA had major boundary changes between 1980 and 1990). Even that one rise does not meet our significance test. Although there is a slight decrease in the averages, they are not large enough to conclude that Puerto Rican assimilation will be forthcoming in the near future.

This section has documented the degree of residential segregation Puerto Ricans face. We found that although levels of segregation are very high in many Rust Belt metropolitan areas, the levels vary both between and within regions.

Table 7-6

1980–1990 Comparative Dissimilarity Indexes for the Ten 1980 MSAs with Largest Number of Puerto Ricans

MSA	1980		1990	
	PR/White	**PR/Black**	**PR/White**	**PR/Black**
New York	72.5	58.1	70.4	55.8
Chicago	80.6	89.0	75.6	86.4
Philadelphia	79.3	76.7	73.9	69.3
Newark	76.4	65.5	74.5	63.6
Jersey City	54.0	73.9	42.5	61.3
Nassau/Suffolk	46.9	64.1	46.1	60.5
Miami	45.5	61.4	39.4	58.4
Los Angeles	53.8	73.8	43.8	60.0
Paterson	77.7	44.8	67.8	48.0
Boston	78.2	58.3	66.7	44.6
Average	66.5	66.6	60.1	60.8

Sources: Massey and Denton 1989, 81; U.S. Census STF 1A.

Response to Proposed Explanation of Puerto Rican Segregation

Now that we have established updated figures, we need to return to the proposed explanations of Puerto Rican segregation and respond to them. As already stated, the New York MSA has been the one traditionally studied in terms of Puerto Rican segregation. This focus, of course, makes sense because New York has historically been the settlement area of choice for Puerto Ricans and still has the largest Puerto Rican population, by far, of all MSAs in the United States. Therefore, we also will take a closer look at the dynamics within the New York MSA, primarily in an attempt to support or refute Massey and Bitterman's (1985) proposed explanation of Puerto Ricans being "poorer and blacker."

We begin our discussion by examining Massey and Bitterman's approach. They looked only at two cities—New York and Los Angeles—making comparisons between 1960 and 1970. During those years the only Hispanics that were counted in the census in New York were Puerto Ricans. In Los Angeles 78 percent of the Hispanics were Mexicans. So their comparison was between Puerto Ricans on one side and mostly Mexicans on the other. Although there are some problems with this method, census data was not as accurate in those years as they are now. Massey and Bitterman stated that in 1970 "70 percent of all Hispanics in New York were Puerto Rican" (1985, 308), so they did not see the presence of other Hispanic groups as a significant problem. By 1980, however, Puerto Ricans made up only 59.8 percent of Hispanics in the New York City MSA (Hispanic Almanac 1984, 101), and by 1990 the percentage dropped to only 49.4 (U.S Bureau of the Census 1991). Also, in 1990 both the Puerto Rican and All Other Hispanic populations numbered more than 900,000 each. Therefore, we can now do a comparative analysis of Puerto Ricans versus All Other Hispanics in a single metropolitan area, which is helpful because we don't have to worry about interference from other regional factors (which could have been present in the previous Los Angeles/New York comparisons). As a reminder, Table 7–7 shows the dissimilarities taken from Appendix 2 for New York.

We can be fairly confident with the dissimilarity indexes for this particular set of comparisons because both minority groups being researched are so large. As Table 7–7 indicates, Puerto Rican/white segregation is still very high at 70.4. It is lower between All Other Hispanics and whites (64.1) but is still in the high range using the less conservative figures. This is not unexpected, because so many of the national groups making up this category are very new to New York and are still self-segregating.

The reverse holds true when we look at dissimilarity indexes between the two Hispanic groups and blacks. It is 55.8 for Puerto Ricans (moderate) and 61.4 for All Other Hispanics (high). We see from these indexes that the Puerto Rican pattern of unusually high segregation from whites and lower segregation from blacks that has been well documented (Jackson 1981; Kantrowitz 1973; Massey 1979; Massey 1981) continues. Also, this phenomenon seems to be unique to Puerto Ricans in that the All Other Hispanics group is less segregated from whites and more segregated from blacks.

Massey and Bitterman's analysis suggested three explanations for this apparent anomaly: low SES, discrimination, and racial heritage. They found that New York Puerto Ricans had lower average SES than Los Angeles Mexicans, that the Puerto Ricans achieved "less spatial assimilation *per unit* of SES" than the Mexicans, and that 8 percent of Puerto Ricans, compared with 1.9 percent of Mexicans, were black (1985, 324, emphasis in original). The racial composition of Puerto Ricans was seen as important because "black Hispanics have a strong effect in promoting more integration with blacks and less with Anglos" (Massey and Bitterman 1985, 324).

We have already addressed the issue of low Puerto Rican SES and have seen how it interacts with segregation. We must agree that lower economic standing certainly contributes to higher segregation, but that alone cannot explain the high levels of Puerto Rican segregation. When we address the idea of racial composition, we do not agree with Massey

Table 7-7

Comparisons of Segregation Levels for Puerto Ricans and All Other Hispanics in the New York MSA, 1990

Dissimilarity with	Puerto Ricans	All Other Hispanics
Whites	70.4	64.1
Blacks	55.8	61.4

Source: U.S. Census 1990 STF 1A.

and Bitterman's findings. In 1990 only 8.2 percent of New York Puerto Ricans identified their race as being black, whereas 18.7 percent of All Other Hispanics did so. This indicates a discrepancy with their findings. Although the percentage of New York Puerto Ricans who were black is basically the same as it was in 1980, the percentage of All Other Hispanics who are black is much higher. According to Massey and Bitterman's argument, this should mean that All Other Hispanics will be more segregated from whites than Puerto Ricans are, but the opposite is actually true. One of two dynamics could be happening here. First, self-identification as being black may not be as much of a liability to "foreign" Hispanics as it is to Puerto Rican "citizens." This could mean that the percentage of Puerto Ricans who are perceived by Anglos as being black (feeding into Anglo discrimination of blacks) could be much higher than the Puerto Ricans' self-identification. On the other hand, it could also mean that we must go further than racial composition, even when combined with SES, to find the real reason for Puerto Rican segregation. Until means other than census self-identification are developed to measure racial composition, we cannot address the issue of any group being "blacker" than the others and use that theory as a basis for explanation.

A helpful analysis was done by Morales (1986). He compared the experiences of Dominicans and Puerto Ricans. He reports that:

> With the exception of the uncounted and undocumented Hispanic workers, Dominicans may be at the bottom of the "other Hispanic" category in terms of socioeconomic indicators. Perhaps since, as a group, Dominicans are darker than other Hispanics, racism may explain their condition. However, Dominicans are also darker than Puerto Ricans, and yet they appear to be doing better.
>
> Dominicans have lower levels of formal education, have poorer English-speaking ability than do Puerto Ricans, and are concentrated in many of the same occupations. However, the 1980 census reveals that Dominicans have not replaced Puerto Ricans in the lowest rung of the economic ladder. On the contrary, as a group, they were economically better off than Puerto Ricans. Dominican labor force participation totals were on par with all New York City residents and well above those for Puerto Ricans. (Morales 1986, 165–66)

These results lead us to believe that although white/black discrimination against Puerto Ricans (especially, the darker ones) certainly provides part of the explanation for their situation, it cannot explain their lower economic levels or higher segregation levels when compared with other Hispanics.

Other 1990 data also cause concern. The ecological argument is based on the assumption that when ethnic groups enter this country, they tend to be poor. As they remain over time and their population becomes more native born, however, they grow economically and will become more mobile socially and spatially. Data in Table 7–8 indicate that Puerto Rican migration has been relatively stable since World War II, with some decline during the 1970s, whereas over half the All Other Hispanic migration occurred from 1980 to the time of the census. This is further reflected in the percentage of native born, 55.5 percent for Puerto Ricans compared with only 27.1 percent for All Other Hispanics.

Not only is the "newness" of the group important in itself (because recent immigrants tend to voluntarily segregate themselves), but also its effect on a group's ability to speak English (and thus have a more

Table 7–8
Comparison of Migration and Language Variables for Puerto Ricans and All Other Hispanics in the New York MSA, 1990

Variables	Puerto Ricans	All Other Hispanics
Time of migration		
1980–1990	22.2%	51.0%
1970–1979	14.0%	25.3%
1960–1969	22.7%	18.0%
1950–1959	26.1%	3.9%
before 1950	15.1%	1.8%
Native-born	55.5%	27.1%
Ability to speak English		
Very well	58.7%	39.0%
Well	23.3%	23.5%
Not well	13.9%	24.5%
Not at all	4.1%	13.0%
Language spoken at home		
English only	7.2%	7.3%
Spanish	92.4%	90.5%
Other	0.4%	2.2%
Linguistically isolated households	26.9%	39.9%

Source: U.S. Census 1990 PUMS, 1-Percent Sample.

open opportunity structure) is equally important. A full 82.0 percent of Puerto Ricans speak English well or very well compared with only 62.5 percent of All Other Hispanics. In addition, although the percentage of households that speak Spanish at home is similar for the two groups, only 26.9 percent of Puerto Rican households are linguistically isolated compared with 39.9 percent of All Other Hispanic households. These language findings make sense given the newness of the All Other Hispanic groups, but they should indicate more segregation for the All Other Hispanic households, not less. All of this data supports the idea that the "paradox" of Puerto Rican segregation continues and has not been adequately explained.

Conclusion

In this chapter we have documented that Puerto Ricans are highly segregated in many Rust Belt cities. We have challenged current thought as laid out by Massey and Bitterman (1985) concerning the causes of this phenomenon. We see that economic mobility is a necessary, though not sufficient, condition for residential mobility. We also see that although racial composition undoubtedly plays a role in explaining Puerto Rican segregation, we must go further than race and class to fully understand the plight of Puerto Ricans.

Throughout this book we have been stating the importance of histories in understanding the well-being of groups. This seems an appropriate time to remember that Puerto Rican history is quite different from that of other groups. We cannot understand their plight without considering the colonial relationship between Puerto Rico and the United States. As a colonized minority citizenry, Puerto Ricans face a unique marginalization that neither affords them the benefits of full citizenship (remember our discussion on the second-class nature of their citizenship) nor allows them to adapt through normal immigrant channels, which presuppose the built-in constraints of deportation threats that the U.S. majority uses to "keep them in line." This marginalization translates into Puerto Ricans being seen as the least desirable group to employ, and lack of employment, as we have seen, is a major factor contributing to Puerto Rican poverty.

Puerto Rican Women and the Labor Force

"If one group can represent the forces that have been related to the 'feminization of poverty' in the United States, it is Puerto Rican women living in the Middle Atlantic region" (Colón-Warren 1996, 105). The following statement sums up our own concerns for Puerto Rican women, but what exactly do we mean by this: "The feminization of poverty has been described as the growing incidence of female-headed families among households below the poverty level, both throughout the world and in the United States" (1996, 108). Our findings so far confirm the high levels of female-headed families as well as the high poverty rates among Puerto Rican families both in the United States and on the island. In 1990, single females headed 29.0 percent of all families in Puerto Rico, and 69.9 percent of those families were in poverty. On the mainland more than one-third of all Puerto Rican families (36.6 percent) were headed by single females, 57.3 percent of which were in poverty.

These data indicated to us the necessity of including a chapter to specifically address the issues of Puerto Rican women as they encounter the U.S. labor market. Grasmuck and Grosfoguel also stress that "the fate of female migrants is not always the mirror image of their male counterparts especially when high rates of family disruption accompany the process. . . . Women's educational and social resources and

121

their access to employment niches do not operate in the same way as men's" (1997, 342).

We are primarily concerned with Puerto Rican communities in the United States, but we believe that to understand the plight of Puerto Rican women here, we must take into consideration the political, economic, and social forces affecting women in Puerto Rico and the United States. Research too often has separated the experiences, but as Ortiz describes it, there are "connections among women's work and the origins of colonial capitalism in Puerto Rico, labor migration and community development in the United States, industrial development and capitalist reorganization both on the island and the mainland, and women's labor struggles in the twentieth century" (A. Ortiz 1996a, 2). Therefore, we will present the profiles of women at different historical times in both places, and we'll peek into the lives of a few *puertorriqueñas* to illustrate our contentions.

Pre–World War II in Puerto Rico

When the United States invaded Puerto Rico, it found a rural people with strong traditional gender roles. A man's primary role was to provide for and protect his family, and his ability to do this was how he defined his masculinity. Women, on the other hand, lived to serve men, raise children, and take care of the home. Teaching and religious vocations were the only recourse for those wanting a "career" (Petra Press 1996). Being a mother was considered a very privileged position. The mother had almost total control over how to raise the children and run the household, and she was "idolized and revered" by the family (Petra Press 1996, 15). These traditional roles, however, did not mean that women never worked outside the home. The United States did an employment survey in 1899, shortly after it "won" the island, and found that many women had jobs, jobs that were primarily an extension of their traditional roles (e.g., sewing, laundering, domestic work). Some were teachers and nurses, a few women were in sales, and sixty were factory workers exclusively in the tobacco industry, but not a single woman worked in the areas of office, needlework, garment manufacturing, or public services (A. Ortiz 1996a, 3–4).

As mentioned in Chapter 3, the United States essentially destroyed the rural agrarian economy of the island, forcing many to move to cities to survive. The cost of living in the cities was much higher, and both the husband and wife often had to find work to make ends meet.

During those early colonial years, women were incorporated into a labor market that was rigidly segregated by gender. They basically had access to "female occupations" and were exploited as they met the needs of "U.S. colonial capitalism" (A. Ortiz 1996a, 4).

By the late 1920s needlework had become an important occupation for Puerto Rican women. They were taught these skills in school, and these jobs fit into who they saw themselves to be as women. Many women worked at home doing piecework, and others worked in shops. Unfortunately, it was very difficult for home needleworkers and those in shops to unite against U.S. manufacturers on issues such as wages. "Thus they were probably the most exploited of all women wage workers during this period" (A. Ortiz 1996a, 5).

By 1930 women worked in more types of jobs. However, there were ramifications for their families. "In a culture that placed so much value on a man's ability to provide for his family, a working wife was often demoralizing, and the resulting conflict put a great deal of strain on many marriages" (Petra Press 1996, 16).

Because it directly affects how Puerto Rican women were incorporated into the U.S. labor market, let's take a closer look at the pre–World War II needlework industry on the island. This industry was organized by U.S. firms facing a crisis caused by World War I that stopped the exportation of "finely sewn and embroidered garments and linens" from European countries (Boris 1996, 36). Because Puerto Rican women were already known for their ability to work with lace and to do intricate embroidery, U.S. firms sent precut, prestamped clothes to contractors in Puerto Rico. Some contractors ran small workshops, but because many of the workers lived in isolated rural areas and the island's road system was not yet developed, most contractors sent batches of the garments to subcontractors in rural areas who then distributed them to the homeworkers. Each level took a share of the profits, so the workers themselves received very little. Although the island's government attempted to end the homework, it had become central to the Puerto Rican economy and "could not be prohibited without causing severe dislocations" (Boris 1996, 35). In 1940, 31 percent of the women still worked at home, sewing and embroidering for wages. However, the insular government was working hard to raise wages, and U.S. firms began to find cheaper labor in other countries: "The organization of the needlework industry thus reflected the dependent status of Puerto Rico, its place as a nascent 'off-shore' production facility for the mainland industry, and its position as a cheap colonial labor market for U.S. manufacturers" (Boris 1996, 38).

Pre–World War II: Coming to the States

Although small groups of Puerto Ricans lived in New York City before the Spanish-American War, it wasn't until the 1920s that a settlement of any consequence developed there. Women played an important role during this time. They were especially helpful in providing information to incoming migrants about how to adapt to their new surroundings. This information service was referred to as "the family intelligence service" (Korrol 1980, 47). During the 1920s and 1930s, the roles of Puerto Rican women in New York City were essentially extensions of their island roles. This is illustrated in the life of Doña Mayda Dominguez.

Mayda was born to a poor family in 1904 in Guayama, Puerto Rico and was the oldest of eight children. She married a man from India who had come to Puerto Rico on business, and in 1934 she and her husband, along with her parents and her three children, moved to Manhattan. It took them forty days to get there by boat, during which time Mayda learned she was pregnant again.

Mayda's husband was very ill with a bad heart (he died at the age of 36), and she had to work. She began by washing and ironing clothes for people in her building. Then she worked in a factory sewing baby clothes during the day and in a Chinese laundry at night, ironing shirts and pants. Her mother took care of her children while she worked. Eight years after coming to New York, Mayda and her family moved from Manhattan to the Bronx. Mayda always worked hard and had a strong sense of family and a warm sense of humor.

When Mayda was forced to work to support her family, she did "women's work"—laundering and sewing. This was common in New York. The women tended to think of themselves as "women of the home (*mujeres de la casa*)" (Korrol 1980, 48), but they were responsible for many activities that brought extra finances into the home. First, they did home piecework, working on "lampshades, hats, artificial flowers and jewelry, as well as embroidering, crocheting and sewing" (Korrol 1980, 49). Piecework offered extremely low salaries because employers counted on the new workers not knowing their rights to minimum wage. This type of work continued through the 1950s.

Another way in which women could supplement the family income was by caring for children. The extended family usually provided that service on the island, but unfortunately the extended family was virtually nonexistent in New York. Women filled in the gap by watching other people's children in their homes.

Women also took in lodgers. New migrants would arrive in New York City and not have a place of their own. They would often look for friends, relatives, or simply others from their hometown with whom to find room and board. Usually these were single men or women, but married couples or whole family units also would board with one another until the new migrants became situated. This arrangement allowed for single women to make the ocean crossing alone, because they knew relatives would meet them once they arrived in New York City.

Most Puerto Rican women in New York during this time earned wages from doing work in their homes. However, "close to 25 percent of those living in New York City participated in the labor force as cigarmakers and domestics, as typists and stenographers, in the needletrades industries as operatives and unskilled workers, in the laundries or restaurants and in the fields as agricultural workers" (Korrol 1980, 54–55). Again, we see this in our story of Doña Mayda: she initially tried to work in the home washing and ironing but then worked outside in the garment industry and in a laundry.

Post–World War II on the Island

The needlework industry on the island declined rapidly after 1945 and just about disappeared after modern clothing factories were introduced in the 1950s. A new area of women's work emerged with a rapid expansion of clerical work during the 1960s and 1970s: "During these years automated clerical work was identified as one of the next links in the chain of twentieth-century modernization projects in Puerto Rico, promising prosperity for workers and an end to the long-standing problem of chronic unemployment on the island" (Casey 1996, 209). In 1990 more than 30 percent of the employed women on the island were clerical workers, making that the occupation with the biggest share of female workers. However, "clerical work has not been a panacea for women workers on the island" (Casey 1996, 215).

Education levels for women on the island are increasing and are higher than those for men. This causes a dual problem. First, it is another factor that hurts male-female relationships. Second, although to former factory workers getting a secretarial job feels like progress, many female college graduates have no choice but to accept clerical positions, and for them these are dead-end jobs. Unemployment among clerical workers is also on the rise. Paradoxically, technology raised the level of prestige for clerical workers, but it also is responsible for eliminating thousands of clerical jobs.

More recently, in part because of their higher education levels, we find that women again are finding alternative sources of employment on the island, in areas such as electronics and pharmaceuticals and also in the managerial and professional sectors (Pérez-Herranz 1996, 143).

Gender stratification persists, exacerbating tensions between men and women. Higher unemployment rates are found among the men than the women, and this is a trend that doesn't seem to be ending as a result of Puerto Rico losing its manufacturing base. "Fomento had succeeded by the 1960s in bringing to Puerto Rico mainly industries that were heavily dependent on women's labor" (A. Ortiz 1996a, 15).

Post–World War II, Migration to the U.S. Picks Up

After World War II the island's *jíbaros* were becoming desperate. The sugar cane industry provided jobs only from January through June, and then the farm workers had no work. Many of them agreed to travel back and forth between the island and the Northeast to be part of the autumn harvest season. The traditional roles were changing, and this change was hard for the men. Women were having a difficult time maintaining an outside job and still doing all the chores necessary to care for their children and run their homes. When husbands were asked to help, they were upset and heated arguments ensued. The men were suffering the humiliation of not being able to adequately provide for their families, causing their wives to have to go off to work. At the same time, many men were away from their families for long periods of time harvesting crops in the United States. All this increased the strain on marriages, often leading to dissolution.

Women also started coming to the United States in large numbers after the war, including Damaris Morales, who was born in Puerto Rico in 1923. As was often the case on the island at that time, Damaris left school and got married when she was quite young—only thirteen years old. At fifteen she had a daughter, and at seventeen, when she was pregnant with her second daughter, her husband left her. Her baby was born on her eighteenth birthday, and she was a single mom with two children and very little education.

Damaris found a job as a seamstress in a factory on the island, and her family helped watch the children for her. After World War II, she heard of the opportunities in New York City, so in 1948 she left her children with relatives and went to New York to stay with an aunt who already lived there and to find a job in the garment district. One year later, when she was somewhat established, she sent for her two girls.

Damaris had very little support from her extended family because most of them were still on the island. Life was not easy for her, but she always worked hard and never went on welfare. By 1972 her daughters were married with families of their own, Damaris's mother was alone in Puerto Rico, and jobs in the garment industry were increasingly difficult to find as more and more companies closed down, so Damaris returned to the island.

Damaris's story is typical. Women in New York City became a source of cheap labor for the garment industry. More and more Puerto Rican women were moving into positions in garment factories rather than doing piecework at home. Even when Puerto Rican participation in the garment industry was at its peak, however, jobs at the better-paying shops were reserved for white women.

At this point, we need to understand the nature of New York City's garment industry. From the turn of the century, it was a place for first-generation immigrants to gain a foothold. Seldom did the second generation want to remain in those types of jobs, so they moved on and left room for the next immigrant group. World War II cut off the supply of

European immigrants to work in the garment industry. The ethnic white workers in the industry at that time were enticed to work in the defense plants being built in the New York area; at the same time, the war meant the production of durable goods declined and there was more demand for garment purchases. All these factors led to the need to find new garment workers. During the war the garment industry primarily turned to blacks and then to Puerto Ricans, who had a reputation for being skilled needleworkers. Puerto Ricans became a large presence in the industry after the war and were actually the predominant ethnic group in some trades (A. Ortiz 1996b).

Puertorriqueñas entered the garment industry at a time when it was being threatened by a number of factors—new technologies, higher overhead costs in the city, and growing foreign imports. The industry's response was to relocate its factories. All these factors limited the ability of Puerto Rican workers to make changes in the industry that would benefit them.

Puerto Rican women were allowed to be members of the International Ladies Garment Workers Union (ILGWU), but the union was another source of discrimination. Union leadership was not interested in protecting the rights of Puerto Rican workers and allowed them to enter only the lowest-paid and least-skilled locals. Their powerlessness in union locals and ILGWU leadership led to a number of ramifications for Puerto Rican women. First, they were completely excluded from all decision making regarding issues that greatly concerned them as workers. Union officials had always pushed for better wages, but at the height of Puerto Rican participation in the industry the union negotiated a number of "sweetheart contracts" with bosses, without the approval of the rank and file, to accept low wage scales. This change in union policy coincided with the entry of nonwhites into the garment industry labor force (Grasmuck and Grosfoguel 1997, 346). Not surprisingly, this created a great deal of distrust between union leaders and Puerto Rican workers.

Second, the union decided to prevent the establishment of federally sponsored training programs in the industry during the early 1960s. These programs would have allowed Puerto Rican women to learn skills and be upgraded from no-skill or low-skill to skilled laborers. The women had no way to effectively oppose this decision. For the first time, the garment industry could not be viewed as a stepping-stone to better opportunities in the future.

A further ramification was that Puerto Ricans had essentially no influence on how union funds were to be spent. The union leadership, which was heavily Jewish and Italian, disbursed funds in ways that would assist their own ethnic groups with little regard for the well-being of the Puerto Rican membership.

The inevitable occurred during the 1960s, and the garment industry went into a steep decline. By the late 1960s, Puerto Ricans were faced with new competition from several new immigrant groups, including Cubans, Haitians, Dominicans, and those from Southeast Asia. Where were Puerto Rican women to work? These women for the most part lacked skills in other occupational areas and suffered from low educational levels and poor English-speaking ability. They could not easily move into other types of jobs, so "many were forced to join the ranks of the permanently unemployed—forever abandoning the hope of using work in the garment industry as a stepping-stone to a better life in America" (A. Ortiz 1996b, 74).

U.S. Puerto Rican Women in Other Industries

We have been reviewing a great deal of information about the garment industry, but not all women were confined to that industry. Remember that in Puerto Rico during the 1960s and 1970s clerical work became a favorite occupation. In New York, the number of clerical jobs also increased. However, these jobs did not present a hopeful alternative for Puerto Rican women, in part because of the women's low educational levels and English-speaking skills and also owing to discrimination factors, which favored white women getting these jobs: "The loss of less skilled female jobs and the expansion of higher skilled female jobs has disproportionately favored native white females. . . . [However,] even when examining women with similar levels of educational attainment, the Puerto Rican female is in a disadvantaged position compared to the native white female" (Cooney and Colón Warren 1979, 292). We will discuss this more fully in the next section dealing with Puerto Rican female labor force participation.

Another area that opened up was bilingual education. It was difficult for Puerto Ricans to become teachers in New York schools, even if they had been good teachers in Puerto Rico, because they could not pass the necessary speech requirements (they usually spoke with heavy accents).

However, beginning in the late 1940s, as a precursor to bilingual education, a few Puerto Ricans were hired as "substitute auxiliary teachers" and worked with students and the community as a bridge (Korrol 1996, 89). When bilingual education finally began in earnest, there was room for some Puerto Rican women who spoke both English and Spanish (even if they had not finished high school) to serve as aides in classrooms.

Remember our story about Doña Mayda? Well, her daughter Aracelis learned her values from her mother. She was married and had a child by the time she was fifteen and never had a chance to finish high school, but family was a priority. Eventually she and her husband had twelve children. Then he left her. Three of the children were already on their own, but she had to raise nine children by herself and, later, one of her grandsons. She had moved to Philadelphia by that time, and she took a job as a bilingual kindergarten aide with the Philadelphia School District. She worked there for twenty-six years, and, as was true of her own mother, she never went on welfare. All twelve of her children finished high school, and nine of them have college degrees. Her fulfillment and delight are in her children, her grandchildren, and her great-grandchildren. Her pride is in teaching them love and respect as her mother taught her.

In the story of Aracelis, we find a woman with low educational attainment who was able to make a difference in the education of other children as well as spurring her own children on to higher levels of attainment. However, New York City lacked enough of this type of job to make much of a dent in the number of Puerto Rican women who were displaced from the garment industry and were now looking for employment.

What happens when employment cannot be found? A dynamic called the discouraged worker syndrome essentially describes that when there is little hope of finding employment, potential workers get so discouraged they leave the workforce completely. This is the next topic of discussion.

Puerto Rican Female Labor Force Participation in the United States

In Chapter 4 we mentioned that the percentage of workers not in the labor force includes students, senior citizens who are retired, disabled people who are unable to work, and wives who choose not to work because their husbands can support their families. It also includes increasing numbers of discouraged workers. We often hear derogatory remarks indicating that Puerto Ricans do not want to work, that they would rather be recipients of welfare. As we shall see, that is really not the case.

After World War II, we found more and more women entering the workforce. In fact, one set of researchers claimed that "one of the most dramatic changes in the post–World War II period is the dramatic increase in female labor force participation" (Cooney and Colón Warren 1979, 281). This was true of whites, blacks, and most other ethnic groups, including Puerto Ricans, but the trend for Puerto Rican women being in the labor force is unique. In 1950 "the participation rate of Puerto Rican females was higher than both whites and blacks. In fact, only the Japanese females had a higher rate than the Puerto Ricans" (Cooney and Colón 1980, 59–60). Puerto Rican females actually participated at a higher rate than all families in the United States combined (Cooney 1979). This agrees with our finding in Chapter 3 that when Puerto Ricans came to the United States, they came with the intent to work. Puerto Rican female labor force participation dropped dramatically, however, especially between 1960 and 1970. Why did this happen, was it the same all over, and did it affect all women in the same ways?

From our earlier discussion, we can certainly understand why women were leaving their former positions in the garment industry. Actually the more accurate way of expressing this would be to say that the positions were leaving them. We also spoke about the problems with entering clerical occupations. We are saying in part that human capital deficiencies prohibited Puerto Rican women from entering certain occupational sectors. But is that really the case? Between 1960 and 1970, Puerto Rican women in New York "had lowered their fertility, increased their education, increased the proportion heading a household, increased the percentage born in the United States, and decreased the proportion in the primary child-bearing ages" (Cooney and Colón Warren 1979, 287). One would think that all of these changes would enhance the population's probability for higher labor force participation rates; instead, the rates went down, at least in New York.

When considering New York, New Jersey, Illinois, and California, researchers found that only in New York did this decrease occur. The problem is that, as we mentioned earlier, because the New York population is so large, when we look at national Puerto Rican figures we find that New York has strongly influenced the figures, so they tend to mirror New York's experiences (Cooney and Colón Warren 1979; Cooney and Colón 1980). Again, the experiences of Puerto Rican women between 1950 and 1970 are different when comparing New York City and Chicago. The huge decline in labor force participation was not noticed in Chicago. What made the difference?

The best explanation can be found in what is called the "job mix." New York had a much more dramatic decline in nondurable operative demand. At the same time, there was a shift in New York toward female white-collar jobs requiring more education. Remember, however, that even though Puerto Rican women's educational levels were rising, discrimination did not allow them access to these new jobs. Also, educational opportunities were not equal as Puerto Ricans "attend highly segregated schools" (Zambrana 1994, 135), which do not give equal training to their students. Rodriguez (1989) was also concerned with the quality of education afforded Puerto Rican children in segregated schools. Our discussion on segregation in Chapter 7 explained how segregation allows room for discriminatory educational practices in terms of quality of education.

Chicago had a more balanced job mix and a higher rate of Puerto Rican female labor force participation. The scale of loss of manufacturing jobs was much larger in New York than in any other area studied. The conclusion that was reached was, "When labor market conditions were favorable, Puerto Rican females *did respond!*" (Cooney 1979, 233).

Another way to look at this issue is to compare Puerto Rican women to Mexican American women who have roughly the same education and fertility characteristics. Mexican American women have increased their participation in the labor force at the same time that Puerto Rican women have decreased their own participation. The two reasons for bringing up this comparison are, first, we want to point out that Puerto Rican citizenship is not necessarily an asset in determining the status of migrant groups. If it were, Puerto Rican women ought to do much better than Mexican American women with similar characteristics because they are all citizens by birth. Although at this point in their history Mexican Americans include a number of generations who are citizens born in the United States, their statistics also include noncitizen immigrants as well as undocumented persons, which should further depress the

Mexican American economic status. If citizenship assisted Puerto Ricans in their economic efforts, then they should be doing better than Mexican Americans, but the opposite is true. As Cooney reminds us, "while Puerto Ricans are not considered foreigners since Puerto Rico is a commonwealth of the U.S., this is more of a technicality than a reflection of reality" (Cooney 1979, 226).

Our second reason for making this comparison has to do with the importance of labor opportunity structure in determining ultimate economic outcomes. Mexican Americans are concentrated in the Southwest, where they have been facing favorable, expanding labor market conditions during the same years that Puerto Ricans have been facing the declining labor market conditions of the Northeast.

Colón-Warren takes us back to labor market conditions. She notes that the "tendency to displace workers through technological development, reorganization of the labor process, the flight of industries to more profitable areas, and the incorporation of additional groups such as minorities and women as labor reserves . . . must be seen as mechanisms that expanded poverty as they have maintained a permanent oversupply of workers whose competition exerts a downward pressure on earnings" (1996, 111). This "oversupply of workers" usually comprises minorities, women, and other oppressed groups who are either out of the labor market altogether or are found in the lowest-paying jobs. In other words, there is segregation in the labor market. "It is through this relegation of women to the lower strata of the working class that poverty is related to gender" (Colón-Warren 1996, 113).

The participation of Puerto Rican females by 1980 was still quite low but was beginning to respond to the rising levels of education. Clerical jobs were beginning to open up, and in 1980, "for the first time, there were more clerical workers than operatives among employed Puerto Rican women" in the Middle Atlantic region (Colón-Warren 1996, 123). However, this was not all good news. Again reflecting our findings of earlier chapters, we remember that the least educated Puerto Rican migrants were relocating to New York City, while at the same time those with higher education were leaving the city to move to other areas in the Northeast or California or back to Puerto Rico. This has the effect of maintaining an increasing number of female-headed families in poverty in New York City.

One other important aspect of Puerto Rican female labor force participation is the difference in participation rates between single and married mothers. There is a much "greater probability that female householders would be out of the labor force" (Figueroa 1991, 186). If full-time work cannot offer a relatively high wage and if day care costs are not relatively low, it doesn't make sense for single mothers to work. Figueroa (1991) found that participation in the labor force was more probable when extended family members or other adults were living in the household, whether or not those other adults worked, because schedules could be arranged to share child care duties.

Before we leave the discussion concerning labor force participation, we should once again recognize the effects of colonialism. Colonies are developed solely for the benefit of the colonizer. A colonized country is exploited by the colonizer for its resources—natural resources, labor resources, military strategic importance, and so forth. When we talk about job opportunity mixes, we tend to think of this in a passive sense—they are just a natural process of economic growth and change. However, we can't lose sight of the fact that Puerto Rican women were purposefully funneled into industries that were already declining. The garment industry, especially, wanted Puerto Ricans to fill in only for the short term so the industry could relocate and reorganize with a semismooth transition. No one was concerned about the well-being of these workers, as was illustrated by the union's decision to prevent setting up training programs. The displacement of Puerto Rican women garment workers was the result of active, not passive, decisions by the industry.

Puerto Rican Women, Poverty, and Welfare

From the discussion on labor force participation, we realize that Puerto Rican withdrawal from the labor force was not voluntary, but rather a response to job displacement. In explaining poverty among Puerto Rican female heads of families, "exclusion from employment does appear to be the fundamental explanation of poverty" (Colón-Warren 1996, 130).

Where do Puerto Rican women turn to care for their families if, as a group, they have virtually no labor opportunities? Cooney (1983) notes that even though job opportunities were not as prevalent for Puerto Rican women, welfare benefits were available in the regions where most of them lived, and they were fairly attractive relative to the level of earnings possible in the low-skilled jobs that remained. Pérez y González describes welfare as follows: "Welfare has come to symbolize the type of dire poverty one does not easily escape from, compounded by the additional stigma of ineptitude and shame. Some Puerto Ricans see the American success story as unrealistic and unattainable due to their immediate circumstances, which require that they use the bulk of their energy and resources to survive from one day to the next, without much to look forward to. Public assistance has served as a safety net for families in crisis" (2000, 71).

A number of considerations enter into a Puerto Rican woman's decision regarding work versus welfare. Colón-Warren (1996) brought up the idea of traditional cultural values. Over the decades, the traditional role of women on the island has been changing. When the greatest influx of Puerto Rican migrant women came to the United States, they were migrating during a time when gender role traditions were still very strong. Also, the magnitude of the influx of Puerto Rican women shortly after World War II meant that the communities were less "Americanized" and would have maintained island traditions better than they do now. Yet their labor force participation was the highest it has ever been in New York. It doesn't make sense that, twenty years after their arrival, their traditional upbringing would all of a sudden make them change their habits of working outside the home.

However, tradition does enter at one level. Torruellas, Benmayor, and Juarbe (1996) interviewed a number of Puerto Rican migrant women, all of whom had worked in the past but were on Aid to Families with Dependent Children (AFDC) at the time of the interviews. Puerto Rican women traditionally did not think of work in terms of "outside work." All female work was work, whether done in their own home for their own families or others or done outside in the workplace. "Incorporating the perspectives of women who are not currently involved in wage labor, but nevertheless consider themselves to be workers . . . challenges us to broaden the very definition of productive labor to include domestic labor" (Torruellas, Benmayor, and Juarbe 1996, 184). Their primary role as homemakers was always considered one in which they performed invaluable work. If they could care for their children and home while holding an outside job, they would. In the absence of being able to earn a wage high enough to care for their children, though, they consider welfare not as a "negation of wage but rather as a resource that has allowed them to take care of their homes, raise their children, and fulfill what they consider is a fundamental cultural, social and productive role" (Torruellas, Benmayor, and Juarbe 1996, 185).

Most migrant women were motivated to come to the United States because they wanted a job and they wanted to advance economically. They did not want to be on welfare. During the years women were so terribly exploited in the garment industry, they still perceived those jobs as a step up. However, between 1960 and 1965 the real earnings for Puerto Rican women in the garment industry declined below the poverty level: "Finally, any incentive to remain in the increasingly undesirable, low-wage, unstable seasonal jobs in [the] garment industry was further weakened. Weekly earnings from apparel manufacture fell from amounting to 160% of welfare benefits to 130% between 1960 and 1970" (Grasmuck and Grosfoguel 1997, 348).

Unfortunately, these women went to work young and never took advantage of educational opportunities. This was shortsighted in that when the economic conditions shifted, they were not prepared to handle that shift. However, there was no reason for them not to believe they could continue and advance in their jobs. These same women were the most unable to relocate to areas with better job opportunities because of the expense of moving:

> Declining job opportunities in the mid-Atlantic region, and the inability to profit from employment in expanding sectors of the economy therefore led these women to view welfare as a means of surviving the negative impact of the economic transformations of the times.
>
> However, mainstream analyses have often blamed unemployment and welfare reliance on individual shortcomings, turning a structural problem into a personal one. (Torruellas, Benmayor, and Juarbe 1996, 191)

We are reminded that systemic constraints, which have been an outgrowth of the colonial relationship between the United States and Puerto Rico, have both limited these women in their ability to find work and driven them to use welfare as a family survival strategy. "Rather than receiving recognition and validation for prioritizing family, the education of their children, and, indeed of themselves, these women were socially stigmatized as 'unworthy' " (Torruellas, Benmayor, and Juarbe 1996, 196). The children of such families usually stayed in school longer and found employment in the formal labor market. Even though Aracelis never went on welfare, for example, we see this strength of commitment in her for her children to stay in school.

Unfortunately, desired results are not always the ones we find. "Puerto Rican children already start with significant problems related to the poverty status of their mothers" (Rosenberg 1991, 203). Rosenberg notes the distinctiveness of Puerto Rican women, who tend to marry early but also go through separation and divorce early, resulting in much younger single mothers. This pattern suggests that "the high percentages of female-headed households found among Puerto Ricans and among blacks are probably not the result of the same family formation and dissolution processes" (1991, 220). Therefore, we should not be recommending the same solutions for this problem for both groups.

Rosenberg continues by warning us that even though we can understand the systemic causes of young mothers being on welfare, we must realize that "their own dependence on welfare may subsequently increase the likelihood that their daughters will be on welfare and perpetuate their high poverty rates" (1991, 221). This is the ultimate tragedy. The strategic solution of using welfare for survival has changed from being a solution to being part of the problem and has profoundly influenced the future of those raised in that environment.

Role of Fathers

One area of family responsibility not yet addressed in this book is the role of fathers in the lives of their children. Landale and Oropesa (2001) did a study on what the primary factor is in determining a Puerto Rican father's involvement in his children's lives. They came up with some interesting findings.

First, the whole concept of female-headed households may have to be viewed differently from one group to another. The usual way of understanding this dynamic is that the women had their children without living with the fathers, or they are divorced or sometimes widowed. However, Puerto Ricans come from the island with a tradition of common-law unions. The reporting mechanisms make no allowance for this type of informal union, and therefore the women are classified as single. Landale and Oropesa note, "Presumably, women and children benefit socially and economically from the partner's presence in the household,

but the benefits may be short-lived because of the instability of informal unions" (2001, 948).

The other finding deals with the critical role of employment in determining a father's involvement in his children's lives: "The father's
employment status is the key predictor of whether the father contributed financially and his level of involvement in the care of the child.
This suggests that the lack of involvement that is evident among many
fathers reflects larger, structurally-induced problems rather than a desire
to abdicate responsibility for their offspring" (Landale and Oropesa
2001, 963). These results reinforce all we have been saying—that Puerto
Ricans want and need to work. The lack of employment damages the
very structure and stability of Puerto Rican families.

Conclusion

We now go full circle and end where we began—by saying that we must
understand the double exploitation Puerto Ricans, and particularly
women, face, which is caused by U.S. business concerns looking for cheap
labor on both the island and the mainland.

Puerto Rican women wanted to work, and they did so in large numbers
as long as jobs were available. Structural changes in the labor market and
discrimination in the workplace, unions, and schools left them unprepared
to fully participate in the new job mix found in New York City.

"Beyond economic dislocation, New York City is also associated with
high rates of family disorganization for Puerto Ricans" (Grasmuck and
Grosfoguel 1997, 352). For single Puerto Rican migrant mothers, welfare became a necessary strategy to consider in caring for their children.
Traditional values associated with work in the home allowed them to
view welfare merely as a resource that allowed them to put their priority where it belonged—with their families. However, as is so often the
case, the cure became the disease, and the Puerto Rican community as
a whole has to deal with the issues of generational dependency and
other physical, emotional, and social ills associated with such large numbers of people growing up in poverty.

As we look at the historical economic changes that have taken place
both on the island and the mainland, we must draw the connections and
understand the lingering effects of these changes—how in the present

these changes continue to haunt us, as evidenced by the huge numbers of women and their children in poverty, and how in the future they will continue to impact the Puerto Rican community as U.S. government and business have combined to leave a legacy of dependency and marginalization in the United States and on the island.

This chapter completes Part II of this book. In every chapter we found further proof that the socioeconomic well-being of Puerto Ricans differs from place to place. We have looked at numerous possible explanations for these variations, many of which have a role to play in the overall problem, but the bottom line points to the necessity of understanding how Puerto Ricans have been able to incorporate into local labor markets. Part III begins to explore these differences.

Viewing Puerto Ricans Within the U.S. Economic Structure

9

Immigrant Incorporation into the U.S. Economy

Through our own statistics and secondary research, we have come to the conclusion that Puerto Rican experiences are not the same in all parts of the country. In fact, they are not necessarily the same in urban areas within the same region of the country. As discussed earlier, it is possible that a certain amount of selective migration is responsible for these differences: if the highly educated move to one location, leaving the less educated in another, areas with the highly educated would likely have higher median incomes. This possibility alone still doesn't explain why Puerto Ricans would move from one area to another, or why Puerto Ricans and Mexicans who have similar educational backgrounds have different socioeconomic outcomes, or even why Puerto Ricans with relatively the same human capital can do better in one city than in another. The answer seems to be found in the ways Puerto Ricans have been incorporated into the labor markets of different areas.

This chapter is laid out in two sections. The first section is a brief look at theories of incorporation of labor. We need some sense of how sociologists have been trying to understand labor incorporation of immigrants/migrants to have a framework for understanding the Puerto Rican experience. The second section of this chapter reviews specific modes of incorporation used by immigrants/migrants and attempts to determine the reasons that Puerto Ricans have or have not been able to take advantage of each mode.

Theories of Incorporation of Labor

Several theories have been put forth to explain the incorporation of immigrants-migrants into the U.S. labor force. We briefly review each of them below.

Assimilation Theory

The traditional theoretical framework used for understanding immigrant incorporation into U.S. labor market structures is that of assimilation. Basically, immigrants start out in low-skill, low-wage, low-security types of jobs, and as they begin to socialize culturally into the U.S. mainstream, they are able to advance into higher-level positions and eventually approach the native white majority in economic level. However, as Portes and Zhou (1992) point out, this theory does not explain why some groups can become acculturated yet still face barriers to economic mobility. This is what led to the use of such terms as "unmeltables" and "colonized minorities."

The assimilation theory has a number of underlying assumptions that we should consider. The first assumption is that immigrants to the United States are homogeneous regarding their backgrounds and purpose for coming to this country. In other words, they have similar characteristics in terms of gender, age, family structure, education, and former work backgrounds and are coming to the United States to make a better life for themselves. If this were true, the assumption is that, for the most part, the groups would follow the same general route toward incorporation. However, we have shown how wrong this assumption is. Most turn-of-the-century Europeans entered the urban centers of the Northeast and Midwest as laborers in the expanding manufacturing sector, and their second and third generations were able to assimilate and disperse both residentially and in terms of types of employment. We have seen that some immigrants still come from the laboring classes wanting to "start at the bottom" and work their way up, but others are highly educated, highly skilled professionals who come to maximize their earnings and professional growth experiences. Others are not economically motivated at all but are political refugees from all strata of life.

A second assumption of the assimilation theory is that U.S. native reception of the new groups will approach uniformity—distrustful and watchful at first but more accepting as acculturation takes place and as the second generation mingles on many levels with the U.S. majority. The literature has always made exceptions concerning blacks, but our history shows that this is also not true of at least some of the Hispanic groups (Mexicans and Puerto Ricans), and it also has not always been true of some Asian groups.

A third assumption is that the U.S. economic structure has remained uniform in terms of its ability to incorporate large numbers of low-skilled workers and set them on tracks toward upward mobility. We have found, however, that laborers are no longer entering an expanding manufacturing economic structure but a declining one. The service industry, which has taken its place, can still incorporate numbers of low-skilled immigrant workers but only in dead-end jobs with little or no hope of upward mobility.

The assimilation theory was helpful in understanding most, but not all, immigration incorporation during the height of industrialization, but it does a very poor job of explaining the experiences of immigrants/ migrants in the current postindustrial age. Therefore, we must look further.

Segmented Labor Market Theories

One alternative approach to understanding an ethnic group's success in the labor market, especially the success of low-skill, low-wage labor, is the split labor market theory (Bonacich 1972). This theory says that the labor market is split along ethnic lines, and it takes on two different forms. One form, the exclusion movement, basically recognizes that the majority group attempts to keep a different ethnic group out of certain segments of the labor market by establishing barriers. We saw this happening in the garment industry, where Puerto Rican women were allowed into only the lower-paid trades while white women held the best positions in "good" shops. The second form of the split labor market theory recognizes that different ethnic groups are necessary to maintain the society by being an exploited or exploitable group used to keep wages low and to threaten organizational efforts. In the garment industry shortly after World War II, Puerto Ricans were used in this way. Once they were politicized to know their rights, new immigrants replaced them in these positions. The weakness of the newer groups to negotiate for higher wages also affects the wages of higher-level groups because they fear that their wages will be driven down or that they'll lose their positions to the lower-wage group. Because the wage/class levels are determined along ethnic lines, this fear builds up antagonism between ethnic groups.

The bottom line is that new groups don't know their rights and are willing to work for very low wages. If the labor market can be segmented by ethnicity, therefore, wages can be kept low by constantly bringing in newer groups. Business wants to maintain the lowest wages possible. Hence, business looks for as cheap and docile a workforce as they can get to effectively compete with other businesses.

A second alternative approach to understanding immigrant incorporation in the labor market comes from the dual labor market literature. In this case, a differentiation is made between the primary and the secondary labor markets. The primary labor market is characterized by stable work conditions, higher wages, scarce skill specifications, and internal labor markets that provide ladders of success within the firm. The secondary, or periphery, labor market is characterized by high turnover rates, low-paying jobs, low-skill jobs, and lack of structured opportunities for promotion within the firm (Sanders and Nee 1987). Morales (1986), in assessing poverty among Puerto Ricans, indicates that to eliminate poverty, mechanisms must be in place to move workers from the secondary to the primary labor market, because the possibilities for upward mobility are limited as long as workers remain in the secondary sector.

Portes relates the dual labor market system to immigration trends. He indicates that:

> Primary labor market immigration generally possesses the following characteristics:
>
> 1. It tends to occur through legal channels and it is promoted or discouraged through explicit changes in the immigration laws.
>
> 2. Workers are primarily hired according to ability rather than ethnicity. . . .
>
> 3. Immigrants tend to have mobility chances comparable to those of native workers. . . .
>
> 4. The function of primary sector immigration is usually to supplement the domestic labor force, rather than to discipline it. (1981, 282–83)

Portes contrasts these characteristics with those of secondary labor market immigration:

> Immigration which is directed to the secondary labor market possesses the opposite characteristics of that absorbed by the primary sector:
>
> 1. Its juridical status is tenuous, ranging from illegal to temporary. . . .
>
> 2. Workers are not primarily hired according to their skills, but according to their ethnicity. . . .
>
> 3. Immigrants tend to be hired for transient and short-term jobs which are not part of a promotion ladder. . . .
>
> 4. The function of secondary sector immigration is not limited to supplementing the domestic labor force but involves disciplining it. . . . The consistent effect of secondary labor immigration is thus to lower the prevailing wage. (1981, 284–85)

Traditionally the role of immigration has been seen as supplementing the supply of low-wage labor. However, the dual labor market provides for both high-wage (or potential growth to high-wage) labor, including professionals, and the more traditional flow of low-wage labor. Grasmuck and Grosfoguel (1997) compare the experiences of five relatively new immigrant groups from the Caribbean—Puerto Ricans, Dominicans, Cubans, Haitians, and Jamaicans—as they have been incorporated into the New York City labor force. If we put their findings within this dual labor market rubric, we would say that Haitians and Jamaicans (in New York but not in other parts of the country) entered the primary labor market, Puerto Ricans and Dominicans entered the secondary labor market, and the Cubans who chose to settle in New York are somewhat in between.

Multiple Modes of Incorporation

Portes and Manning have taken a different approach to understanding modes of incorporation. They recognize that groups cannot be lumped together as low-skill and high-skill because these groups include numerous categories, each of which operates in a different way. For instance, low-wage labor immigration could be a result of temporary labor contracts (we saw this in effect at times for both Mexicans and Puerto Ricans), undocumented entries including Mexicans eluding officials at the U.S.-Mexican border and Dominicans who make their way to Puerto Rico by boat and then come to the United States as "Puerto Ricans," and legal immigration which includes those who intend to make the United States their new home ([1986]1991, 321). We also have "brain drain" immigration, which consists of professionals, technicians and craftsmen usually bound for the primary labor market and generally not residentially segregated.

Besides primary and secondary sectors, Portes (1981) and Portes and Manning ([1986]1991) talk about middleman minorities who act as a buffer between the white majority and minorities by taking the risks associated with being merchants in inner-city low-income or high-crime areas. They also bring out the importance of the ethnic enclave economy. Both of these issues will be discussed later.

When looking for explanations of how a particular group is incorporated into the U.S. labor force, Portes and Borocz (1989) add the dimension of the relationship between sending and receiving countries. The nature of this relationship certainly affects how a group is incorporated, but it can also affect the reasons that a group left its homeland in the first place and why it chose the United States as its destination.

Role of Discrimination

The inclusion of receptivity of the host country as one of the dimensions leading to mode of incorporation brings us to the issue of discrimination and how it works. Morales (1986) embraces the idea that inequality is a vital element in keeping the U.S. economic system working. The United States condones and perpetuates the exploitation of vulnerable groups and relegates some groups to a semipermanent state of remaining poor. This is exactly what we see happening with Puerto Ricans. He states that "poverty is transmitted as an economic necessity" (1986, xvii). Betancur, Cordova, and Torres state this a little more explicitly: "Although the system requires a reserve army of workers, the colonial version assigns that role to specific ethnic and racial groups, and established mechanisms to keep them in place" (1993, 110).

Unfortunately, most discussions on discrimination relate to blacks only. It is assumed that some groups, such as Puerto Ricans, that include large percentages who identify themselves on the census as being black are victims of white discrimination against blacks. However, Rodriguez found that this was not true. She reported a study spanning the years 1950–1970 that found that "within each occupational group,

Puerto Rican males and females are paid less than black or white males or females" (1980, 32). In a later work, she found that Puerto Ricans who identified themselves in 1980 as blacks or as whites fared just about the same in terms of their economic status, but those who identified themselves as "other" or wrote in "Spanish" did much worse. As a group, those who called themselves "Spanish" were "more disadvantaged than those who identify as White or Black. They are less employed in the government sector, have fewer upper-level occupations, less college education, more unemployment, greater poverty, work fewer hours and weeks, and are more concentrated in declining manufacturing areas" (Rodriguez 1989, 69). Throughout this book we have been espousing the idea that there is more to understanding ethnic relations in this country than simply plugging groups into a white or black mold. Here again we see that more is going on than simply white discrimination against blacks. Ethnicity or "foreignness" also seems to fit in.

Now, let's move on to examine the ways in which new groups gain entrance into the U.S. labor market structure.

Modes of Incorporation

This section concentrates on entrepreneurship, middleman minorities, the ethnic enclave, government employment, welfare, and the informal labor market as they relate to the incorporation of Hispanics. It also explores the concepts of ethnic queues and ethnic niches as they relate to opportunities and mobility.

Entrepreneurship

Immigrants have long used self-employment as an initial means of entering the U.S. economic system. Self-employment as a whole has been declining since 1950, but entrepreneurship is still a means utilized by the foreign-born to make a go of it in this country (Waldinger 1986; Light [1984]1991). The questions we must ask are: Why do immigrants gravitate toward self-employment? Why are some immigrant groups more likely to become self-employed than others? What types of enterprises do immigrant groups begin? and Why have Puerto Ricans not utilized this means more than they have?

One reason immigrants tend to go into entrepreneurship is that they recognize how disadvantaged they are in the secondary labor market. Another reason is that some groups come from homelands that cultivate the values and motivations necessary to encourage business enterprise. Light notes that this includes a socialization process that produces adults who prosper in business. He terms this the "orthodox" approach to understanding immigrant business enterprise ([1984]1991, 309). A third reason for going into private business is part of what is called the "reactive" approach. Even though running small shops may be looked down at by the native whites, it is still quite attractive when compared to opportunities in the immigrants' homeland. Also, the immigrant proprietor can be at an advantage in an ethnic community, where issues of loyalty and trust play a part. Those who do not plan to stay in the United States demonstrate another type of reactive approach. They don't mind working long hours, seven days a week, because their goal is to amass as much money as possible as quickly as possible so they can return to their homeland.

Regardless of their reasons for entering entrepreneurship, for a group to be successful it must have access to two particular types of resources. First is ethnic resources, including making use of language and cultural barriers and ethnic tastes to establish a privileged position in terms of markets and labor sources. It also entails preferential hiring of coethnics as well as support of other immigrant ventures.

The second type of needed resources is cultural or material class resources. Cultural class resources are obtained through the socialization process, which transmits values, attitudes, knowledge, and skills that promote a business mentality. Material class resources include human capital and investment capital. Class resources are important; when ethnic resources supplement class resources, however, achievement is more predictable.

Waldinger expands on this framework by including the "interaction between the opportunity structure of the host society and the social structure of the immigrant group" (1986, 250). This depends on "(1) a niche in which the small firm can viably function; (2) access to ownership positions; (3) a predisposition toward small business activity, and (4) a group's ability to mobilize information resources in organizing the firm" (1986, 250). Waldinger's main point is that, regardless of the resources an immigrant group has, "if ownership positions are equally coveted by immigrants and nationals, then the former are not likely to win out" (1986,

258). Therefore, we need to look at the types of enterprises generally available to the immigrant entrepreneur.

The first place in which immigrants can be competitive is their own ethnic community, where their knowledge of tastes and buying preferences allows them an advantage in providing such items as culinary and other cultural products. They also find room in developing businesses that specialize in immigrant adaptation problems as well as in such service businesses as travel agencies, law firms, realtors, and accountants. Their edge in these areas comes from trust. "Trust is an important component of the service, and the need for trust pulls the newcomer toward a business owner of common ethnic background" (Waldinger 1986, 260). However, if businesses remain focused on the ethnic community, growth potential is limited.

To branch out from the ethnic community, immigrant entrepreneurs need, again, to find areas where they have access to ownership. The types of business open to them are those with low economies of scale, those with the risks of instability and uncertainty, and those servicing a small or differentiated market.

Even within an industry, we find what is called "economic dualism" (Piore 1980). This can be illustrated by looking at the construction business in New York City. Balmori (1983) describes how New York's construction business is separated between new construction and additions/alterations. New construction is reserved primarily for native whites, whereas immigrant groups (Dominicans, in Balmori's study) can enter the industry in the secondary sector of additions/alterations (rehabs). In this situation Dominican enterprise is not confined to the Dominican community, but because its jobs are relatively small and can be completed quickly, a greater likelihood for layoffs and uncertainty in obtaining contracts exists.

Now, we turn to the question of why we do not find more Puerto Rican entrepreneurs. In Part I, we found that before the Spanish-American War Puerto Ricans included many merchants who joined the Cubans in establishing a benevolent society called *Sociedad Benéfica Cubana y Puertorriqueña*. These merchants were not just involved in local trade but had built up trade with the islands as well. However, the U.S. victory over Spain and its subsequent takeover of Puerto Rico drastically changed the makeup of Puerto Rican immigrants.

In the late 1930s, enough Puerto Rican businesses existed to establish the Puerto Rican Merchants' Association. Most of these businesses catered to the ethnic community and included *bodegas* or *colmados* (grocery stores), small cafés, bars, restaurants, *botánicas* (shops selling herbs and religious icons), and travel agencies (Fitzpatrick 1987, 49).

Post–World War II Puerto Rican immigrants were primarily rural and urban laborers, many of whom were brought to the United States through labor contracts. In an agrarian society, business acumen was not a part of most Puerto Ricans' socialization, nor did Puerto Ricans have financial resources. However, they did continue to be involved in small businesses servicing the ethnic community, primarily in New York City: "There were 6500 *bodegas* in the New York area in 1985. It is estimated that 50 percent of the food marketing of Hispanics takes place through the *bodega*. They have the *personalismo* of Hispanic neighborhood institution with all its local conveniences and accommodations to people in poor areas" (Fitzpatrick 1987, 49).

Despite the low level of class resources, ethnic resources were high and led to the proliferation of ethnic-oriented small businesses. Why, then, has entrepreneurship not flourished and become a means for eventual mobility in the greater labor structure for Puerto Ricans as it has with other groups?

One possible explanation is that ethnic solidarity, necessary for the success of ethnic businesses, relies on the idea of having a fairly stable geographic ethnic community. Early Post–World War II Puerto Ricans looked to Spanish Harlem in Manhattan to find residence. These laborers became "an important source for the economic solvency of marginal landlords in New York" (Sánchez 1986, 212). They were easily exploitable residents who could be packed into dilapidated and overpriced apartments. However, as the economic transition to professional services took place, these same landlords, "especially those with large holdings in downtown Manhattan, began to see Puerto Ricans as an obstacle to property speculation and development rather than as easy prey" (Sánchez 1986, 213). They began a massive eviction effort, emptying their buildings and either rehabbing or selling their properties to take advantage of the gentrification efforts necessary to incorporate the many new professionals moving into the city. Besides gentrification, "East Harlem was prevented from becoming an even greater population base of Puerto Ricans because of the vast program of slum clearance and public housing which broke up the Puerto Rican concentrations as soon as they were formed and prevented new concentrations from forming" (A. Torres 1995, 70).

Puerto Ricans, forced to move, relocated primarily to the Bronx and Brooklyn. During the 1970s, Puerto Ricans faced another massive relocation force dubbed the "Burning of the Bronx" by Fitzpatrick (1987). He states that "the two districts of the South Bronx with the highest Puerto Rican population lost 57 percent of their housing units between 1970 and 1980, most of them destroyed in the epidemic of deliberately set fires. This resulted in a massive dispersal of the Puerto Rican population" (Fitzpatrick 1987, xii).

The extent of this movement is further described by Rodriguez:

> The proportion of Puerto Ricans whose residences had not changed from 1975 to 1980 was the lowest of all groups: 51%, compared with 74% of Whites and 63% of Blacks. When almost half a population experiences residential change, there is more going on than changes in tastes, income, or even untabulated upward mobility. The high proportions of Puerto Ricans who moved in the Bronx and Brooklyn are indicative of the housing destruction and abandonment in these areas. . . . The Bronx and Brooklyn, the two boroughs where the *majority* of Puerto Ricans live, have also been major areas of housing devastation. Between 1970 and 1980, these two boroughs accounted for more than 80% of the net loss of housing units in the *entire country*. (1989, 107)

Rodriguez goes on to describe the "psychic despair" felt by those who daily suffered the loss of both people and places that were important facets of their world: "Those who remained in the South Bronx were forgotten by the city and stigmatized by their place of residence. In addition, they had to pay the social and economic costs of housing abandonment, depopulation, and commercial and industrial flight. They had to work harder to live less well. They had to walk farther for food and transportation; they had to travel farther for all their needs" (1989, 110). Both formal and informal activities joined forces to wreak havoc on a community. Not only were businesses destroyed in the fires, but also with so many homes being destroyed, the people frequenting the remaining businesses were moving away and thus eroding the ethnic market so necessary for the survival of ethnic enterprises. Rodriguez puts all this into perspective as she states, "Sadly, it appears to some today that these entrepreneurial efforts never occurred; that, indeed, there is a lack of entrepreneurial interest or skill on the part of Puerto Ricans and that this distinguishes the Puerto Rican migration from other migrations" (1989, 111).

Puerto Ricans did have a history of entrepreneurship. Between Manhattan evictions and South Bronx fires, though, Puerto Rican businessmen lost their base and, subsequently, their heart for entrepreneurship.

Middleman Minorities

Some ethnic entrepreneurs have been referred to as "ghetto merchants" (Portes and Borocz 1989). Basically, they provide business services in high-risk areas characterized by frustration and poverty. "Distinct in nationality, culture, and sometimes race from both the superordinate and subordinate groups to which they relate . . . they can be used by dominant elites as a buffer to deflect mass frustration and also as an instrument to conduct commercial activities in impoverished areas" (Portes and Manning [1986]1991, 321). It is important to stress that these statements refer to commercial enterprises only. Starting businesses in depressed areas requires minimal initial capital while, at the same time, circumventing discriminatory practices that would not allow for a start-up of the same type of business in a different area. "Immigrants accept the risks entailed by such ventures in exchange for the opportunity to share in the financial benefits of high retail prices and usury in lower class neighborhoods" (Portes and Borocz 1989, 622).

The idea of these immigrants is to amass a great deal of money through self and familial sacrifice to either return to their homelands or to leave the risky area with a better competitive edge with which to enter the general market. A prime example of this approach is Chinese or Korean merchants in predominantly black neighborhoods. Another possibility is Dominican merchants in Puerto Rican neighborhoods.

To understand why Puerto Ricans have not taken up middleman status, we must remember that they are the ones living in the lower-class, segregated neighborhoods where middleman minorities make their living. Also, their U.S. citizenship does not allow them to be as manipulated as foreign immigrants, so they are not granted the same opportunities, nor are they content with accepting the same limitations as immigrants are.

Ethnic Enclave

Much has been written about the ethnic enclave, especially since the development of the Cuban enclave in south Florida. Some have debated whether or not immigrants can really do better in the enclave labor market than they would in the secondary labor market. Part of the problem leading to this debate is how to define an ethnic enclave. One way to define it is to focus on the geographic community (see Wilson 1984). Sanders and Nee (1987) studied Cubans living in Miami and Hialeah, the two cities in which the Cuban enclave is found. They found that self-employed Cubans in the enclave did well but that private-sector employees did not do as well as their counterparts outside the enclave.

One basic problem in the way Sanders and Nee outlined their analysis was that they defined the enclave as where people lived rather than where they worked. By doing this, all Cubans who do well enough financially to move out of the cities but still maintain their business or employment in the cities are not counted as part of the enclave. A better definition is given by Portes: "Enclaves consist of immigrant groups which concentrate in a distinct spatial location and organize a variety of enterprises serving their own ethnic market and/or the general population. Their basic characteristic is that a significant proportion of the immigrant labor force works in enterprises owned by other immigrants" (1981, 290–91).

By using this definition, we would include all Cubans who work in the two cities regardless of where they live, and we would exclude Cubans living in the two cities but working elsewhere. Portes and Jensen (1989) did a study using this definition and found that those who lived outside the enclave but worked in it did comparatively better than those who worked outside the enclave.

Although the ethnic enclave does provide immigrants with an alternative to trying to fit into the primary or secondary labor markets, it cannot be utilized by all, or even most, groups. Portes and Manning list three prerequisites for the emergence of an ethnic enclave economy: ". . .first, the presence of a substantial number of immigrants with business experience acquired in the sending country; second, the availability of sources of capital; and third, the availability of sources of labor" ([1986] 1991, 329). It is easy for us to understand the development of the Cuban enclave within this framework. They certainly had a large number of immigrants, and they were and still are concentrated geographically. Also, the early waves of refugees included numerous professionals and others with both human and financial capital, to say nothing of the fact that the U.S. refugee package assisted them in upgrading their human capital characteristics. Finally, the first wave did include many laborers, but it was really the later waves that brought the necessary source of labor to maintain the enclave.

As with middleman minorities, the ethnic enclave depends on entrepreneurship. However, there are a number of distinctions between the two modes of incorporation. First, middleman minorities are exclusively commercial, whereas the enclave includes a sizable productive sector. Second, middleman minorities complement native enterprise by filling in problematic areas, and enclave enterprises compete with existing domestic firms. Third, the enclave is spatially concentrated, but middleman minorities are scattered among other groups (Portes and Manning [1986]1991, 329–30).

Puerto Ricans have not been able to establish an enclave even though they have had a large enough presence in New York City to have done so. They have a good continuing source of labor, but they have had neither the social nor the economic resources Cubans brought with them to enable them to enter entrepreneurship at the levels required to establish an enclave economy.

Government Employment

Government employment has become a safety valve for African Americans suffering from structural unemployment in the private sector. However, the same has not been true for Puerto Ricans. Rodriguez reports: "In 1970 only 12 percent of Puerto Ricans were employed by the government, compared to 23 percent of blacks, while local government employed only 7 percent of Puerto Ricans as compared with 15 percent of blacks" (1980, 39). The New York City Commission on Human Rights in 1973 was so appalled at the underrepresentation of Puerto Ricans in New York City government that it made specific recommendations regarding recruitment of Puerto Ricans. Puerto Ricans were the only ethnic group so recognized (Rodriguez 1980, 39). The U.S. Commission on Civil Rights reported that "underrepresentation of Puerto Ricans in public service work is a major discriminatory barrier and undermines the basic concept of equal opportunity" (1976, 81). A survey done by the New York City Commission on Hispanic Concerns in 1986 found that the situation had improved somewhat with 19 percent of Puerto Ricans as compared to 29 percent of blacks being employed by city government, but there was still concern that, despite the implementation of affirmative action programs, Puerto Ricans were not better represented in government (Rodriguez 1989).

The 1980s saw a retrenchment policy in New York City as a result of its 1975–1976 fiscal crisis, which precluded further expansion of this sector for almost a decade (Torres and Bonilla 1993, 101). This policy affected Puerto Rican employment in government severely. "There were no new hires, and many were let go. Those last hired became those first fired and, to the extent that Puerto Ricans were in local government, they tended to be among those last hired" (Rodriguez 1989, 95). Besides their propensity for being laid off, Puerto Ricans, "compared to African Americans . . . appeared less able to exercise the political power necessary to establish and preserve a sizable niche in the public sector" (Torres and Bonilla 1993, 101).

One reason for the low representation of Puerto Ricans in government may be their low level of educational attainment. Government positions require the passing of civil service examinations as well as a certain level of educational credentialing.

Welfare and the Informal Economy

If Puerto Ricans are underrepresented in the primary sector, face jobs that are being downgraded or eliminated in a restructured secondary sector, recognize that entrepreneurship is out of reach for most, and do not find government employment taking up the slack, how do they cope economically? Welfare and entrance into the informal labor market seem to be the major avenues for survival.

When faced with the possibility of unemployment, welfare does provide Puerto Ricans an alternative to accepting what has been termed "demeaning, degrading, poorly paid, physically demanding, dead-end jobs that fail to offer even an 'illusion of mobility' " (Morales 1986, 73). Rodriguez describes the role of welfare in a contracting economy as a "response to structural and sectoral unemployment. In addition to taking up the slack in the economy it also provides jobs for clerical and higher skilled workers—the welfare establishment—while it cools out what may otherwise be an unbearable and explosive situation for the unemployed. At the same time, it tends to subsidize the low-wage industrial sector and the landlord class, which is a direct beneficiary of welfare rent payments" (1980, 42–43). Despite the desire of Puerto Ricans to work, they have been forced to rely on welfare. Dependence on welfare, in both the United States and Puerto Rico, has established a marginalized population with little hope of breaking the cycle.

One way of getting ahead when no legitimate routes are apparent is to join the informal market or underground economy. This category includes illegally operated firms in legitimate industries that pay wages "under the table" as well as firms producing unlawful goods and services. It also encompasses various forms of hustling and criminal activities such as selling drugs.

Neither welfare nor entering the informal sector is a viable long-term means for Puerto Ricans to combat their economic crisis. We must look to other concepts to find reasonable alternatives.

Ethnic Queues

The ethnic queue is a process by which persons are stratified in the labor market according to ethnicity. In essence, just so many jobs are available at each level within an industry. The newest immigrant group starts at the bottom and cannot move up to the next level until the group currently occupying that level vacates it either by moving up higher themselves or by leaving the market (e.g., the suburbanization of white laborers).

In an expanding labor market, all the groups eventually move up in the queuing until they approach equity with native workers. However, when the largest migration of Puerto Ricans entered the U.S. job market in New York, the New York economy was actually contracting rather than growing. The reason there was room for Puerto Ricans initially was that a great deal of movement was taking place out of the local labor market of groups higher up in the queue. However, it was only a matter of time before the dynamics of a contracting market and the influx of Puerto Ricans crossed and caused a large surplus of Puerto Ricans with no place to enter, let alone move if they were already in the queue. Puerto Ricans were recruited to fill jobs that were temporary. These jobs were being phased out, but native groups vacated them before the transition was complete. Therefore, a temporary workforce was necessary to keep the economic "machinery" going while the transition was in process. Puerto Ricans have been credited with helping New York hold on to the garment industry. If it had not been for cheap Puerto Rican labor, more firms would have chosen to leave, and those that stayed would have had to institute production reductions.

Education also plays a role in the queuing. Teachers have been conditioned to accept the concept of the ethnic queue and are teaching and enforcing its ideology and reality on Puerto Rican students. Rodriguez reports, "This has taken various forms, such as resistance to special programs such as bicultural and bilingual education and reliance on tracting [sic] and special schools to take care of 'problem students' " (1974, 145). How can students be honed to fit industrial queuing when the market no longer provides that type of mobility? Yet again we find factors involving incorporation into the U.S. labor market that do not work for Puerto Ricans in the same way they worked for earlier immigrant groups.

Ethnic Niches

One possible means of compensating for all the barriers to incorporation is found in the idea of ethnic niches. An ethnic niche is "a particular mechanism that allow[s] groups to cope with modest skills and employers' prejudice. . . . [by establishing] an employment environment in which members of a particular group are overrepresented" (Model 1993, 162). However, niches worked better for white groups than for blacks and Hispanics. "As a result, white ethnics moved up; peoples of color did not" (Model 1993, 162). Finally, blacks and Hispanics were able to establish some niches, but these only offset discrimination and not weak job skills. Government employment is such an area, as discussed earlier. Affirmative action made being a minority an asset, but poor education and test results were still a liability.

Niches can provide a number of economic advantages to an ethnic group: "a simplified job search, the benefits of unionized jobs, and opportunities for upward mobility" (Model 1993, 167). Puerto Ricans had such a niche in the garment industry. Unfortunately, the downgrading of that industry caused the loss of that niche, and it is difficult to develop niches in a postindustrial economy. Model reports that "Puerto Rican men have been least successful of all groups . . . in securing a helpful niche" (1993, 186) while newer arrivals have been more successful despite the economic structural changes.

Once again, we go back to the importance of entrepreneurship. Model reports that a large proportion of new immigrants are better educated and wealthier. They "play a pioneering role in establishing ethnically owned small businesses, which offer the only viable niches in a deindustrializing society" (1993, 192).

This discussion begins to point to the absolute necessity of upgrading the educational attainment of Puerto Ricans, yet education itself is problematic. Not only are teachers tracking students into low-skill areas, but also, as we noted earlier, returns to education in the Northeast are very low for Puerto Ricans relative to those of native whites.

Conclusion

Ethnic groups have been able to approach the U.S. labor market through a number of means and "make it" in the United States. However, we have reviewed each of these means, and without exception we have found hindrances to Puerto Ricans making effective use of any of them. In Chapters 10 and 11, we will compare experiences in different U.S. urban areas and look for those dynamics that seem to make a difference in how Puerto Ricans are faring.

10

Puerto Rican Incorporation into New York

Puerto Ricans entered the New York labor market at the worst possible time—the onset of deindustrialization. We have established that Puerto Ricans were disadvantaged when trying to use any of the usual means for immigrant groups to be incorporated into the labor market. Add to that the fact that they, as citizens, were not as exploitable as some other groups and therefore even had a hard time keeping the low-skill menial labor jobs they began with, and the result is a marginalized, dependent ethnic group.

We do not find the same dismal story, however, for Puerto Ricans in all areas of the United States. We have seen how different regions and even different urban areas within the same region have been kinder to Puerto Ricans. Now we want to try to understand why.

Because New York City is still the metropolitan area that contains by far the largest number of Puerto Ricans in the United States, we begin by taking a closer look at that city and trying to understand its labor dynamics as they relate to globalization and restructuring. Next we will examine various industries and determine how globalization affected their development. Finally, we will review two groups with which Puerto Ricans are often compared—African Americans and Dominicans—to see how their paths are similar and how they are different as they all mix within the labor market of New York City.

161

Effects of Globalization and Restructuring

New York made the transition from a goods to a services economy earlier than did the rest of the United States: "In 1950 the New York City economy was characterized by a fairly diversified industrial base. Manufacturing . . . [with] 29.8% of the total, led all sectors. Services . . . accounted for 24%. . . . By 1983, the manufacturing share of employment had fallen by half to 15% and that of services almost doubled to 44%" (Torres and Bonilla 1993, 89).

New York, an old world center, faced a drastic decline in employment levels and population size, growth in inner-city poverty, old and inefficient building structures, and a decaying infrastructure. It was disproportionately affected by the relocation of jobs to the South and overseas. Grasmuck and Grosfoguel reported a loss of 450,000 manufacturing jobs between 1960 and 1980. "The scale of this loss, a decline of 67% between 1966 and 1991, was wholly disproportionate to the losses in other central cities" (1997, 346).

In the midst of this decline, New York also had a large immigrant influx and exhibited major growth in some sectors. To understand how this could be, we need to take a closer look at the economic structure and its various needs for labor.

Rodriguez tries to understand the disappearance of jobs for Puerto Ricans in light of the development of a global economy. International migrants are drawn into the global system and compete with domestic workers at the same time businesses are moving operations to developing countries to take advantage of cheap labor. Puerto Rican job loss is being "ensconced in an international matrix of forces that weave their way back to determine the fates of regional economies" (1989, 969).

New York City has been a center for headquarters and finance for a long time. However, its role is now quite different from what it was in earlier times. It has become a world-class city with a large concentration of producer services. Also, it attracted a great deal of foreign investment after 1976, which played a significant role in the growth and recovery of certain sectors of the economy. These foreign investors favor old, declining manufacturing centers with high unemployment.

The availability of a skilled industrial work force politically weakened by the closing of factories is one factor promoting foreign investment in manufacturing. So too is the large presence of a politically powerless immigrant labor pool that can either replace native supplies of low-wage workers, who became highly politicized in the 1960s, or occupy the new jobs created by the transformation of the industrial structure. (Sassen-Koob 1985, 308)

When we talk of Puerto Ricans as being highly politicized, we must remember the era. During the 1960s the United States was going through civil and labor rights struggles. Puerto Ricans began to claim social and labor rights, but the garment industry owners were not willing to give in to those claims. After all, new immigrants were on the scene who were willing to work for less, so the employers had little reason to surrender to the demands of Puerto Ricans. In manufacturing the city was simultaneously looking at the closure or migration of plants and the expansion of a downgraded manufacturing sector that required different forms of production and different organization of the work process (Sassen-Koob 1985, 309–13). New niches were available for unskilled workers, but the reorganization, or "loosening of worker–employer ties," has given an advantage to unskilled immigrants while damaging the institutional arrangements that Puerto Ricans and other resident unskilled labor looked to for security and shelter. How, exactly, does the growth of production services and the expansion of the downgraded manufacturing sector work to affect low-income job availability in New York?

Effects of Restructuring on New York's Industries

Not all restructuring was in the form of downgrading. We must remember that while manufacturing was being downgraded, the service sector was coming into its own. We begin this section by looking at production services, one of the growth industries in the city. Then we will look at downgraded manufacturing, with a special review of the garment and footwear industries.

Production Services

Growth in production services has provided a "critical mass of very high-income workers" (Sassen-Koob 1984, 157). This, in turn, has led to both residential and commercial gentrification. We saw the effects of residential gentrification on the Puerto Rican community as it was displaced from Manhattan.

Production services not only provide for high-income workers, they also provide low-income jobs both directly and indirectly. Directly, there is a need for janitors, receptionists, doormen, and other low-wage workers that may involve night and weekend shifts. These jobs have few if any skill and language requirements and are generally not unionized. In short, these jobs "promote disenfranchisement among workers and could conceivably be held by foreign language, powerless workers" (Sassen-Koob 1986, 97).

Indirectly, the lifestyles of high-income workers require people to cater to their demands for goods and services that are not usually mass-produced or sold through mass outlets. Among other tasks, this includes a need for people to walk dogs, clean homes, watch children, and park cars. Many of these jobs are not even counted in major industry statistics because they fall into the underground, or informal, economy. Immigrants provide a suitable supply of labor for these jobs because they are willing to accept low wages as well as to staff generally undesirable positions.

Downgraded Manufacturing

One of the major features of a downgraded manufacturing sector is the expansion of sweatshops and industrial homework as means of production. "[In 1982] there were 15 times as many apparel 'sweatshop' firms operating . . . as in 1970, and . . . these firms accounted for about 50,000 jobs, or almost all of the recorded job loss in the legalized apparel industry from 1970 to 1980" (Sánchez 1986, 218).

In addition to sweatshop and homework expansion, the technological transformation of the work process and a rapid growth of high-tech industries that offered a large number of low-wage jobs in production have also contributed to the downgrading of the manufacturing sector. This downgrading has affected the garment, toy, footwear, and electronics industries (Sassen-Koob 1984).

The downgraded manufacturing sector often utilizes the same industries that used to have organized plants and reasonable wages. However, these industries have been reorganized, and the new forms of production and organization work against labor.

We tend to associate "backward jobs" with low-growth or undeveloped economies. Paradoxically, though, there is also a place for them in "the most dynamic sectors of highly advanced industrialized economies" (Sassen-Koob 1984, 164).

New York's Garment and Footwear Industries

We have already addressed at length the garment industry and the exploited but crucial role Puerto Ricans played in that industry. Now we take yet another look at this industry.

New York's garment industry was one of the first industries to undergo internationalization. It did this through a variety of means. First, large, rather automated operations were developed primarily in the Southwest, and these operations incorporated jobs that New York City used to have. Second, there was a loss of medium-sized operations that were typically unionized and really made up the core of the city's industry. Third, there was the growth of sweatshop and homework forms of production mentioned earlier.

> The larger shops with standardized production were the ones most likely to move. The less-mechanized branches, as well as the industry's marketing and design operations, have remained in New York City. . . . branches that are more tied to fashion, have higher seasonal requirements, and demand more tailoring skill have remained in the north. . . . Highly specialized finishing work also remains in New York City. (Sassen-Koob 1985, 309–10)

At the close of World War II, garment workers were predominantly Jewish and Italian. Because relative hourly wages declined, there were seasonal swings in employment, and the industry was being regarded as having low prestige, these white groups dropped out of the industry's effective labor supply to be replaced by Puerto Ricans. As mentioned before, Puerto Ricans have been credited with saving the industry from losing more jobs and firms than it did. During the 1970s wages fell, working conditions deteriorated, there was more pronounced seasonality, and weekly wages diminished. Although Puerto Ricans started out in sweatshops and doing homework, they had become unionized and received benefits and were not willing to go back to the previous informal economy. This allowed room for Asian and Hispanic immigrants to enter the industry.

Mass production using cheap labor is preferred when producing standardized products, and firms with such requirements left New York City. When the demand is not standardized and is susceptible to unpredictable variations, enterprises must be small with low capital barriers (Waldinger 1985, 324). Because only a portion of apparel demand is susceptible to standardization, there is still room for New York to compete in the production of unstandardized goods (Waldinger 1985, 329). New York's garment industry "now functions simply as a spot market, specializing in such unstable components of demand as short-lived style items and overruns on certain standard goods" (Waldinger 1984, 63).

New York's restructured garment industry offers another example of economic dualism. Manufacturers are firms that "design clothing, purchase the textiles out of which clothes are made, and then merchandise the finished goods" (Waldinger 1985, 326). They remain controlled by the white native population. To minimize risk factors, "New York firms have moved textile-cutting departments and inexpensive pleating operations to specialized firms, and have closed in-house sewing operations in favor of separate sewing contractors" (Waldinger 1985, 331).

The specialized firms act as contractors only, sewing or finishing garments as specified by manufacturers, and this is where immigrant enterprise flourishes. However, the restructuring works to minimize risks for them, too. Contractors do not have to have the capital to pay for raw materials, nor do they have to accept the risk of accumulating inventory. Their primary role is one of recruiting and organizing labor. Because of ethnic networks, they are ideally suited to perform that task. This whole arrangement sounds very much like the original arrangements in Puerto Rico, where U.S. businesses sent the materials to contractors who then farmed it out to homeworkers either directly or through subcontractors.

Although group solidarity and a willingness to take risks are important for immigrant enterprise success, we must remember that immigrant owners need a niche in which the small firm is viable. Thus, immigrant enterprise within the garment industry competed to secure protected market niches. Dominicans were pleaters, Chinese from Hong Kong became sewers and stitchers, and Taiwanese became knitters (Waldinger [1986–87]1991, 345). As immigrants gained strong job attachments in the industry, native black and native Hispanic ties to the industry were weakened, and Puerto Ricans lost their major industrial niche.

The garment industry was not the only one to be restructured. The footwear industry was also affected but in a slightly different way. In this case, the large factories, which primarily serve the domestic market, are mostly mechanized and stayed in the area. Medium-size plants that were mostly unionized have experienced disproportionate closings. Sweatshops and industrial homework have also expanded in this industry. Competition from imported footwear has hurt the industry, but indirectly the loss of footwear jobs is offset by the increase in jobs associated with import trade (Sassen-Koob 1985, 313).

These two industries have been described to provide examples of how an increasing flow of low-wage immigrant labor can be incorporated into a city's economy while at the same time the native low-wage labor has been largely excluded.

Puerto Ricans and Other Minorities

The helpfulness of Puerto Rican citizenship has been drawn into question in discussions in a number of chapters in this book. It is often difficult, however, to understand exactly what we mean when we say that citizenship has not only *not* been helpful but has actually been a hindrance to the Puerto Rican community. Let's try to sort this out by drawing two sets of comparisons, both within the context of New York City. First we will look at the Puerto Rican experience compared with the experience of another native marginalized group—African Americans. Our primary purpose for highlighting the distinctions between these two groups is to further buttress our contention that they cannot be lumped into a single research program, that the theoretical framework for understanding what has happened to African Americans in our northern cities cannot be used to effectively understand the problems Puerto Ricans face. Even though the discussion centers on two minority groups of color that are citizens of the United States, their separate histories and unique characteristics led them to different socioeconomic outcomes, with Puerto Ricans falling behind African Americans. We will see how Puerto Ricans' "foreign" qualities, especially language, have operated to put them at a disadvantage when compared with African Americans.

Our second set of comparisons will be with Dominicans. Both Dominicans and Puerto Ricans are from Caribbean Spanish-speaking islands. Both are made up of a mixture of Spanish, African, and indigenous Indian heritages, leaving them with large numbers of people recognized by the white majority as being racially black. Because Dominicans have not been in this country for very long, we don't know exactly where they will settle in the layers of ethnic stratification. However, we will see that their immigrant status, and even the fact that their population includes large numbers of undocumented immigrants, has worked to their advantage in the changing New York labor market, allowing them to take advantage of opportunities that are not available to Puerto Ricans as a result of their politicized position as citizens.

Puerto Ricans and African Americans

Before the diaspora from Puerto Rico began flooding New York City, African Americans had a significant established community several decades old. This prior migration in large numbers gave African Americans an important advantage over Puerto Ricans: "From a purely chronological standpoint, African Americans attained earlier entry into the labor market and had a longer period of time to build the indigenous social, political, and cultural organizations that would strengthen their community structure" (A. Torres 1995, 65).

In addition to the earlier establishment of the African American community, we need to look at the pace with which the two communities were developed. African Americans made no huge rush into the city. Their development took place over a number of decades. However, Puerto Ricans came in overwhelming numbers in the post–World War II period. These large numbers were almost too much for the prewar community to effectively absorb. We saw in Chapter 8 that the prewar women occupied important roles in the community because they were information conduits for new arrivals. However, for these conduits to work, the size of new waves of arrivals had to be reasonable enough for a gradual incorporation into the community: "The rapid pace of Puerto Rican migration during the late 1940s and early 1950s apparently upset the necessary equilibrium between arriving migrants and settled community. The previously established community was not sufficiently consolidated to provide leadership and influence, given the speed and size of the new migration" (A. Torres 1995, 68).

When the economic structural changes came about in New York, these two groups were in a very different position in terms of integrating into the new order. Puerto Ricans, especially the women, were much more heavily concentrated in occupations that were declining than

African Americans were. This meant they had more to lose when jobs were lost in these areas. Also, Puerto Ricans could not make a significant inroad into the expanding service and clerical occupations primarily owing to education and language issues, including that many did not speak English and those who did speak English often spoke with pronounced and "undesirable" accents. African Americans, however, were able to take advantage of these areas. Their native tongue was English, and they were already beginning to see the advantage of education as a means of bettering themselves economically. Finally, African Americans, unlike Puerto Ricans, were able to enter the governmental sector early on. Again, we see the stumbling blocks of lack of education and "foreign" language orientation. When that sector began to decline as a result of the city's fiscal problems, African Americans had seniority and their jobs were more protected than those of the relatively small number of Puerto Ricans who entered the sector much later.

These are only a few of the differences that lead to the conclusion that the Puerto Rican experience must be examined by taking into consideration its own historical realities, rather than superimposing theories developed out of the African American experience. Timing and size of migration, labor concentrations in a limited number of industries, and language issues provided distinct barriers that impeded Puerto Ricans' progress in the new economic order in New York City. Additionally their "foreignness," especially in terms of language, meant their citizenship could not be counted on even in competition with the highly discriminated against African American community.

Puerto Ricans and Dominicans in New York

Immigrants from the Dominican Republic did not start to come to New York City in large numbers until the mid-1960s, twenty years after the initiation of the Puerto Rican flow of migrants. This meant they were facing an even more depressed labor market than Puerto Ricans did when they first came. However, we must remember that it was also a time ripe for low-skill, low-wage immigrant labor.

Over the last twenty-five years, the size of the Dominican population in New York City has increased to the point where Dominicans are now the third largest minority there (A. Torres 1995, 119). Although the 1990 census enumerated more than 330,000 Dominicans in New York, their numbers are most probably over 500,000, the undercount owing in large part to the presence of undocumented immigrants.

In some ways the incorporation of Dominicans resembles that of Puerto Ricans. They are largely rural and come from a poverty-stricken homeland. They also entered the labor market to fill economic sectors most in need of low-wage labor. At the time the Dominicans began to arrive, low-skilled manufacturing jobs in the secondary market were declining. Puerto Ricans were losing jobs, and, as mentioned earlier, were not willing to take giant steps backward to work in sweatshops or do piecework at home to remain in the garment industry. This left room for a number of immigrant groups, including Dominicans, who would be a more docile workforce and would be willing to work for extremely low wages.

The issue of the various modes of incorporation was mentioned in Chapter 9. Would Dominicans be able to take advantage of entrepreneurship or middleman economies? How well would they be able to establish and take advantage of immigrant niches in the labor market?

Dominicans did take the challenge of entrepreneurship. The restructuring of the garment industry made room for numerous small firms. As we have seen in our previous analysis, Dominicans developed a niche in the specialty subcontracting area of pleating. They own small ethnic-specific factories employing pressers and pleaters—all Dominican immigrants. The firms built in flexibility designed to meet the needs of their workers and relied heavily on family member involvement. This involvement is useful to supply "the organizational resources needed to adjust to sudden shifts in demand and meet deadlines . . . [and to allow] firms to maintain output despite irregularities in worker attendance and punctuality" (Waldinger 1984, 66).

These small firms are often criticized for taking on the characteristics of sweatshops, which ultimately translates into exploiting their own people. However, Waldinger found something different:

> While it is true that owners' informal ties to the broader immigrant community initially provide them with privileged access to a cheaper source of labor—a crucial advantage in competing against non-immigrant firms—recruiting through the immigrant network also stabilizes work relationships in a context of loosely defined work roles. This means workers acquire those managerial and production skills which permit them to move into entrepreneurial positions. For workers employed in the immigrant firm, the

opportunity to acquire these skills compensates for low pay and provides the motivation to learn a variety of jobs. (Waldinger 1984, 70–71)

Besides owning small, high-risk factories in the garment industry, we also find Dominicans owning small contracting firms, again in the high-risk sectors of that industry (Balmori 1983), as mentioned earlier.

Although Dominicans, as with Puerto Ricans, found it difficult to develop permanent niches in the economy, they have been able to take advantage of entrepreneurship. They have also assumed the role of a middleman minority in Puerto Rican communities. How does that work?

Remember, small businesses flourished in the Puerto Rican barrios during the 1950s and 1960s, but we no longer find many in these neighborhoods, especially those owned by Puerto Ricans. In Chapter 9 we mentioned how the population base to support these small businesses was destroyed by the manipulation of the communities inhabited by Puerto Ricans. This situation led to most Puerto Rican entrepreneurs becoming discouraged and leaving their shops. Speaking the same language and sharing many of the same customs as Puerto Ricans, Dominicans have filled the gap by establishing small businesses in the Puerto Rican community. This gets a little tricky. Dominican-owned small businesses in the Dominican community are considered entrepreneurship. However, Dominican-owned small businesses in the Puerto Rican community are really part of a middleman economy that takes the risk of running businesses in depressed areas where the majority owners don't want to be. We mentioned in Chapter 9 how a good example of this is Korean businesses in black communities. It is not as easy for an outsider to identify Dominicans in Puerto Rican communities as middlemen, but the principle is still the same. Even though they are in another group's territory, "their markets are still limited to economically depressed ethnic enclaves" (A. Torres 1995, 120).

Although it is too soon to determine the fate of Dominicans in New York, it appears as though they may be going down the same route as Puerto Ricans because they are showing signs of extreme poverty and social stress. We will have to wait to see how Dominicans fare relative to Puerto Ricans in the long run, but for now we see that their lack of citizenship has opened up some doors that have been closed to Puerto Ricans specifically because of their citizenship and because they have been politicized to recognize and demand their rights. Also, the Dominicans' different history in the New York political and economic systems has not led them to be discouraged entrepreneurs, as are Puerto Ricans, but rather has encouraged them to enter this mode of labor incorporation.

Both of our comparisons lead us to the same conclusion—U.S. citizenship has at the very least not been a help to Puerto Rican labor incorporation and has most probably been a hindrance. In comparison with African Americans, Puerto Ricans' "foreignness" has disadvantaged them. Unlike the Dominican experience, their citizenship and subsequent politicization has disadvantaged them.

Conclusion

New York has become the home of the very rich and the very poor. It is a world-class city composed of native whites, native minorities, and numerous immigrant groups who are all trying to improve their economic conditions. Its restructuring affords little hope for those who are marginalized and barely hanging on. It is not just the loss of jobs, because the number of other jobs has increased, but it is the type of jobs that have been lost that has caused so much of a problem for low-skilled groups. No longer can they enter an expanding industrial market with built-in ladders to upward mobility. Now they must be content to enter dead-end jobs or partake of welfare just to survive.

Puerto Ricans have felt the brunt of all this reorganization, but it has not been just bad luck. We have seen how political forces, owners of residential property, business owners, and educators have all contributed to the disadvantaged position of Puerto Ricans. Our final comparisons with African Americans and Dominicans make it clear that citizenship has not been helpful in ameliorating conditions in New York.

One of the ways in which we have seen Puerto Ricans coping with the bleakness of the New York labor market is to relocate if they possibly can. We have seen throughout this book that the situation in New York is not necessarily replicated in other areas. Chapter 11 investigates other cities in an attempt to determine the differences between those cities and New York and how the approaches those cities have taken have affected their Puerto Rican communities.

11

Puerto Rican Incorporation into Areas Other Than New York

t is now time to leave New York and look at other areas in the United States to see how Puerto Ricans have adapted to labor markets elsewhere. The major problem in approaching this topic is the scarcity of research done in local areas outside of New York. There are probably a number of reasons for this lack of research. First, we must remember that New York has held such a prominent place in Puerto Rican migration to the United States that most researchers are drawn there. Even in 1990 most other Puerto Rican communities were relatively small. Other than New York, only the Chicago and Philadelphia metropolitan areas (not even just the cities) had more than 100,000 Puerto Ricans.

Chicago's 131,000 Puerto Ricans are the second largest Puerto Rican concentration in the United States. However, of the total 735,000 Hispanics in the metropolitan area, almost 500,000 are Mexican. The Mexican community is older, more stable, and larger than the Puerto Rican community. Therefore, most research efforts have focused on the Mexican population or on how the Mexican and Puerto Rican communities combine, or don't combine, efforts in confronting Chicago's political and economic systems.

Philadelphia's metropolitan area, with the third largest Puerto Rican population, presents a different picture. Puerto Ricans make up 69.0 percent of the total Hispanic population of the area, and in the city itself they represent a full 76.1 percent of the Hispanic population. Some efforts have been made to look at Puerto Rican adaptation in Philadelphia. However, one characteristic of Philadelphia's Puerto Rican community is its invisibility, meaning that it has been virtually ignored in the midst of political decisions determined to meet the needs of the almost equal-size white and black communities. Also, because Puerto Ricans make up such a large percentage of Philadelphia's Hispanic population, researchers tend to look at Hispanic aggregate figures without distinguishing between the experiences of the different national origin populations.

We have established that Puerto Ricans do much better in metropolitan areas in the South and the West, but for that area, too, we have found difficulty in locating research. Miami has the largest Puerto Rican community in Florida, with 73,000, but it houses close to a million Hispanics, including 564,000 Cubans. The census asks Hispanics to categorize themselves as Mexican, Puerto Rican, Cuban, or Other Hispanic, and 293,000 Hispanics in Miami were from the "Other" category. Many of them are Colombian. It makes sense that Hispanic research in the Miami area would concentrate on the Cuban enclave and the influx of Central and South Americans there.

The same problem exists in California, except that it is even more exaggerated. Take Los Angeles, for example. Los Angeles is home to 3,351,000 Hispanics, 2,527,000 of which are of Mexican descent. Another 738,000 are in the "Other" category, primarily from Central and South America. There are only 40,000 Puerto Ricans. We surmise that it might even be difficult to find what we would call a Puerto Rican community. The segregation figures we calculated for Chapter 7 indicate that segregation between Puerto Ricans and other Hispanics is extremely low in all the MSAs in the West. Therefore, we would expect a great deal of mixing. Again, primary research interests have been focused on the Mexican and other Hispanic populations and on how all the groups mix.

There is a pragmatic concern with doing research on the smaller cities. The type of research needed to develop detailed labor market incorporation histories would probably be approached only if a large work could be published. This means one of two things—either doing the research toward a dissertation (and a number of dissertations have been written with just this idea in mind) or publishing a book. The problem is that, until recently, no large market for books on Puerto Rican incorporation in small cities has existed. One of the major points of this book is that just such research needs to be done.

With all this in mind, we will try to at least begin to explore the lives of Puerto Ricans in areas of the United States outside New York. We start by looking at the two major cities of Chicago and Philadelphia. We will then turn to a number of smaller cities. Finally, we will include a short mention of the continuing flow of Puerto Rican agricultural migrants.

Large Cities

Chicago

Felix Padilla found the same paucity of research on Puerto Ricans in local communities that we have been addressing. He referred to Puerto Ricans in Chicago as part of a "forgotten minority," because "although Puerto Ricans have lived in this midwest metropolis for almost five decades, a systematic study of their way of life is still lacking today" (1987, 2). This was especially surprising to Padilla because Chicago is home to the Chicago School with all its research emphasis on immigrant/migrant adaptation.

As we mentioned earlier, Puerto Ricans have not been found in large numbers in Chicago for nearly as long as Mexicans have been there. Before World War II very few Puerto Ricans lived in Chicago—only 240 in 1940 (Padilla 1987, 56). After the war and until 1960, the migration route was one that came to Chicago via New York City. "However, after 1960, direct air service between Chicago and San Juan began to introduce a completely uninitiated Puerto Rican to the city" (Ropka 1973, 51). Padilla calls this the "second great shift of surplus labor from the Island to the United States" (1987, 56), the first being the large movement to the Northeast, primarily New York.

There were two major factors in the migration from the island to Chicago. First, as was the case with many other cities, labor recruitment took place. In 1946, Castle, Barton, and Associates from Chicago worked with the insular government to recruit migrant workers to Chicago. "This initial group of Puerto Rican workers were contracted for employment in

domestic and foundry work" (Padilla 1987, 58). The second factor was
that the news had gotten back to Puerto Rico that jobs were beginning
to be scarce in New York and maybe workers should consider going to
Chicago and other cities that had not yet been hit with the loss of jobs.

The early Puerto Rican migrant was undereducated and underskilled.
Unlike Mexicans in Chicago, Puerto Ricans did not have a tradition in
agriculture or construction in the United States. They also didn't have experience in heavy industry or mining. Therefore, the jobs Puerto Ricans
took were not ones in competition with Mexican laborers. Ropka (1973)
reports that Puerto Ricans took any jobs they could get, and many were
employed in the restaurant business. "Starting as busboys, sweepers and
kitchen help, some become waiters with much improved earning power"
(Ropka 1973, 54). They were also found as messengers and deliverymen,
in stock rooms and packaging areas of stores, and in janitorial work.
Learning English was the most important factor for Puerto Ricans to advance. Padilla describes the Puerto Rican in Chicago's economic order:

> [It] was primarily in specific occupations and industries abandoned and/or
> not desired by "old-ethnic labor." Puerto Rican workers came to do the dirty
> work . . . the work no other group was willing to perform. Puerto Rican
> workers were not used by employers or management to undercut wages of
> other ethnic labor. Unlike black and Mexican labor before them, to cite two
> analogous cases, Puerto Ricans were not even considered as strike-breakers
> during times of management and labor disputes. Puerto Ricans in Chicago
> serve as a "non-competing group." (Padilla 1987, 10)

To cope with the economic circumstances facing them, Puerto Rican
families had to alter their traditional patterns of employment. Women
had to enter the labor market because the men could not adequately
meet the needs of their families. Most Puerto Rican women in Chicago
became assemblers, laundry and dry cleaning operatives, packers and
wrappers, or spinners and weavers. Just as in New York, they tended to
take positions that were an extension of their duties in the home.

The reception given to Puerto Ricans by Chicago's white population
was based on racial prejudices and stereotypes. First depicted as a docile
immigrant group, the population grew and the stereotypes changed to
very lurid descriptions. These stereotypes allowed the majority culture to
rationalize their discrimination and justify the inferior status that they assigned to Puerto Ricans. "Racial discrimination, the movement of jobs

to locations outside Chicago, and rigid educational requirements kept the Puerto Rican labor force out of the primary labor market and fixed into occupational classifications in the declining and stagnant sectors of the economy where many still remain today" (Padilla 1987, 110).

As the Puerto Rican population grew and became more conspicuous, the whites' attitude of indifference turned to hostility. Interestingly, ethnic antagonism was not found in the workplace: "A distinctive aspect of the jobs available to the Puerto Rican working class was that both white and black Americans tended to reject them in favor of more desirable employment" (Padilla 1987, 115).

Because Puerto Ricans were doing work nobody else wanted to do, "racial/ethnic antagonisms between Puerto Ricans and whites, in particular, became related to social, political, and community issues" (Padilla 1998, 70). The two biggest areas of antagonism came in the form of housing discrimination and police injustice.

When Puerto Ricans first came to Chicago, they chose to settle in or near the center of the city and were interspersed among whites and sometimes blacks. They did not begin to develop a *barrio* of their own until the early 1960s (Padilla 1998, 68).

In June 1966, an act of police brutality sparked the first Puerto Rican riot in the United States. Padilla describes the feelings of the community at that time. He saw that the riot "demonstrated the depth of Puerto Rican discontent, the extent of Puerto Rican anger and hate, and the ease with which Puerto Rican anger and hate could flare into violence" (1987, 155). This was a very significant event in that it led to the establishment of a number of Puerto Rican institutions within the community that are still operating today for the welfare of the people. It also

> helped to shift the philosophy of their struggle. In the post-riot period the dominant pattern of Puerto Rican adaptation to Chicago's larger society began to give way to, or at least coexist with, a more politicized and direct social action pattern of interest-group articulation. Barrio leaders began to focus on more militant ways to erase the cycle of poverty, unemployment, and poor education. (Padilla 1998, 74)

During the 1970s the Puerto Rican working class was still at the bottom of Chicago's occupational ladder, but the barrio residents were becoming more diversified in terms of socioeconomic status. A professional elite composed of a Puerto Rican middle class was beginning to have impact in the community. Puerto Ricans, especially those born and raised in Chicago, were recognizing the importance of higher education. However, going to college was not easy. Colleges and universities also had to be challenged to meet the needs of its Puerto Rican constituency.

Another problem with going to college was the preparedness of Puerto Ricans to study at that level. "[Studies] indicated very explicitly how the schools in Chicago were failing to educate Puerto Rican children . . . for each of the years 1969 and 1970, the cumulative drop-out, or more accurately, push-out rate for this Spanish-surnamed population was 71.2 percent" (Padilla 1987, 210).

Even with more Puerto Ricans taking advantage of educational opportunities, the job situation in Chicago is depressing at best. Most Puerto Ricans have little hope of changing their place in the labor pecking order. However, in the early 1980s they began to look to politics to bring about changes and also as a source of employment.

Chicago did not develop in the same way as many other Rust Belt cities. Although still relegated to the lowest occupational rungs of the ladder, Puerto Ricans were not highly concentrated as manufacturing laborers, so no drastic dislocation was caused by deindustrialization. The community coped through a variety of mechanisms, some of which are helpful (like going on to college) and others, such as gang formation, that are more destructive. Now, we take a look at another large city— Philadelphia—which has the third largest Puerto Rican community in the country.

Philadelphia

It is difficult to untangle the sparse research on how the initial Puerto Rican settlement in Philadelphia began. Taller Puertorriqueño's oral history study states, "There was no one single pattern of migration to Philadelphia. But, on the whole, Puerto Ricans tended to first settle in other parts of the country, mainly the Jersey farms, and then turn to Philadelphia for permanent residence. Furthermore, one member of a family would arrive in the United States and afterwards send for the rest of the family" (Taller Puertorriqueño 1979, 42). However, Ericksen and colleagues determined that the first significant flow of migrants during the 1940s came primarily from the urban middle class in Puerto Rico. Then, by the late 1940s and early 1950s, this group was overwhelmed by the much larger number of unskilled and poorer migrants who came directly from the rural areas of Puerto Rico (1985, 21). Whalen (2001) did an in-depth historical study through interviews and examination of documents from those early years. She found that the normal pattern was for the men to come to work on farms in the area and the women to come to work in the city's garment industry or come on a labor contract as a domestic.

Although we cannot pin down the exact characteristics of the first migrants, we do know that the largest numbers did not come straight from the island but followed at least three secondary migration patterns. First, as early as 1943 we find Puerto Ricans entering the area through labor contracts with Campbell Soup Company. Campbell's was located in Camden, New Jersey, across the Delaware River from Philadelphia, and had begun using the resources of the War Manpower Commission to recruit Puerto Rican laborers. Often laborers would then move to Philadelphia to settle (Taller Puertorriqueño 1979; Ericksen et al. 1985). Second, many workers came over on agricultural labor contracts, and at the end of their contract period they formed a small but steady flow of Puerto Ricans into Philadelphia. And third, a flow of migrants into Philadelphia was initiated by families coming from New York City. These flows all led to a large increase in Philadelphia's Puerto Rican community in the 1950s.

The first enclave of Puerto Ricans in Philadelphia during the 1940s and 1950s was found in the Spring Garden area (Taller Puertorriqueño 1979, 41). Once this community had begun to take shape in the city, the residents formed "a classic pattern of 'chain migration' " (Ericksen et al. 1985, 20) as they assisted new migrants in finding jobs and housing. These migrants "began to serve as a magnet that attracted other Puerto Ricans to the area" (Taller Puertorriqueño 1979, 43). Especially helpful in this regard was the size of the homes in the Spring Garden area. They were large enough to allow residents to bring extended family over from the island to stay with them until they could get settled, or they could use the extra space to take in lodgers to supplement their income. Unfortunately, those nice large homes close to Center City Philadelphia attracted young professionals, and gentrification displaced the Puerto Ricans from their original community. Now they are primarily located in the North Philadelphia section, which is "an area of heavier blight, transient residents, and welfare families" (Taller Puertorriqueño 1979, 45).

Once Puerto Ricans arrived in Philadelphia, what kind of labor market did they find? Ericksen and colleagues point out that the community began to "consolidate itself by attracting predominantly unskilled, manual and agricultural workers from Puerto Rico at precisely the time when the local labor market began a long-term decline in the availability of unskilled occupations" (1985, 22). The loss of these types of jobs has hurt the chances of Puerto Ricans who want to find occupational mobility. In fact, this loss is directly related to the fact that Puerto Ricans to this day are still found concentrated in the lowest occupational and income levels of the city.

A 1954 study done for the Commission on Human Relations found that Puerto Rican men "were largely employed in 'private household and service' jobs (waiter, dishwasher, bus boy, guard, bartender, janitor, etc.) and 'operative' jobs (bus driver, machine operator, etc.)" (Siegel, Orlans, and Greer 1954, 34). The women, on the other hand, were primarily found as "operatives" in various clothing factories. Some Puerto Rican men worked for small nonunion contractors who paid lower wages. However, not many made it into the large unionized construction companies. One of the drawbacks was the union entrance fee of about $100. Also, very few were found in heavy industry or the skilled trades, "despite their marked dexterity and industriousness" (Metauten 1959, 13).

Entrepreneurship thrived in the ethnic community as signs in Spanish indicated the existence of a *bodega*, a restaurant, a travel agency, or a money transfer enterprise. These businesses, however, were and still are confined to the Hispanic community.

A later study by Taller Puertorriqueño found that "most Puerto Ricans moving to Philadelphia are involved in the secondary labor market. Especially important are hotel and restaurant jobs and unskilled factory jobs" (1979, 47). These jobs allow room for non–English-speaking laborers but no room for advancement or training. As we have seen elsewhere, education was seen as the key to moving into the primary labor market. Most educated Puerto Ricans (in the late 1970s) could be found in community organizations, government, education, human services, or communications.

In the early period of migration, employers were anxious to find labor for menial tasks, and they were delighted to have Puerto Ricans be a part of their workforce. However, having Puerto Ricans work for you and having to live near Puerto Ricans were two different things, and there was a great deal of hostility. Whalen (2001) notes the alarm and hostility with which neighbors and community professionals reacted to the newcomers. Siegel, Orlans, and Green recount the story of how a group of whites in 1953 "stormed the home of a Puerto Rican family, damaging the apartment and injuring a child. The police and other observers were in agreement that the near-riot which resulted from the attack made on the family was an outgrowth of prejudice against the Puerto Ricans in the neighborhood, and that there was no specific cause for the outbreak of violence between the two groups" (1954, 50).

The commission's report, which was precipitated by those tense conditions between whites and Puerto Ricans, found that less than half the whites even knew that Puerto Ricans were citizens of the United States. This lack of knowledge about Puerto Ricans was also discovered when employers complained to the government that Puerto Ricans broke labor contracts. They wanted the government to deport the Puerto Ricans.

Although most of the studies done on Puerto Rican incorporation into Philadelphia were primarily interested in the early establishment period, we do know that the decline of manufacturing has deeply hurt the community. Winpenny describes this decline: "The process of Philadelphia's deindustrialization lumbered along with a deadly and unrelenting cadence" (1996, 1). From 1970 to 1994, Philadelphia lost 263,000 jobs, 30 percent of its tax base, and over 20 percent of its population. It is true that the regional area has picked up with a burgeoning bio-tech industry in the suburbs and a lot of "high tech or brain-driven industrial development throughout the Delaware Valley" (Winpenny 1996, 2), but these do not help the plight of the city.

To understand why the city lost so much industry, Winpenny lays out a number of explanations and connects them to specific industries:

> Global restructuring . . . sounded the death knell for most of the city's steel industry and ship building . . . the flight of capital and jobs to Mexico made a difference in electronics. . . . The staggering migration of northern industry to the Sunbelt to escape unions and higher wages explains the loss of textile, carpet, and clothing firms. . . . Shifts in consumer taste devastated Stetson Hats and ultimately buried Curtis Publishing and the *Evening* and *Sunday Bulletin*. (1996, 8–9)

Not only do the regional job expansions not assist the city's dwindling tax base, but also they do not represent options for a large marginalized,

unskilled labor force. The scale of manufacturing job loss has put Philadelphia's Puerto Rican community at a tremendous disadvantage and has
left them once more to be an unemployed dependent population.

Smaller Cities

Lorain, Ohio

Lorain, Ohio, is a smaller-size metropolitan area of 256,000 people. Its
15,000 Hispanics, including 11,000 Puerto Ricans, make up a relatively
small portion of that population. In the city itself, however, Hispanics,
most of whom were Puerto Ricans, made up roughly 20 percent of the
population (Arroyo 1998, 58).

The first group of Puerto Ricans to arrive in Lorain came after World
War II in October 1947. These Puerto Ricans came directly from the island after having been contracted by U.S. Steel as an experiment. They
were all single men and were housed in barracks owned by U.S. Steel.
Most of them did unskilled manual labor in a new coke plant that had
just been built in Lorain: "By 1951 there were 3,200 [Puerto Ricans in
Lorain], of which 2,000 were single men" (Arroyo 1998, 59).

There were relatively few problems until the early 1950s, when U.S.
Steel stopped housing the Puerto Ricans who then had to look for housing elsewhere. They were exploited and had to live in "shameful conditions" (Arroyo 1998, 60). The National Tube Company (which became U.S. Steel) was one of the major employers of Puerto Ricans
between 1947 and 1951, but by 1953 they were no longer employing any
Puerto Ricans. This caused a dispersion to Youngstown and Cleveland.
However, a Ford Motor plant opened in Lorain and took up the employment slack, resulting in a stable community. Another stabilizing factor was the 1952 formation of a Puerto Rican Catholic church named *La
Capilla del Sagrado Corazón* (Chapel of the Sacred Heart) (Arroyo 1998,
63). "Lorain during the 1960s and 1970s was one of the most extraordi-
nary and most stable Puerto Rican communities in the nation" (Fitzpatrick 1987, 66–67). In 1970,

> 55 percent of the families owned their homes. No other area approached that
> statistic. . . . Over 50 percent worked in the Ford Motor Company and U.S.
> Steel in good, solid jobs where they have had the stabilizing factor of union
> membership. Median family income was the second highest for Puerto Rican

communities. . . . Nationwide, 25 percent of all Puerto Ricans are at least partially dependent on public welfare; on the basis of 1975 estimates, the figure in Lorain was only 3.3 percent. (Fitzpatrick 1987, 67)

This stable community was also hit by the economic transformation. Arroyo (1998) notes that in the mid-1980s there were really two different Puerto Rican populations: an older, very stable population and a younger population characterized by welfare and its need for social services. Since the 1980s, as the slump in heavy industries affected Lorain, many older residents have migrated to find employment elsewhere. In 1990 the median family income for Puerto Ricans in Lorain had fallen from second place among Puerto Rican communities in the country to ninth place out of the forty metropolitan areas we have been looking at in this book. This "remarkable community . . . has been deeply shaken by the decline of the steel and automotive industries" (Fitzpatrick 1987, 196) and is now struggling to survive.

Perth Amboy, New Jersey

Perth Amboy and New Brunswick are the two central cities of the metropolitan area called Middlesex, Somerset, and Hunterdon in New Jersey. The whole area's population of 1,022,000 includes 75,000 Hispanics representing a good mix of national origins. Two groups, Puerto Ricans with 32,000 and "Other" Hispanic with 31,000 make up the bulk of it. As with many of our smaller cities, we will have to rely on only one research study to glean some insights into the Puerto Rican community. Fred Golub did a study of Perth Amboy that was published in 1956. Although his work is so old, we can get some ideas as to the formation of the community, but we will obviously not be able to comment on its adaptation to the economic transformation hitting the Middle Atlantic states.

Perth Amboy is situated about seventeen miles south-southwest of Newark, New Jersey. It developed with a heterogeneity of national backgrounds that made it "possibly the best city in the State of New Jersey for integration of Puerto Ricans" (Golub 1956, 6), although they faced "the same social prejudices [as earlier immigrant groups], reenforced [sic] by the element of color bias" (1956, 1). Very few Puerto Ricans (less than 500) lived in Perth Amboy before 1949. Then the migration picked up, so that there were about 3,000 by 1955. If you recall, both men and women were a part of the migration that went to New York City. However, it was different with Perth Amboy. The first migrants were men who had been agricultural workers and relocated to the city to fill the need for unskilled manual labor. As they found work and saved some money, they brought their families over to join them. They also encouraged others to come. At the time of the study, "one-half of the Puerto Ricans in Perth Amboy [came] from a single area, the San Sebastian area of Puerto Rico" (1956, 6).

Job patterns varied by gender. Male Puerto Ricans worked at any job they could find, including washing dishes and washing cars, as long as it gave them an income. The women, however, were more concentrated industrially. Heavy industry provided good opportunities at the time because there was a shortage of unskilled labor in Perth Amboy and there were relatively few African Americans there with whom to compete. The men entered the heavy industry positions, but the women were more likely to enter the consumer goods industries and fill jobs more in keeping with their previous work experiences.

Golub's study indicated that Puerto Ricans were not displacing other workers, for two reasons. First, they held a marginal position in the labor market—they were the last hired and first fired when unemployment was high. Second, they tended to take jobs that non–Puerto Ricans were not as likely to seek, jobs left available when previous immigrant groups were upgraded or their children became mobile enough to enter skilled, white-collar, or professional jobs.

According to Golub, Puerto Ricans made up 6 to 7 percent of the total population. One of the patterns he was trying to ascertain was the use of welfare. He found that when unemployment was high (e.g., in March 1954, through February 1955), Puerto Ricans made up 12.6 percent of the total population on welfare. However, in 1951 and 1952 when unemployment was low, they made up less than 2 percent of the caseload. Golub's conclusion was, "Puerto Ricans are not drawing excessively on public insurance and welfare benefits, except as their job patterns create above-average need for them. When opportunities are available, Puerto Ricans would rather work than collect public benefits" (1956, 14). This agrees with our discussion on Puerto Ricans in New York. They wanted to work!

Milwaukee, Wisconsin

Although not on the scale of a Chicago or Philadelphia, Milwaukee is a larger city with close to 1.5 million residents in 1990. Its Hispanic community is relatively small—only 51,000 altogether including close to 29,000 Mexicans. The Puerto Rican population in 1990 was less than 16,000. Jose Torres did his dissertation in 1980 on Puerto Rican men in Milwaukee. He, too, had to face the lack of prior research on Puerto Rican incorporation in U.S. society: "Despite the fact that Puerto Ricans have been migrating and settling in Milwaukee for more than a quarter of a century, bringing with them a language and a culture different from that of the dominant society, the Puerto Rican community has received little attention in the local literature" (1980, 50). He also bemoans the fact that the Puerto Rican people in Milwaukee are "largely ignored or misunderstood, particularly by the makers of policy and the holders of power" (1980, 40).

Puerto Ricans initially came to Milwaukee in the late 1930s and early 1940s. These early migrants were male agricultural laborers who came from other cities in the Midwest and rural areas in Michigan. They originally came primarily from rural areas of Puerto Rico and had few or no skills, but they were needed as workers in the factories near Milwaukee.

The major migration to Milwaukee didn't start until after World War II, and it was characterized by an increase of Puerto Rican workers who came directly from the island and from other cities. This was precipitated by Milwaukee employers' participation in the major postwar recruitment of Puerto Ricans, particularly to foundries and tanneries. Although Milwaukee is small in comparison to other cities, migration between 1950 and 1952 amounted to about 2,000 Puerto Ricans.

Migration patterns turned around in 1953 in response to an economic recession, and Milwaukee found more Puerto Ricans returning to Puerto Rico or moving to other cities than were entering their city. Another turn around occurred in the period of 1955–1960 when employment opportunities improved slightly and families made the move to Milwaukee. Even during this period, the outlook for Puerto Ricans was not very good. The city's demand for labor decreased and all working groups faced high unemployment. "Puerto Rican unemployment was estimated to be as high as 40% in comparison to 6% for the total labor force during 1958" (J. Torres 1980, 45), and the migration flow began to decline again after 1960.

Puerto Ricans continued to respond to labor opportunities with periods of inmigration and periods of return migration. This makes sense when we consider that availability of employment was one of the most important factors in determining a Puerto Rican's move to Milwaukee. Then from 1972 to the time of Torres's study (1980) they once more were making the move from other U.S. cities to Milwaukee.

Over time, it was found that employed Puerto Ricans had incomes comparable to those of non–Puerto Ricans. The problem was that many more Puerto Ricans were on welfare, their labor force participation was lower, and they still had the most undesirable jobs. This agrees with our findings that Puerto Ricans who have jobs do fairly well, but the problem is that there just are not enough jobs.

The history of Puerto Ricans in Milwaukee tends to be very sensitive to labor issues. Cyclical migration has been brought up before, but we see in Milwaukee that the relative position of the whole Puerto Rican community tended to ebb and flow in response to the city's labor opportunity structure. Torres concludes that "for the most part, the conditions of Puerto Ricans in Milwaukee . . . have improved very little in the last 25 years" (1980, 56).

Allentown and Bethlehem, Pennsylvania

Situated right beside each other, Allentown and Bethlehem are two central cities in the Allentown, Bethlehem, and Easton MSA. With a 1990 population of 687,000, this is a medium-size metropolitan area. Included in the entire MSA are 29,000 Hispanics, 21,000 of whom are Puerto Rican.

We have only sketchy information on Allentown, but it does not seem to have developed in the same way as neighboring Bethlehem. The massive work by the Lehigh County Historical Society notes, "There would be a treasure for future Allentown historians if a few scribes among the Hispanics . . . would record what brought these latest groups to this city and what their early struggles have been" (Hellerich 1989, 550). We do know that 90 percent of Allentown's Hispanics came directly from rural areas of Puerto Rico or from another U.S. city. This means that the Puerto Rican community is growing through a constant influx from other areas, as opposed to large natural growth. Also, on the basis of the 1990 population, estimates were that by the year 2000 Hispanics (primarily Puerto Ricans) would make up 15 to 20 percent of Allentown's population.

We have recognized the importance of education for economic mobility. School records indicate that during the 1975–76 school year, Hispanic students outnumbered black students for the first time, and "within a decade, there were double the number of Hispanics compared with blacks in city schools" (Hellerich 1989, 547).

The historians pointed a finger at the people's desire to return to Puerto Rico and their relatively low educational attainment and have "blamed the victim" in the sense that they have said the people were "placing greater uncertainties and burdens upon themselves than were faced by many immigrants in the past" (Hellerich 1989, 548). However, Antonsen in 1997 characterized Allentown's school district as one that "segregates the students in a series of 'Tracks' with Latinos trapped in the lowest levels. Although Latinos comprise more than 40 percent of Allentown's student body, the school district employs approximately 1.7 percent Latinos in any capacity. Allentown's nine member School Board contains not a single Latino" (Antonsen 1997, ii).

As for employment, a 1978 report indicated, "Nearly all Hispanics who were employed worked in manual labor in factories, housekeeping and farm labor. . . . An Hispanic 'professional' community was virtually non-existent" (Hellerich 1989, 547). However, during the middle 1980s efforts were being made to bring Hispanic professionals to the city, and by 1987 there were a few Hispanic physicians and lawyers in Allentown.

The economy of Allentown was also changing, as with most areas in the Northeast. Typically, there was a decline in manufacturing jobs—in both heavy manufacturing and textiles—and a corresponding expansion in the nonmanufacturing economic sectors. The problem is that, educationally, Hispanics were not able to take advantage of those new jobs.

Antonsen sums up the situation for Puerto Ricans in Allentown by saying that "Allentown's power structure is united in its denigration, repression, and exploitation of the city's Latinos" (1997, ii).

Because of the sketchy nature of our information on Allentown, we cannot be sure exactly how it developed, but we have a much better source for Bethlehem. Antonsen (1997) did a comprehensive study on the development of Bethlehem's Puerto Rican community.

Migration to Bethlehem took place in two distinct waves. The first wave began shortly after World War II. This wave included farm laborers who came during the late 1940s and through the 1950s to work on farms surrounding Bethlehem. Many of these workers stayed on during the off-season and worked in the factories. It also consisted of laborers enticed by the recruitment efforts of Bethlehem Steel and numerous other industries to work in the factories. Finally, this first group included some middle-class people who were educated and able to provide leadership to the community.

The first wave continued through the early 1970s. Coming from rural areas of Puerto Rico, especially Patillas and Corozal, they found stable employment that provided them with at least some upward mobility. Industrial jobs that could be filled by unskilled but industrious workers such as those from the island were plentiful. "By 1960, the industrial sector's textile and metal industries produced 56.1 percent of all the area's jobs" (Antonsen 1997, 23). The primary employer in the area was Bethlehem Steel, and many Puerto Ricans worked in the steel plant. Most of these were relegated to the Coke Works, one of its hottest sections.

When this first wave of migrants came, they were met by a small but established colony of Mexicans who, because of the common language, helped them adapt, especially within the Bethlehem Steel mill.

One thing immediately noticeable is that the effects of the economic transformation from manufacturing to service industries did not take place as early in Bethlehem as it did in New York. Employment opportunities were still good in the early 1970s. One more point should be made. As we have been finding in all areas, Puerto Ricans came seeking work (Antonsen 1997, 25). Also, the settlers sent word back home about the opportunities present in Bethlehem.

The children from this first wave were able to take advantage of the economic advances of their families. One manifestation of their social mobility was a fourfold increase between 1970 and 1980 in the percentage of Hispanic students who went to college. "By the late 1980s, several of the children of the first wave became community leaders" (Antonsen 1997, 5). This indicates a stability within the community—not like the case in Milwaukee, where the population was constantly on the move between Puerto Rico, Milwaukee, and other U.S. cities.

> The availability of secure and relatively well paying blue-collar employment was the key variable that enabled the early Puerto Rican settlers in Bethlehem to improve the quality of their lives. Steady employment with its resulting stable income proved more important than education in insuring upward class mobility for the early settlers and their children. (Antonsen 1997, 38)

The second migration wave began in the late 1970s and represented different background characteristics. Rather than coming from rural areas of Puerto Rico, the new migrants were more likely to be coming from urban areas of the island. Also, an increasing percentage were not from the island at all but from New York's *barrios*. This wave had fewer two-parent families and instead had a higher percentage of single mothers. Not only were these migrants different from those of the first wave, but also when they arrived in Bethlehem they faced a declining industrial sector. They had a hard time doing as well as the first wave or the children of the first wave, and by 1990, "about forty percent of the Puerto Rican community of Bethlehem was living in poverty" (Antonsen 1997, 81). In essence this second wave, which moved from urban slums either in New York or on the island to find better opportunities, was sorely disappointed and seemed to be going down an economic slide. They were not as able to compete for jobs in the expanding service, retail, government, and other white-collar sectors for many of the same reasons cited in our discussion of New York.

This mismatch of labor skills and labor opportunities led the Puerto Ricans in Bethlehem to rely on welfare. "In 1991, 39.9 percent of the Hispanics [in Bethlehem] received public assistance, compared to 26.8 percent of the African Americans, and 4.52 percent of the other residents" (Antonsen 1997, 87). Once again we find an industrious migrant group desirous of work and willing to work hard being relegated to a marginalized position of dependency.

New England Cities

New England states, and especially Connecticut and Massachusetts, have been the home of Puerto Ricans since the antebellum period (Cruz 1998, 3). We don't think of Puerto Ricans as having been in the United States that long except for the New York City community, but as a public television show entitled "Puerto Rican Passages" pointed out, Puerto Ricans resided in Bridgeport, Connecticut, in 1844 and in New Haven, Connecticut, in 1861. Of course, they were the exceptions, but they represented the beginning of New England interaction with Puerto Ricans. In its program script, the Connecticut Public Television and Radio reports, "In 1936 in New Haven, the nucleus of the modern Puerto Rican community arrived when the New Jersey branch of the Winchester Repeating Arms Company transferred eight Puerto Rican employees" (1997, 6). The script continues by indicating, "During World War II, Puerto Ricans played a major part both in the armed services and war related work. They were recruited to work in places such as Electric Boat in New London and Remington Arms in Bridgeport" (1997, 6–7). However, after World War II while Operation Bootstrap was restructuring the economy on the island, the Puerto Rican government worked with U.S. state government officials, including those from Connecticut, to recruit workers. The Shade Tobacco Growers Agricultural Association (STGAA) recruited thousands of laborers for Connecticut and Massachusetts to work in apple orchards and tobacco farms. Morales points out that labor contracts had been negotiated between Puerto Rico and Massachusetts since 1948, but Puerto Rican migrant workers had been recruited there even earlier than that: "The first migrations of Puerto Ricans to Massachusetts were into the Connecticut River Valley for work on tobacco farms. First brought into the Hartford, Connecticut, area, the use of these workers spread up the Connecticut River Valley into Massachusetts" (1986, 78).

During the 1950s Connecticut was drawing one-quarter of its population from New York. However, just as we saw with Perth Amboy and Milwaukee, there were also direct connections between towns in the United States and towns in Puerto Rico. Aguada, Puerto Rico, sent migrants to Meriden, Connecticut; Loiza was linked to the city of New Haven; and Orocovis was partnered with Waltham, Massachusetts. In fact the New England cities preferred migrants from the island because those who had been in New York were more knowledgeable and would stoop to do what they considered demeaning and dead-end migrant farm labor only until they could get better employment.

Many of the migrant workers did not go back to Puerto Rico after the term of their contract was over but migrated to one of the nearby cities to go into manufacturing. During the 1960s many of the Puerto Rican communities began in the towns situated near the agricultural areas. "Puerto Ricans worked in Guilford foundries, toiled in Meriden's silver industry, sweat in the brass mills of Waterbury, produced tools in New Britain factories and labored in Willimantic's textile mills" (Conn. Public Television and Radio 1997, 14). Meriden, Connecticut, was known as a model community and provided steady jobs at factories including the International Silver Company.

By the early 1970s, 100,000 Puerto Ricans lived in Connecticut, but its industries, including thread, silver, and defense, started to decline. Puerto Rican unemployment in Willimantic rose to 28 percent. As jobs decreased, the use of entitlement programs increased. However, residents of one of the housing projects in New Britain were interviewed, and they all said they preferred working to welfare (Conn. Public Television and Radio 1997, 25). The Connecticut State Committee to the U.S. Commission on Civil Rights reported in 1973 that Puerto Ricans in Connecticut were among the state's "most disadvantaged citizens. They suffer from poverty, illness, unemployment, and poor housing" (1973, v).

Morales (1986) uses Waltham, Massachusetts, as a case study and draws a bleak picture. Puerto Ricans went to Waltham because they wanted to work. When they couldn't find jobs, they got discouraged. Feeling insecure and hopeless, they would talk of moving from Waltham, going on welfare, or just letting unemployment benefits run out and trying once more to find a job. They presented a mini-picture of the larger New York City community.

Let's take a quick look at aspects of Puerto Rican incorporation into three of Connecticut's cities—New Haven, Hartford, and Bridgeport.

New Haven

In 1970 Puerto Ricans were said to be "grossly unemployed, underemployed and usually limited to low level, unskilled jobs with little hope for advancement" in New Haven (Conn. State Committee 1973, 1). The Connecticut State Committee to the U.S. Commission on Civil Rights (hereafter referred to as the Committee) found an insignificant number of Spanish-speaking employees in high-level jobs. They were also grossly underrepresented in government positions. In eleven city government departments, there were no minority group employees. No

Spanish-speaking persons worked in the mayor's office or in the personnel department of the civil service committee.

The school system looked the same. The school population was 7.2 percent Puerto Rican, but only fifteen of its 1,260 teachers were Puerto Rican.

The city's health department also excluded Spanish-speaking residents. It had five Puerto Ricans out of 104 employees and not one of them was at the professional level. "The omission of Spanish speaking professional personnel may result in poor communication between the person who needs medical assistance and the person who provides medical assistance. The result is a probable barrier to adequate health care for Puerto Ricans in New Haven" (Conn. State Committee 1973, 3).

The police force had a unique way of excluding Puerto Rican officers—Puerto Ricans tend to be short, but officers had to be at least five feet, eight inches in height. The Department of Welfare also lacked Puerto Rican workers, which hurt many of its clients who were Puerto Rican because they might not have had equal access to the services that could help them break the poverty cycle.

In summary, the Connecticut State Committee found that in 1970, "No Spanish speaking person occupies a policy-making position in any city agency. Most are employed in the category of menial labor, while others are skilled workers and others are in service positions. In short, of the 114 jobs which Spanish speaking persons hold within city government, all are low-paying and devoid of policy-making responsibility" (Conn. State Committee 1973, 4).

One of the problems with relying on secondary research for studies as we have done here is that we are limited to the angle of the authors and their time frame. All of the government involvement information presented is from the early 1970s, and undoubtedly much of it has changed. However, even though it is very dated, it does give us a picture of how Puerto Ricans were treated in New Haven at that time.

Hartford

At first glance Hartford looks like quite a different story. However, the report we located on Hartford was published in 1998, twenty-five years after the report on New Haven. In the early 1970s, Hartford's Puerto Rican citizenry was not represented any better than that in New Haven.

In fact, the frustrations caused by bearing the brunt of all the economic woes of the city and being powerless to speak against oppression came to a head in the late summer and fall of 1969 with a number of Puerto Rican riots. At that time about 20,000 Puerto Ricans lived in Hartford, and the community was "demographically significant but unrepresented" (Cruz 1998, 65).

Puerto Ricans began coming to Hartford in large numbers in the 1950s. These migrants included farm laborers, skilled workers, and also a few professionals: "The Puerto Ricans coming into Hartford in the 1950s were from diverse backgrounds. Some were from the semi-isolated mountain regions of the island who came to work the tobacco farms. Others came from larger towns, such as Ponce in the south, with skills that were mismatched to the jobs they took upon arrival" (Cruz 1998, 37).

We find the labor settlement history in Hartford similar to that of other Connecticut towns—migrants coming to work the fields and deciding to stay. However, the attitude of the white majority was not welcoming. In fact city officials called Puerto Ricans "a problem" in 1954, even though they represented no serious crime over the three prior years, and in 1953 fewer than 20 Puerto Ricans were on the welfare rolls (Cruz 1998, 47–48).

Over the next two decades, the Puerto Rican population increased dramatically. Hartford, the insurance town, historically had a pretty good mix of jobs all along. As late as 1965, the numbers of manufacturing and service jobs were almost even, but this started changing by the early 1970s as manufacturing jobs declined and service jobs increased.

One of the problems the Hartford Puerto Rican community faced was housing displacement in the 1970s. This split the community into two sections, which effectively caused suspicions between the sections. Of course, coalition-building and political mobilization were much harder under these conditions.

More jobs were being lost. Cruz describes what was going on:

> In 1982, one thousand workers had been sent packing following the dissolution of a Connecticut General subsidiary. In 1990, Aetna had reduced its workforce by eliminating twenty-six hundred positions. Two years later, Travelers announced that it would lay off five thousand workers by 1994. In this context, it was not hard to understand why one of every ten buildings in Hartford was abandoned in 1995 or why in the short span between 1990 and 1994 the city lost 11.1 percent of its population. (1998, 155)

By 1990 Hartford's Puerto Rican population was 27 percent of its total population, which was the highest concentration of Puerto Ricans anywhere in the country.

Bridgeport

The Connecticut State Committee also reported on Bridgeport in 1973. They called it the "center of industry and employment for the surrounding area" (1973, 17). However, as with New Haven and Hartford, Bridgeport was not responding to the needs of its Puerto Rican citizens.

The facet of incorporation singled out for a closer look by the Committee was education. Bridgeport found its Puerto Rican students dropping out in large numbers. It desperately needed Puerto Rican guidance counselors, yet they had none. As one student explained his experiences, "A Spanish speaking student comes into the room. Immediately that person is considered dumb without even being given a chance" (Conn. State Committee 1973, 18). Students felt rejected by their teachers, and the school system provided few programs designed to meet their needs, so they dropped out. A number of plans were devised to bring in Spanish-speaking teachers, but funding was never sufficiently allocated to allow for more than superficial implementation of those plans. Part of the problem is that the Board of Education had no Puerto Ricans, so the community did not have a forum from which to present the needs of its children.

Hawaii

We have constantly talked about how Puerto Rican migration primarily began after World War II. However, labor contracts were in effect almost from the moment of U.S. colonization.

The first migrations began in 1900. The Hawaii Sugar Planters' Association recruited sugarcane workers at a time when Puerto Rican workers were hurting as the result of a destructive hurricane in 1899. Eleven expeditions were made from Puerto Rico to Hawaii running from November 22, 1900, through October 11, 1901. Generally, the expeditions entailed a boat ride from Puerto Rico to New Orleans, a train trip from New Orleans to San Francisco, another ocean voyage from San Francisco to Honolulu, and finally a ride on a small inter-island steamer to Lahaina on the island of Maui (Souza 1998, 27–28). For a variety of reasons, many of the Puerto Ricans changed their minds during the long train ride and tried to escape, but agents from the Association would capture any escapees and put them back on the train. However, sloppy transfer procedures in San Francisco allowed almost half the Puerto Ricans to escape to begin settlements near San Francisco.

Those who finished the trip were put into a camp where they received housing, fuel, medicine assistance, and work. A family would receive either room in a barracks with outdoor cooking space, or a tiny cottage in a camp. Plantations had workers from many nationalities, each one with its own camp. The plantation owners used language as "an effective way to control the workers. . . . [They brought] in different ethnic groups so that no one group would have too much power" (Souza 1998, 28).

The Puerto Ricans who went to Hawaii tended to stay there because the trip back to Puerto Rico was both difficult and expensive. After a while workers were able to move out of the camps into single cottages, and some even succeeded in owning little homes.

Their children adapted to the new surroundings by learning to play new musical instruments and participating in sports. In fact, "in the 1940's and 50's there was an active Puerto Rican Athletic Club" (Souza 1998, 33). Other organizations were also formed, including the Puerto Rican Heritage Society of Hawaii, whose main purpose is "to promote and to preserve the cultural heritage of Puerto Ricans of Hawaii by focusing on their adaptation to life in Hawaii, by examining their role in the Hawaiian society and by researching their cultural and historical base" (Souza 1998, 33).

It is difficult to gather statistical data about Puerto Ricans in Hawaii. One reason is that, as in Puerto Rico, there is a great deal of intermarriage, which makes ethnic identification confusing. For example, someone whose lineage includes Japanese, Hawaiian, Puerto Rican, and maybe something else would not necessarily choose Puerto Rican as his or her ethnicity.

San Francisco and Other Cities in California

As we just discovered in our discussion of the Hawaiian settlements, the San Francisco community was started by those who refused to go to Hawaii. As with the Hawaiian community, it was important to have organizations to preserve culture and language in all the California settlements from San Francisco south to San Diego. Piñeiro states, "There is a very strong sense of *puertorriqueñismo* [Puerto Ricanness] in the area" (1998, 38).

Although the Puerto Rican community is one of California's fastest-growing communities, Piñeiro reports that "the resources available to the Puerto Rican community have been very limited and not adequate for providing programs to alleviate the most pressing needs in the community" (1998, 39). Puerto Ricans have been called "a minority within a minority of about six million Hispanics" (Piñeiro 1998, 40).

During the 1980s, as we have documented in other chapters, "skilled and unskilled workers have been migrating to California. There is also a great migration of professionals directly from Puerto Rico" (Piñeiro 1998, 42). Recruiters are still going to the island, but they are no longer seeking laborers. Companies such as Hewlett-Packard, General Electric, and IBM are recruiting directly from the University of Puerto Rico. As Piñeiro explains:

> One reason for this is that there are not enough engineers in California for the jobs available right now [mid-1980s], so they are recruiting from every possible source. The other reason is that these companies receive money from the Department of Defense, and part of that contractual agreement is that they have to have affirmative action. Puerto Rico is producing quite a few professionals which helps these companies in two ways: first, they bring resources that the companies need, and second, when they hire Puerto Ricans they are complying with the Federal Government. (1998, 42)

Besides these imported professionals, Puerto Ricans have been impacting California's educational institutions at all levels.

Rural Areas

We have primarily been focusing on urban settlement patterns of Puerto Ricans in the United States. However, we should not ignore that rural settlements still exist. In fact, we still find the annual migration of workers to U.S. farms: "It is estimated that, even today, about twenty thousand Puerto Rican workers come to the mainland each year to harvest such crops as tobacco in Connecticut, fruits and vegetables in New York and New Jersey, and sugar beets in Michigan" (Petra Press 1996, 23).

How have conditions been for Puerto Rican farm workers in the United States? Unfortunately, agriculture is just one more industry that has exploited Puerto Ricans.

After World War II, Puerto Rican farm laborers were recruited as contract labor by the Glassboro Growers Association, a New Jersey farmers' association, to pick strawberries, peaches, and table vegetables. Farmers generally violated the contracts in that they "did not respect the minimum wage or number of hours, and often deducted the cost of transportation from the workers' wages" (M. Pérez 1998, 82).

When the laborers' contracts were over, many Puerto Ricans moved into nearby cities rather than return to the island. The Vineland, New Jersey, Puerto Rican community is one that grew primarily through this movement of farm workers. This community became quite stable, with a large proportion of home owners. It also did not forget its past and united with the farm workers' struggle.

Numerous organizing efforts have tried to confront the farmers with varying success. M. Pérez says that "wherever there is oppression, there is struggle, and even though the farm workers have been oppressed, they have been trying to develop a strong organization for a long time" (1998, 85). The Meta organization (*Ministerio Ecuménico de los Trabajadores Agrícolas*) was begun in the early 1970s by Episcopal ministers and was responsible for both organizing and educating farm workers. In 1975, ATA (*Asociación de Trabajadores Agrícolas*) was started in Hartford by pro-independence activists and did a great deal of work in Hartford and in New Jersey. It tried to be recognized by the government of Puerto Rico to be the "workers' representative in contractual matters" (M. Pérez 1998, 85), but after a number of years with no success, the ATA disappeared.

In the late 1970s the workers tried to get César Chávez to help in their organizing efforts, but he was not able to come because of problems being faced by his own union. Finally, in 1979, CATA (*Comité de Apoyo de los Trabajadores Agrícolas*) was formed through the efforts of activists and many workers themselves. This group was in an intense struggle in the south Jersey area during the mid-1980s. One of its members, David Velazquez, pointed out that "history is being made at all times by people who have to respond to injustice, not because of their principles, but because of the need to survive" (M. Pérez 1998, 87).

And so they continue to struggle against the overwhelming influence of the employers' lobbyists, who persist in discriminating against Puerto Rican farm workers.

Conclusion

Obviously, much more needs to be done in terms of developing up-to-date city or metropolitan area case studies that focus on the history of labor incorporation. Although hit by the effects of the move into post-industrialization at different times, even in different decades, most of the cities we have talked about are in the Rust Belt regions and have similar trajectories. Our two discussions about Hawaii and California are a beginning, but they are sketchy in terms of labor incorporation patterns. Case studies from areas where Puerto Ricans are doing much better will be tremendously helpful in trying to understand the factors on which we should focus to improve the situation for Puerto Ricans wherever they are located.

Despite that many of the studies utilized in this section were written quite a while ago and many of them did not have labor incorporation as their research focus, we believe that the differences noted in local labor markets do support our overall thesis that the local labor context has a large impact on how well Puerto Ricans do in any particular area. In all areas, however, we continue to find discrimination and marginalization. We must keep this in mind so we don't succumb to the temptation of thinking a simple relocation can solve the woes of Puerto Rican people.

12

Conclusion

We began our journey toward understanding the nature and causes of Puerto Rican poverty with a number of objectives in mind. Our first objective was to show that it is necessary to look at Puerto Ricans as a distinct group, rather than combining them with all the other Hispanic national groups. To address this issue, we told the histories of the three major Hispanic national groups—Mexican, Cuban, and Puerto Rican—so that we would understand how different the forces were that shaped their entrance into the United States and their interaction with the majority power structure. We found that the groups were regionally situated and that Mexicans and Puerto Ricans were dispersing, whereas Cubans were becoming more concentrated. Data from the 2000 census is beginning to trickle out, but Hispanic data is still very general and not disaggregated by national group. We can say, however, that Hispanics as a whole seem to be diffusing. Of a total of 3141 counties in the United States, 2990 "have shown some increase in their Hispanic populations during the 1990s, and in about a quarter of all counties that increase exceeded 1000 persons over the past decade" (Frey 2000, 20–21).

We also wanted to get a picture of where Puerto Ricans stand when compared with Mexicans and Cubans. We began by comparing income, poverty, and female-headed family variables and concluded that Puerto Ricans are definitely worse off than the other two groups. We then looked at two different sets of possible explanations for their condition. The first set dealt with characteristics found within the group itself—nativity, English language ability, and education. This was a bit confusing, because we would assume that Puerto Ricans would be the lowest in all three of these categories, but that just wasn't the case. Mexicans had lower education; Cubans had lower numbers of U.S. born, and both Mexicans and Cubans were worse off than Puerto Ricans linguistically. We concluded that these "human capital" variables are important, but they do not take us far enough to understand what is happening. Therefore, we looked at a second set of variables intended to depict the labor opportunity structures faced by each of the groups. This is where we found some help, because Puerto Ricans had higher unemployment and lower labor force participation than the other two groups. We began to realize that analyzing labor structure would be a more helpful direction to take. One interesting finding that we noted was that Puerto Ricans who had wage income did not do that badly compared to the other groups. In other words, those who worked were doing all right. The problem seemed to be that too many Puerto Ricans were not working at all.

Our second objective was to take a different approach to studying Puerto Ricans. Most studies have been done using national totals or using New York as a case study. We believed that if we compared a number of metropolitan areas across the country that had fairly decent-sized Puerto Rican communities, we would discover that Puerto Ricans do not have the same experience in all locales and that in fact they have drastically different experiences both between and within regions of the United States. Using the same set of variables that we used for our first objective, we found that the experiences varied a great deal. The South and the West offer much better prospects for Puerto Rican well-being than does the Northeast or Midwest. Not only that, but we saw much larger variations within the two Rust Belt regions, variations that confirmed that the economic transformation from a manufacturing to a service economy has unevenly affected the metropolitan areas of the Rust Belt according to their former dependence on manufacturing as their economic base. We also discovered that the financial returns of education for Puerto Ricans at all levels of education were not nearly as great as for the white majority and that the increases in income between levels of education showed different patterns depending on region.

As a part of this objective, we wanted to begin sorting out the internal migration patterns to determine whether Puerto Ricans were doing better in some areas because they had better opportunities there or because Puerto Ricans moving to the West and South had better human capital and would have been better off no matter where they were. We did find some evidence that selectivity was taking place in migration patterns, but tentatively we can say that the levels of selectivity could not explain the degree of difference we found between regions.

Before leaving this objective, we took a tangent and looked at two specific issues—residential segregation and feminization of poverty. We found tremendously high levels of segregation among Puerto Ricans in many of the Rust Belt metropolitan areas, but this was not the case in the West and South, where the levels were moderate to low. We made two important discoveries in Chapter 7. First, Puerto Rican segregation patterns fit neither the pattern for turn-of-the-century European immigrants nor the pattern for blacks. In addition, we found that black segregation was much more steeped in color discrimination but that Puerto Rican segregation was more of an economic ploy on the part of the white majority to ensure the presence of a labor reserve. This was very necessary during the deindustrialization stages so that the effects of this economic process would be more gradual and not cause as drastic a dislocation as it would have otherwise.

In our discussion on the feminization of Puerto Rican poverty, we determined that the major problem was decline in female labor force participation. Over and over we heard how Puerto Ricans came to the United States to *work!* During the early decades, that's exactly what they did. However, with the decline in manufacturing, particularly in the garment industry, it seemed as though they had little chance to work. Grasmuck and Grosfoguel (1997, 348) describe it this way: "The 'ethnic recycling' that characterized the garment industry at an earlier period with one group entering and after one or two generations moving out and *up*, became, in the Puerto Rican case, one of entering and then moving out—and staying out—*out* of the labor force altogether."

Our final objective was to spur our thinking beyond the black-white dichotomy, to recognize that Puerto Ricans must be studied within their own historical and cultural framework rather than being forced into a mold made for another group. This has been a real problem in the past.

Pérez y González talks about the uniqueness of Puerto Rican struggles: "[T]heir colonial situation, U.S. citizenship, and linguistic, cultural, and religious differences set them apart from the dominant groups" (2000, 75). Andrés Torres warns us about the dangers of trying to understand Puerto Rican poverty through theoretical frameworks designed to explain African American poverty. In discussing New York City he says, "Today, with residents arriving from all over the globe, the city hears the sentiment expressed ever more vociferously that we must begin to reconceptualize race relations beyond black and white" (1995, 5). He makes three salient points in this regard. First, if all we are interested in is how whites and blacks have different experiences and outcomes, then poverty is viewed as an African American dilemma only. "The Puerto Rican 'problem' is given scant, usually patronizing, attention in the general scheme of policy discussions" (1995, 5). Second, we are faced with an important paradox—why do Puerto Ricans suffer greater inequality and powerlessness than blacks do, when blacks suffer a greater burden of racism? Finally, Torres points to the fact that not only are Puerto Ricans culturally distinct but also they are a multiracial community, which greatly complicates things if we are determined to deal only with black and white.

One of the relatively recent research programs to understand the high levels of concentrated poverty in the black ghettos of U.S. major cities is that of the "underclass." This is one of the theoretical tools that has been tentatively offered to understand the plight of Puerto Ricans. Torres and Rodriguez leave no doubt as to their opinion of its suitability:

> The term *underclass* conveys—even to those who are quite distant from such discussions—an immediate, pejorative sense of class, that is, a position outside of or beneath the regular class structure. . . . the word means so many things to so many people, it is not a very efficient term. Moreover, it is disparaging and stigmatizing. It is one matter to use imprecise terminology; it is another to employ offensive vocabulary. (1991, 255)

Underlying Themes

In our introduction we also laid out a number of underlying themes that would keep popping up as we went through our analysis. The first theme was the importance of New York City to the entire Puerto Rican experience. It would be difficult to overemphasize New York's role in Puerto Rican adaptation to the U.S. labor structure. We've talked about the sheer size of the New York Puerto Rican community, and that is important, but even more important is its influence on most other Puerto Rican communities in the nation (and in Puerto Rico). It began the deindustrialization process sooner than did other cities, and the effects were severe for Puerto Rican people.

One of the other underlying themes was the special circumstances of Puerto Rican women, and we saw that they were especially hurt with the restructuring going on in New York. Using welfare as a strategy to be able to continue their "work" at home with their families, what was held out as a cure became a disease that has entrenched many in a life of dependency and marginalization.

Our other two underlying themes tend to go together. We noted that the Puerto Rican experience in the United States could not be divorced from that on the island and that we were really looking at two halves of the whole. As a part of this understanding, we recognized the colonial status of the island and the second-class citizenship forced on its people. U.S. business concerns destroyed the indigenous economy of the island and substituted a system that could work only with massive migration off the island—and that is exactly what happened. However, the marginalization that to this day does not allow these U.S. citizens to vote for the president or have anything more than a nonvoting representative in Congress has followed them to the mainland, where their citizenship has been shown to be more of a hindrance than a help in securing labor niches and a chance for economic mobility. Denis sums this up as follows: "The Puerto Rican working class is in fact the object of a double exploitation that also has no geographic escape. This exploitation goes on both in Puerto Rico and in the metropolis, like the two faces of the same reality" (1980, 43).

Now that we have revisited what we wanted to accomplish, we will finish by looking at some of the major issues that came out of our analysis and begin to discuss policy recommendations where possible.

Issues and Policy Recommendations

We have discovered a number of issues, but two of them seem to overwhelm or interact with the rest: the lack of jobs and the low level of education of Puerto Ricans. Connected to these are issues of wages, segregation, and understanding how family responsibilities fit in for the many single mothers.

Puerto Ricans distrust policy decisions because they seldom are made with Puerto Rican welfare in mind. What they have experienced is

> the underfunding of essential public services such as education, health care, mental health services and transportation. These realities have coalesced with the reduced funding for enforcement of civil rights legislation, the erosion of the safety-net to the unemployed and the poor, the shift of public monies to corporate subsidies in spite of corporate downsizing, the contracting out of work to low wage workers here and abroad, and the reluctance of corporations to reinvest in the inner cities. (Boricua First! 1996, 11)

Torres and Rodriguez (1991) warn us that policy debates become political issues, and often the politics drive policy agendas and recommendations more than the needs. As this relates to Puerto Ricans, there is reason to believe "a corporate-political agenda of economic, social, and political suppression is undermining the living standards of an entire generation of workers, while denying future generations a decent living" (Boricua First! 1996, 11). With these warnings in mind, let's discuss the issues.

Jobs and Earnings

Torres and Rodriguez remind us that "roughly one half of the poverty in the United States . . . consists of persons who are actively connected to the labor force" (1991, 248). This means that people are working but are still suffering from poverty. This could be true for a number of reasons. First, there is the problem of underemployment. This occurs when a person either works too few hours per week or too few weeks per year (as in seasonal work). Underemployment is difficult to determine; however, we know that someone who works only twenty hours a week at minimum wage will not be able to survive, let alone take care of a family.

A second contributing factor of being both employed and in poverty has to do with discrimination. Rivera-Batiz and Santiago (1997) highlight the fact that Puerto Rican men and white men with the same human capital characteristics do not receive the same wages—the Puerto Rican man's wages will be lower.

Three types of recommendations can probably be made in this area. The first deals with minimum wage. The minimum wage levels are reviewed so seldom that people working for the minimum will effectively receive less money even after a raise in minimum wage level than they did before because of cost of living increases. If the wage rate lags behind, it needs to be raised immediately. Second, jobs need to be created—real jobs for people with real possibilities of progressing. And third, not only should those jobs be created, but training Puerto Ricans for those jobs also must be a priority.

Family Responsibilities

Closely connected to the issue of jobs is the problem of Puerto Rican women who are out of the labor force and on welfare. Welfare reform guidelines will force these women back into the workforce, at least on a part-time basis. However, policies are never neutral—they either help or hurt people. Our discussion throughout this book indicates that a special focus ought to be placed on single mothers. To help them transition into meaningful outside labor, we must develop "a better understanding of why they have thus far not joined the labor force, and why they have not found reasonably well-paying jobs" (Rosenberg 1991, 222). The whole concept of family and "work" needs to be understood, and provisions need to be built into the policies so that Puerto Rican mothers can fulfill their responsibilities at home and outside. The needs of immigrant/migrant women must be taken into consideration when developing policies because "family instability often accompanies the process of migration itself and many immigrant children increasingly depend on the socioeconomic position of their mothers" (Grasmuck and Grosfoguel 1997, 358).

Along with understanding the plight of female-headed families, we must remember that the lack of jobs is the primary reason that fathers are not a part of their children's lives.

Housing

For women to go to work, one of the biggest issues is child care. Culturally, Puerto Rican women were raised to rely on extended family, but this is not always accessible in the United States. We found that women who had another adult living in the home, whether a husband, an extended family member, or simply a boarder, were more likely to work outside the home. Figueroa points out a creative avenue of combining housing needs with child-care needs. She proposes that housing programs be designed to provide large enough homes that those who would like to bring extended family in to live with them will have the room to do so. Remember that even though it was unplanned, Puerto Ricans moving into homes in their initial enclave in Philadelphia were able to do just that, and family members did come for a variety of reasons.

Another point to make regarding housing is that policies need to be enforced to stop the purposeful segregation of Puerto Ricans in depressed and oppressed communities.

Education

Education is an area in which we ought to be able to make a difference, but we don't. A big part of this problem has to do with the high level of segregation in the schools. Boricua First! points us to a study in 1994, which found that "Latinos attend the most segregated schools of all groups, with schools in the Northeast the most segregated of all" (1996, 47). The new labor structure requires a more highly educated and trained workforce, and yet we systemically exclude Puerto Ricans from the very possibilities of being prepared for open positions. There are a number of recommendations primarily offered by Boricua First! (1996) and by Rivera-Batiz and Santiago (1997) that address educational needs at all levels. First, for any level of education, policies should address curriculum issues so that multicultural curricula are put into schools and diversity is celebrated. Also, for any level of education, parents need to know how to redress the intense segregation in their children's schools. If they are not externally segregated into separate schools, students are effectively segregated within schools by being overrepresented in special tracks or special-education programs. Students who do get assigned to the regular tracks seldom find any encouragement to go to higher tracks, which could be helpful in eventual college experience. Counselors need to be held accountable for effectively guiding students to go on to college if they so desire. Puerto Rican students need to have improved math and science education. This is primarily so they will have the skills to compete at the college level. Students who are in vocational education ought to be guided into effective ways of integrating into the workforce. Worker apprenticeship programs would be especially helpful.

When the time comes to consider college, students are often thrown for a loop when facing high-level standardized tests. "Test bias can mean that the test is measuring divergence from white, upper-middle class language, cultural experiences, and learning style more than it is measuring academic skills" (Boricua First! 1996, 46). This means that communities must determine what type of tests they think would be fair for their children. Finally, retention in college is a real problem, and a system of counseling needs to be established that will continue with undergraduates and even follow students into applying for graduate school.

Final Words

The immensity of the situation facing Puerto Ricans in the Northeast tempts us to get discouraged, throw up our hands, and say, "It's no use. Nothing will work." But that just isn't true. The policy implications touched on earlier are superficial at best. Much more needs to be done. But it is possible to change things around. One situation that ought to be avoided at all costs is the embracing of any more policies that are not well thought out and, therefore, end up making the situation even worse.

Whenever we speak about policy recommendations, we must be aware that we are really dealing with symptoms rather than causes, putting Band-Aids on sores rather than aggressively attacking the cancer. By this we mean that when we talk about a lack of jobs for Puerto Ricans or their dependency on public assistance, we tend to deal with policies that are geared either for developing additional jobs suitable to the skill levels in the Puerto Rican community or increasing the educational and skill level of Puerto Ricans so they will be better able to compete for the jobs that already exist. This ignores the underlying fact that the lack of jobs didn't "just happen." The plight of Puerto Ricans in the United States (as well as on the island) has been orchestrated through a colonial system that promotes discrimination at numerous levels. Business manipulation has effectively taken a hard-working national group and is holding them on the side in case they're needed. Educational systems are tracking Puerto Ricans to gain skills for nonexistent jobs. Housing discrimination is segregating the effects of poverty in concentrated areas in many of our Rust Belt cities. The end results of all this is that we now have a generation of younger women who no longer know a community of workers but rather exist in a state of dependency. This needs to stop. Changes to assist individuals are helpful, but the overall problem will not be eradicated until major efforts are made to impact the systemic injustices leading to and being perpetuated by intense poverty.

Appendices

Appendix 1
Selected MSAs by Region

Northeast
Allentown, PA
Atlantic City, NJ
Bergen/Passaic, NJ
Boston, MA
Bridgeport, CT
Buffalo, NY
Hartford, CT
Jersey City, NJ
Lancaster, PA
Lawrence, MA
Middlesex/Somerset/
   Hunterdon, NJ
Monmouth/Ocean, NJ
Nassau/Suffolk, NJ
New Britain, CT
New Haven, CT

New York, NY
Newark, NJ
Orange County, NY
Philadelphia, PA
Reading, PA
Rochester, NY
Springfield, MA
Trenton, NJ
Vineland, NJ
Waterbury, CT
Worcester, MA

Midwest
Chicago, IL
Cleveland, OH
Detroit, MI
Lorain, OH

Milwaukee, WI

South
Ft. Lauderdale, FL
Miami, FL
Orlando, FL
Tampa, FL
Washington, DC
West Palm Beach, FL

West
Honolulu, HI
Los Angeles, CA
Oakland, CA
Riverside, CA
San Diego, CA

Appendix 2
Dissimilarity Indexes for Selected MSAs, 1990

MSA/PMSA Name	Dissimilarities				
	PR/Wht	PR/Blk	All Other Hisp/Wht	All Other Hisp/Blk	PR/All Oth Hisp
Northeast					
Allentown, PA	68.4	42.2	38.3	27.5	40.8
Atlantic City, NJ	56.7	51.1	45.5	50.2	30.5
Bergen/Passaic, NJ	67.8	48.0	54.4	47.1	24.5
Boston, MA	66.7	44.6	51.2	50.0	35.7
Bridgeport, CT	75.6	33.1	48.5	39.3	35.0
Buffalo, NY	70.8	74.5	36.0	68.9	52.3
Hartford, CT	79.3	53.5	46.4	53.9	42.9
Jersey City, NJ	42.5	61.3	48.1	78.3	43.7
Lancaster, PA	72.0	19.9	*	*	*
Lawrence, MA	78.7	**	71.3	**	13.6
Middlesex/Somerset/ Hunterdon, NJ	58.8	49.7	44.2	44.6	25.9
Monmouth/Ocean, NJ	44.5	43.0	27.2	50.7	27.7
Nassau/Suffolk, NY	46.1	60.5	43.5	51.7	33.2
New Britain, CT	61.9	30.4	*	*	*
New Haven, CT	64.8	52.6	38.5	44.4	40.8
New York, NY	70.4	55.8	64.1	61.4	40.7
Newark, NJ	74.5	63.6	62.5	65.7	39.1
Orange County, NY	39.0	27.6	41.2	25.4	22.0
Philadelphia, PA	73.9	69.3	41.4	61.6	48.9
Reading, PA	75.4	29.4	*	*	*
Rochester, NY	66.7	40.1	36.0	47.7	47.9
Springfield, MA	70.0	56.5	40.2	51.5	38.3
Trenton, NJ	68.0	47.1	43.8	50.3	37.6

MSA/PMSA Name	Dissimilarities				
	PR/Wht	PR/Blk	All Other Hisp/Wht	All Other Hisp/Blk	PR/All Oth Hisp
Vineland, NJ	47.8	51.4	*	*	*
Waterbury, CT	67.7	34.5	*	*	*
Worcester, MA	64.4	46.7	46.1	49.5	35.8
Northeast Average	64.4	46.7	46.1	49.5	35.8
Midwest					
Chicago, IL	75.6	86.4	61.5	82.8	52.6
Cleveland, OH	71.0	87.6	34.5	75.3	50.5
Detroit, MI	63.9	81.1	37.1	81.1	38.3
Lorain, OH	67.0	49.8	*	*	*
Milwaukee, WI	69.2	71.7	51.4	78.0	26.8
Midwest Average	69.3	45.3	46.1	79.3	42.1
South					
Ft. Lauderdale, FL	30.1	59.7	25.3	61.6	14.1
Miami, FL	39.4	58.4	51.9	76.7	35.2
Orlando, FL	33.3	62.2	22.1	58.5	20.0
Tampa, FL	43.8	59.6	48.0	64.6	30.6
Washington, DC	33.3	56.4	42.8	60.9	36.2
West Palm Beach, FL	41.6	64.1	42.4	60.9	23.1
South Average	36.9	60.1	38.8	63.9	26.5
West					
Honolulu, HI	41.8	25.5	29.2	47.4	20.3
Los Angeles, CA	43.8	60.0	61.3	59.5	31.5
Oakland, CA	43.9	56.5	38.7	53.1	23.8
Riverside, CA	30.6	27.4	36.1	36.5	28.7
San Diego, CA	37.8	34.8	45.7	44.6	31.1
West Average	39.6	46.2	42.2	48.2	27.1

*The All Other Hispanics number less than 5000, so indexes are not included in figuring regional averages.

**The Blacks number less than 5000, so indexes are not included in figuring regional averages.

Source: U.S. Bureau of Census 1990 PUMS, 1-Percent Sample.

Works Cited

Antonsen, Peter J. 1997. *A History of the Puerto Rican Community in Bethlehem, PA, 1944–1993.* Bethlehem, Pa.: Council of Spanish Speaking Organizations of the Lehigh Valley.

Aponte, Robert. 1991. Urban Hispanic Poverty: Disaggregations and Explanations. *Social Problems* 38:516–28.

———. 1993. Hispanic Families in Poverty: Diversity, Context and Interpretation. *Families in Society: The Journal of Contemporary Human Service* 74(9):527–37.

Arroyo, William. 1998. Lorain, Ohio: The Puerto Rican Experiment: A History Unexplored. In *Extended Roots: From Hawaii to New York: Migraciones Puertorriqueñas a los Estados Unidos*, 2nd ed., ed. Oral History Task Force, 57–63. New York: Centro de Estudios Puertorriqueños.

Azieri, Max. 1981–82. The Politics of Exile: Trends and Dynamics of Political Change among Cuban-Americans. *Cuban Studies/Estudios Cubanos* 11(2)/12(1):55–78.

Bach, Robert L. 1987. The Cuban Exodus: Political and Economic Motivations. In *The Caribbean Exodus*, ed. Barry B. Levine, 106–30. New York: Praeger.

Balmori, Diana. 1983. *Hispanic Immigrants in the Construction Industry: New York City, 1960–1982.* New York: New York University, Center for Latin American and Caribbean Studies. Occasional Paper No. 38.

Bean, Frank D. and Marta Tienda. 1987. *The Hispanic Population of the United States.* New York: Russell Sage Foundation.

Betancur, John J., Teresa Cordova, and Maria de los Angeles Torres. 1993. Economic Restructuring and the Process of Incorporation of Latinos into the Chicago Economy. In *Latinos in a Changing U.S. Economy: Comparative Perspectives on Growing Inequality*, eds. Rebecca Morales and Frank Bonilla, 109–32. Newbury Park, Calif.: Sage Publications.

Bonacich, Edna. 1972. A Theory of Ethnic Antagonism: The Split Labor Market. *American Sociological Review* 37(5):547–59.

Bonilla, Frank and Ricardo Campos. 1981. A Wealth of Poor: Puerto Ricans in the New Economic Order. *Daedalus* 110(2):133–76.

Boricua First! 1996. National Puerto Rican Leadership Agenda. Paper presented to the 104th Congress, March 29.

Boris, Eileen. 1996. Needlework Under the New Deal in Puerto Rico, 1920–1945. In *Puerto Rican Women and Work: Bridges in Transnational Labor*, ed. Altagracia Ortiz, 33–54. Philadelphia: Temple University Press.

Borjas, George J. 1983. The Labor Supply of Male Hispanic Immigrants in the United States. *International Migration Review* 17(4):653–71.

Boswell, Thomas D. and James R. Curtis. 1983. *The Cuban-American Experience: Culture, Images, and Perspectives*. Totowa, N.J.: Rowan & Allanheld Publishers.

Casey, Geraldine J. 1996. New Tappings on the Keys: Changes in Work and Gender Roles for Women Clerical Workers in Puerto Rico. In *Puerto Rican Women and Work: Bridges in Transnational Labor*, ed. Altagracia Ortiz, 209–33. Philadelphia: Temple University Press.

Colón-Warren, Alice. 1996. The Impact of Job Losses on Puerto Rican Women in the Middle Atlantic Region, 1970–1980. In *Puerto Rican Women and Work: Bridges in Transnational Labor*, ed. Altagracia Ortiz, 105–38. Philadelphia: Temple University Press.

Connecticut Public Television and Radio. 1997. Puerto Rican Passages. An unpublished script for a program aired 13 September 1997 at 8 p.m. EST, channel 35, Philadelphia.

Connecticut State Committee to the U.S. Commission on Civil Rights. 1973. *El Boricua: The Puerto Rican Community in Bridgeport and New Haven*. U.S. Commission on Civil Rights.

Contreras, Raoul Lowery. 1998. House Votes Again Reveal Anti-Hispanic Tendencies. *Philadelphia Inquirer*, 9 March, A-13.

Cooney, Rosemary Santana. 1979. Intercity Variations in Puerto Rican Female Participation. *Journal of Human Resources* 14(2):222–35.

———. 1983. Nativity, National Origin, and Hispanic Female Participation in the Labor Force. *Social Science Quarterly* 64(3):510–23.

Cooney, Rosemary Santana, and Alice Colón. 1980. Work and Family: The Recent Struggle of Puerto Rican Females. In *The Puerto Rican Struggle: Essays on Survival in the U.S.*, eds. Clara E. Rodríguez, Virginia Sánchez Korrol, and José Oscar Alers, 58–73. Maplewood, N.J.: Waterfront Press.

Cooney, Rosemary Santana, and Alice Colón Warren. 1979. Declining Female Participation among Puerto Rican New Yorkers: A Comparison with Native White Nonspanish New Yorkers. *Ethnicity* 6:281–97.

Cortese, Charles F., R. Frank Falk, and Jack K. Cohen. 1976. Further Considerations on the Methodological Analysis of Segregation Indices. *American Sociological Review* 41(4):630–37.

Cruz, José E. 1998. *Identity & Power: Puerto Rican Politics and the Challenge of Ethnicity*. Philadelphia: Temple University Press.

Denis, Manuel Maldonado. 1980. *The Emigration Dialectic: Puerto Rico and the U.S.A.* New York: International Publishers.

Dietz, James L. 1986. *Economic History of Puerto Rico: Institutional Change and Capitalist Development*. Princeton, N.J.: Princeton University Press.

Dominguez, Virginia R. 1975. *From Neighbor to Stranger: The Dilemma of Caribbean Peoples in the United States*. New Haven, Conn.: Yale University, Antilles Research Program.

Duncan, Otis Dudley and Beverly Duncan. 1955. A Methodological Analysis of Segregation Indexes. *American Sociological Review* 20(2):210–17.

Ericksen, Eugene P., David Bartelt, Patrick Feeney, Gerald Foeman, Sherri Grasmuck, Maureen Martella, William Rickle, Robert Spencer, and David Webb. 1985. *The State of Puerto Rican Philadelphia.* Philadelphia: Temple University, Institute for Public Policy Research.

Estrada, Leobardo F., F. Chris García, Reynaldo Flores Macía, and Lionel Maldonado. 1981. Chicanos in the United States: A History of Exploitation and Resistance. *Daedalus* 110:103–31.

Fazlollah, Mark. 1993. Blacks Gain Sway in Two Suburbs. *Philadelphia Inquirer,* 22 November, B-1, B-3.

Fernandez, Roberto M., Ronnelle Paulsen, and Marsha Hirano-Nakanishi. 1989. Dropping Out among Hispanic Youth. *Social Science Research* 18(1):21–52.

Figueroa, Janis Barry. 1991. A Comparison of Labor Supply Behavior among Single and Married Puerto Rican Mothers. In *Hispanics in the Labor Force: Issues and Policies,* eds. Edwin Melendez, Clara Rodriguez, and Janis Barry Figueroa, 183–202. New York: Plenum Press.

Fitzpatrick, Joseph P. 1987. *Puerto Rican Americans: The Meaning of Migration to the Mainland.* Englewood Cliffs, N.J.: Prentice-Hall.

Frey, William H. 2001. Census 2000. *American Demographics* 23(6):20–33.

Gann, L. H., and Peter J. Duignan. 1986. *The Hispanics in the United States: A History.* Boulder, Colo.: Westview Press.

Gill, Richard T., Nathan Glazer, and Stephen R. Thernstrom. 1992. *Our Changing Population.* Englewood Cliffs, N.J.: Prentice Hall.

Golub, Fred T. 1956. *The Puerto Rican Worker in Perth Amboy, New Jersey.* New Brunswick, N.J.: The Institute of Management and Labor Relations, Rutgers University.

González, Luis Manuel. 1964. The Economic Development of Puerto Rico from 1898 to 1940. Ph.D. diss., University of Florida.

Goode, Judith, and JoAnne Schneider. 1994. *Reshaping Ethnic and Racial Relations in Philadelphia.* Philadelphia: Temple University Press.

Grasmuck, Sherri, and Ramón Grosfoguel. 1997. Geopolitics, Economic Niches, and Gendered Social Capital among Recent Caribbean Immigrants in New York City. *Sociological Perspectives* 40(30):339–63.

Grebler, Leo, Joan W. Moore, and Ralph C. Guzman. 1970. *The Mexican-American People: The Nation's Second Largest Minority.* New York: Free Press.

Hellerich, Mahlon H., ed. 1989. *Allentown 1762–1987: A 225-Year History,* v. 2. Allentown, Pa.: Lehigh County Historical Society.

Hispanic Almanac. 1984. *See* Hispanic Policy Development Project.

Hispanic Policy Development Project. 1984. *The Hispanic Almanac.* New York: Hispanic Policy Development Project.

History Task Force, Centro de Estudios Puertorriqueños. 1979. *Labor Migration Under Capitalism: The Puerto Rican Experience.* New York: Monthly Review Press.

Holbik, Karel, and Philip L. Swan. 1975. *Industrialization and Employment in Puerto Rico, 1950–1972.* Austin: University of Texas at Austin.

Institute for Puerto Rican Policy (IPR). 1993. *Datanote on the Puerto Rican Community,* no. 13.

Jackson, Peter. 1981. Paradoxes of Puerto Rican Segregation in New York. In *Ethnic Segregation in Cities*, ed. Ceri Peach, Vaughan Robinson, and Susan Smith, 109–26. London: Croom Helm.

Jahn, Julius, Calvin F. Schmid, and Clarence Schrag. 1947. The Measurement of Ecological Segregation. *American Sociological Review* 12(3):293–303.

Kantrowitz, Nathan. 1973. *Ethnic and Racial Segregation in the New York Metropolis: Residential Patterns among White Ethnic Groups, Blacks, and Puerto Ricans*. New York: Praeger Publishers.

Kihss, Peter. 1953. Puerto Rican Will to Work Stressed. *New York Times*, 25 February, L-18.

———. 1954. Survey Finds New Jobs in City Exceed Influx of Puerto Ricans. *New York Times*, 16 January, L-1, L-8.

Korrol, Virginia Sánchez. 1980. Survival of Puerto Rican Women in New York Before World War II. In *The Puerto Rican Struggle: Essays on Survival in the U.S.*, eds. Clara E. Ridríguez, Virginia Sánchez Korrol, and José Oscar Alers, 58–73. Maplewood, N.J.: Waterfront Press.

———. 1983. *From Colonio to Community: The History of Puerto Ricans in New York City, 1917–1948*. Westport, Conn.: Greenwood Press.

———. 1996. Toward Bilingual Education: Puerto Rican Women Teachers in New York City School, 1947–1967. In *Puerto Rican Women and Work: Bridges in Transnational Labor*, ed. Altagracia Ortiz, 82–104. Philadelphia: Temple University Press.

Landale, Nancy S. and R. S. Oropesa. 2001. Father Involvement in the Lives of Mainland Puerto Rican Children: Contributions of Nonresident, Cohabiting and Married Fathers. *Social Forces* 79(3):945–68.

Levine, Barry B. 1987. Surplus Populations: Economic Migrants and Political Refugees. In *The Caribbean Exodus*, ed. Barry B. Levine, 5–14. New York: Praeger.

Light, Ivan. [1984]1991. Immigrant and Ethnic Enterprise in North America. In *Majority and Minority: The Dynamics of Race and Ethnicity in American Life*, 5th ed., ed. Norman R. Yetman, 307–18. Boston: Allyn and Bacon. (First printed in *Ethnic and Racial Studies* 7[2] [1984].)

Lucas, Isidro. 1978. *Aquí Estamos*. Chicago: Chicago United.

Maldonado, Edwin. 1979. Contract Labor and the Origins of Puerto Rican Communities in the United States. *International Migration Review* 13(1):103–21.

Maldonado, Rita M. 1976. Why Puerto Ricans Migrated to the United States in 1947–73. *Monthly Labor Review* 99:7–18.

Massey, Douglas S. 1978. On the Measurement of Segregation as a Random Variable. *American Sociological Review* 43(4):587–90.

———. 1979. Residential Segregation of Spanish Americans in United States Urbanized Areas. *Demography* 16(4):553–63.

———. 1981. Hispanic Residential Segregation: A Comparison of Mexicans, Cubans, and Puerto Ricans. *Sociology and Social Research* 65(3):311–22.

———. 1986. The Social Organization of Mexican Migration to the United States. *Annals of the American Academy of Political and Social Science* 487:102–13.

Massey, Douglas S., and Brooks Bitterman. 1985. Explaining the Paradox of Puerto Rican Segregation. *Social Forces* 64(2):306–31.

Massey, Douglas S., and Nancy A. Denton. 1988a. The Dimensions of Residential Segregation. *Social Forces* 67(2):281–315.

————. 1988b. Suburbanization and Segregation in U.S. Metropolitan Areas. *American Journal of Sociology* 94(3):592–626.

————. 1989a. Residential Segregation of Mexicans, Puerto Ricans, and Cubans in Selected U.S. Metropolitan Areas. *Sociology and Social Research* 73(2):73–83.

————. 1989b. Hypersegregation in U.S. Metropolitan Areas: Black and Hispanic Segregation along Five Dimensions. *Demography* 26(3):373–91.

————. 1993. *American Apartheid: Segregation and the Making of the Underclass.* Cambridge, Mass.: Harvard University Press.

Massey, Douglas S., and Mitchell L. Eggers. 1990. The Ecology of Inequality: Minorities and the Concentration of Poverty, 1970–1990. *American Journal of Sociology* 95(5):1153–88.

McCoy, Terry L. 1987. A Primer for U.S. Policy on Caribbean Migration: Responding to Pressures. In *The Caribbean Exodus,* ed. Barry B. Levine, 242–59. New York: Praeger.

Metauten, Raymond. 1959. *Puerto Ricans in Philadelphia.* Philadelphia: Commission on Human Relations.

Mills, C. Wright. 1959. *The Sociological Imagination.* New York: Oxford University Press.

Mills, C. Wright, Clarence Senior, and Rose Kohn Goldsen. 1950. *The Puerto Rican Journey.* New York: Harper and Brothers.

Model, Suzanne. 1993. The Ethnic Niche and the Structure of Opportunity: Immigrants and Minorities in New York City. In *The "Underclass" Debate: Views from History,* ed. Michael B. Katz, 161–93. Princeton, N.J.: Princeton University Press.

Morales, Julio. 1986. *Puerto Rican Poverty and Migration: We Just Had to Try Elsewhere.* New York: Praeger.

Neidert, Lisa J., and Marta Tienda. 1984. Converting Education into Earnings: The Patterns among Hispanic Origin Men. *Social Science Research* 13:303–20.

Nelson, Candace, and Marta Tienda. 1985. The Structuring of Hispanic Ethnicity: Historical and Contemporary Perspectives. *Ethnic and Racial Studies* 8(1):49–74.

Ortiz, Altagracia. 1996a. Introduction. In *Puerto Rican Women and Work: Bridges in Transnational Labor,* ed. Altagracia Ortiz, 1–32. Philadelphia: Temple University Press.

————. 1996b. *"En la Aruja y el Pedal Eché la Hiel":* Puerto Rican Women in the Garment Industry of New York City, 1920–80. In *Puerto Rican Women and Work: Bridges in Transnational Labor,* ed. Altagracia Ortiz, 55–81. Philadelphia: Temple University Press.

Ortiz, Vilma. 1986. Changes in the Characteristics of Puerto Rican Migrants from 1955 to 1980. *International Migration Review* 20(3):612–28.

Padilla, Felix. 1985. *Latino Ethnic Consciousness: The Case of Mexican Americans and Puerto Ricans in Chicago.* Notre Dame, Ind.: University of Notre Dame Press.

————. 1987. *Puerto Rican Chicago.* Notre Dame, Ind.: University of Notre Dame Press.

————. 1998. A Brief History of Puerto Ricans in Chicago, 1950–1970. In *Extended Roots: From Hawaii to New York: Migraciones Puertorriqueñas a los Estados Unidos,* 2nd ed., ed. Oral History Task Force, 65–77. New York: Centro de Estudios Puertorriqueños.

Pastor, Robert. 1987. The Impact of U.S. Immigration Policy on Caribbean Emigration: Does It Matter? In *The Caribbean Exodus*, ed. Barry B. Levine, 242–59. New York: Praeger.

Peoples Press. 1977. *Puerto Rico: The Flame of Resistance*. San Francisco: Peoples Press.

Pérez, Lisandro. 1984. Migration from Socialist Cuba: A Critical Analysis of the Literature. In *Cubans in the United States*, eds. Miren Uriarte Gastón and Jorge Cañas Martínez, 12–21. Boston: Center for the Study of the Cuban Community.

Pérez, Martín. 1998. Living History: Vineland, New Jersey. In *Extended Roots: From Hawaii to New York: Migraciones Puertorriqueñas a los Estados Unidos*, 2nd ed., ed. Oral History Task Force, 79–87. New York: Centro de Estudios Puertorriqueños.

Pérez y González, María E. 2000. *Puerto Ricans in the United States*. Westport, Conn.: Greenwood Press.

Pérez-Herranz, Carmen A. 1996. Our Two Full-Time Jobs: Women Garment Workers Balance Factory and Domestic Demands in Puerto Rico. In *Puerto Rican Women and Work: Bridges in Transnational Labor*, ed. Altagracia Ortiz, 139–60. Philadelphia: Temple University Press.

Petra Press. 1996. *Cultures of America: Puerto Ricans*. Tarrytown, N.Y.: Benchmark Books.

Piñeiro, Jorge. 1998. Extended Roots: San Jose, California. In *Extended Roots: From Hawaii to New York: Migraciones Puertorriqueñas a los Estados Unidos*, 2nd ed., ed. Oral History Task Force, 37–43. New York: Centro de Estudios Puertorriqueños.

Piore, Michael. 1980. The Technological Foundations of Dualism and Discontinuity. In *Dualism and Discontinuity in Industrial Society*, eds. Suzanne Bergen and Michael Piore. Cambridge, Eng.: Cambridge University Press.

Portes, Alejandro. 1981. Modes of Structural Incorporation and Present Theories of Labor Immigration. In *Global Trends in Migration: Theory and Research on International Population Movements*, eds. Mary M. Kritz, Charles B. Keely, and Silvano M. Tomasi, 279–97. Beverly Hills, Calif.: Sage Publications.

Portes, Alejandro and Jószef Borocz. 1989. Contemporary Immigration: Theoretical Perspectives on Its Determinants and Modes of Incorporation. *International Migration Review* 23(3):606–30.

Portes, Alejandro and Leif Jensen. 1989. The Enclave and the Entrants: Patterns of Ethnic Enterprise in Miami Before and After Mariel. *American Sociological Review* 54:929–49.

Portes, Alejandro, and Robert D. Manning. [1986]1991. The Immigrant Enclave: Theory and Empirical Examples. In *Majority and Minority: The Dynamics of Race and Ethnicity in American Life*, 5th ed., ed. Norman R. Yetman, 319–32. Boston: Allyn and Bacon. (First printed in *Competitive Ethnic Relations*, ed. Susan Olzak and Joane Nagel. Orlando, Fla.: Academic Press, 1986.)

Portes, Alejandro, and Cynthia G. Truelove. [1987]1991. Making Sense of Diversity: Recent Research on Hispanic Minorities in the United States. In *Majority and Minority: The Dynamics of Race and Ethnicity in American Life*, ed. Norman R. Yetman, 402–19. Boston: Allyn and Bacon. (First printed in *Annual Review of Sociology* 13[1987].)

Portes, Alejandro, and Min Zhou. 1992. Gaining the Upper Hand: Economic Mobility among Immigrant and Domestic Minorities. *Ethnic and Racial Studies* 15(4): 491–522.

Poyo, Gerald E. 1984. Cuban Communities in the United States: Toward an Overview of the 19th Century Experience. In *Cubans in the United States*, eds. Miren Uriarte-Gastón and Jorge Cañas Martínez, 44–64. Boston: Center for the Study of the Cuban Community.

Reimers, David M. 1981. Post–World War II Immigration to the United States: America's Latest Newcomers. *Annals of the American Academy of Political and Social Science* 454:1–12.

Reischauer, Robert D. 1989. Immigration and the Underclass. *Annals of the American Academy of Political and Social Science* 501:120–31.

Rivera-Batiz, Francisco L., and Carlos E. Santiago. 1996. *Island Paradox: Puerto Rico in the 1990s*. New York: Russell Sage Foundation.

Rivera-Batiz, Francisco L., and Carlos Santiago. 1997. *Puerto Ricans in the United States: A Changing Reality*. Washington, D.C.: The National Puerto Rican Coalition.

Rodriguez, Clara E. 1974. *The Ethnic Queue in the U.S.: The Case of Puerto Ricans*. San Francisco: R and E Research Associates.

———. 1980. Economic Survival in New York City. In *The Puerto Rican Struggle: Essays on Survival in the U.S.*, eds. Clara E. Rodríguez, Virginia Sánchez Korrol, and José Oscar Alers, 31–46. Maplewood, N.J.: Waterfront Press.

———. 1989. *Puerto Ricans Born in the U.S.A.* Boston: Unwin Hyman.

Ropka, Gerald W. 1973. The Evolving Residential Patterns of the Mexican, Puerto Rican and Cuban Population in the City of Chicago. Ph.D. diss., Michigan State University.

Rosenberg, Terry J. 1991. Work and Family Responsibilities of Women in New York City. In *Hispanics in the Labor Force: Issues and Policies*, eds. Edwin Melendez, Clara Rodriguez, and Janis Barry Figueroa, 203–22. New York: Plenum Press.

Rosenberg, Terry J., and Robert W. Lake. 1976. Toward a Revised Model of Residential Segregation and Succession: Puerto Ricans in New York, 1960–1970. *American Journal of Sociology* 81(5):1142–50.

Sakamoto, Arthur. 1988. Labor Market Structure, Human Capital, and Earnings Inequality in Metropolitan Areas. *Social Forces* 67(1):86–107.

Sánchez, José Ramón. 1986. Residual Work and Residual Shelter: Housing Puerto Rican Labor in New York City from World War II. In *Critical Perspectives on Housing*, eds. Rachel G. Bratt, Chester Hartman, and Ann Meyerson, 202–20. Philadelphia: Temple University Press.

Sanders, Jimy M., and Victor Nee. 1987. Limits of Ethnic Solidarity in the Enclave Economy. *American Sociological Review* 52:745–73.

Santiago, Anna M., and George Galster. 1995. Puerto Rican Segregation in the United States: Cause or Consequence of Economic Status? *Social Problems* 42(3):361–89.

Sassen-Koob, Saskia. 1984. The New Labor Demand in Global Cities. In *Cities in Transformation: Class, Capital, and the State*, ed. Michael Peter Smith, 139–71. Beverly Hills, Calif.: Sage Publications.

———. 1985. Changing Composition and Labor Market Location of Hispanic Immigration in New York City, 1960–1980. In *Hispanics in the U.S. Economy*, eds. George J. Borjas and Marta Tienda, 299–322. Orlando, Fla.: Academic Press.

———. 1986. New York City: Economic Restructuring and Immigration. *Development and Change* 17:85–119.

Siegel, Arthur, Harold Orlans, and Loyal Greer. 1954. *Puerto Ricans in Philadelphia: A Study of Their Demographic Characteristics, Problems and Attitudes.* Philadelphia: Commission on Human Relations.

Souza, Blase Camacho. 1998. Boricuas Hawaiianos. In *Extended Roots: From Hawaii to New York: Migraciones Puertorriqueñas a los Estados Unidos,* 2nd ed., ed. Oral History Task Force, 25–35. New York: Centro de Estudios Puertorriqueños.

Taeuber, Karl E., and Alma F. Taeuber. 1965. *Negroes in Cities: Residential Segregation and Neighborhood Change.* Chicago: Aldine Publishing.

———. 1976. A Practitioner's Perspective on the Index of Dissimilarity. *American Sociological Review* 41(5):884–89.

Taller Puertorriqueño. 1979. *Batiendo La Olla ("Stirring the Pot"): Oral History Project.* Philadelphia: Taller Puertorriqueño.

Tienda, Marta. 1985. The Puerto Rican Worker: Current Labor Market Status and Future Prospects. In *Puerto Ricans in the Mid '80s: An American Challenge,* ed. National Puerto Rican Coalition, 63–91. Alexandria, Va.: National Puerto Rican Coalition.

Tienda, Marta, and Leif Jensen. 1988. Poverty and Minorities: A Quarter-Century Profile of Color and Socioeconomic Disadvantage. In *Divided Opportunities: Minorities, Poverty and Social Policy,* ed. Gary D. Sandefur and Marta Tienda, 23–61. New York: Plenum Press.

Torres, Andrés. 1995. *Between Melting Pot and Mosaic: African Americans and Puerto Ricans in the New York Political Economy.* Philadelphia: Temple University Press.

Torres, Andres, and Frank Bonilla. 1993. Decline Within Decline: The New York Perspective. In *Latinos in a Changing U.S. Economy: Comparative Perspectives on Growing Inequality,* eds. Rebecca Morales and Frank Bonilla, 85–108. Newbury Park, Calif.: Sage Publications.

Torres, Andres, and Clara E. Rodriguez. 1991. Latino Research and Policy: The Puerto Rican Case. In *Hispanics in the Labor Force: Issues and Policies,* eds. Edwin Melendez, Clara Rodriguez, and Janis Barry Figueroa, 247–63. New York: Plenum Press.

Torres, Jose B. 1980. Acculturation and Psycho-social Adjustment among Puerto Rican Men in a Midwestern City: Milwaukee, Wisconsin. Ph.D. diss., University of Wisconsin.

Torruellas, Rosa M., Rina Benmayor, and Ana Juarbe. 1996. Negotiating Gender, Work, and Welfare: Familia as Productive Labor among Puerto Rican Women in New York City. In *Puerto Rican Women and Work: Bridges in Transnational Labor,* ed. Altagracia Ortiz, 184–208. Philadelphia: Temple University Press.

U.S. Bureau of the Census. 1991. Census of Population and Housing, 1990: Summary Tape File 1C on CD-ROM, machine-readable data files. Washington, D.C.: U.S. Bureau of the Census producer; Ann Arbor, Mich.: Interuniversity Consortium for Political and Social Research distribution, one year after production year.

———. 1992. Census of Population and Housing, 1990, United States: Public Use Microdata Sample: 1-Percent Sample, computer file. Washington, D.C.: U.S. Bureau of the Census producer; Ann Arbor, Mich.: Interuniversity Consortium for Political and Social Research distributor, one year after production year.

———. 1993a. *1990 Census of Population and Housing: CPH-R-1B, Guide, Part B, Glossary.* Washington, D.C.: U.S. Government Printing Office.

————. 1993b. *1990 Census of Population: Social and Economic Characteristics, Puerto Rico, 1990 CP-2-53*. Washington, D.C.: U.S. Government Printing Office.

————. 1993c. *Statistical Abstract of the United States: 1993*, 113th edition. Washington, D.C.: U.S. Government Printing Office.

————. 1993d. *1990 Census of Population: Persons of Hispanic Origin in the United States, 1990 CP-3-3*. Washington, D.C.: U.S. Government Printing Office.

————. 2001a. *The Hispanic Population in the United States: Population Characteristics, March 2000, P20-535*. Washington, D.C.: U.S. Government Printing Office.

————. 2001b. *Profiles of General Demographic Characteristics, 2000 Census of Population and Housing, United States*. Washington, D.C.: U.S. Government Printing Office.

U.S. Commission on Civil Rights. 1976. *Puerto Ricans in the Continental United States: An Uncertain Future*. Washington, D.C.: U.S. Commission on Civil Rights.

Waldinger, Roger. 1984. Immigrant Enterprise in the New York Garment Industry. *Social Problems* 32(1):60–71.

————. 1985. Immigration and Industrial Change in the New York City Apparel Industry. In *Hispanics in the U.S. Economy*, eds. George J. Borjas and Marta Tienda, 323–49. Orlando: Academic Press.

————. 1986. Immigrant Enterprise: A Critique and Reformulation. *Theory and Society* 15:249–85.

————. [1986–87]1991. Changing Ladders and Musical Chairs: Ethnicity and Opportunity in Post-Industrial New York. In *Majority and Minority: The Dynamics of Race and Ethnicity in American Life*, 5th ed., ed. Norman R. Yetman, 333–52. Boston: Allyn and Bacon. (First printed in *Politics and Society* 15[4] [1986–87].)

Whalen, Carmen Teresa. 2001. *From Puerto Rico to Philadelphia: Puerto Rican Workers and Postwar Economies*. Philadelphia: Temple University Press.

Williams, Byron. 1972. *Puerto Rico: Commonwealth, State or Nation?* New York: Parent's Magazine Press.

Wilson, Kenneth L. 1984. The Interrelationship Between Culture and Economy: Reflection on the Future of the Cuban American Community. In *Cubans in the United States*, eds. Miren Uriarte-Gastón and Jorge Cañas Martínez, 102–10. Boston: Center for the Study of the Cuban Community.

Winpenny, Thomas R. 1996. The Subtle Demise of Industry in a Quiet City: The Deindustrialization of Philadelphia, 1965–1995. Unpublished paper.

Winship, Christopher. 1977. A Revaluation of Indexes of Residential Segregation. *Social Forces* 55(4):1058–66.

Zambrana, Ruth E. 1994. Puerto Rican Families and Social Well-Being. In *Women of Color in U.S. Society*, eds. Maxine Baca Zinn and Bonnie Thornton Dill, 133–46. Philadelphia: Temple University Press.

Index

acculturation, 145
adaptation, xvi, 9, 174, 175, 183, 195, 202
Aetna, 193
affirmative action, 159, 196
African Americans, xvi, 4, 13, 156, 157, 161,
    167, 172, 184, 189; compared with Puerto
    Ricans in New York, 168–169. *See also*
    blacks
agrarian sector, 9
agrarian society, 152
Aguada (P.R.), 190
Aid to Families with Dependent Children,
    135
Alabama, 21
Allentown, 186–187
Anglo majority, 14, 31
Anglos, 5, 39, 117, 118
annexation, 10, 15, 30
anomaly, 110, 112, 117
Arizona, 16, 38
Arkansas, 21
Asociación de Trabajadores Agrícolas, 197
assimilation, 41, 104, 107, 108, 115, 117, 144
assimilation pattern, 10
assimilation theory, 144, 145
Atlantic City, 77, 79
Autonomous Charter, 34

barrio(s), 19, 171, 177, 189
Batista regime, 23, 24
Batistianos, 24
Bay of Pigs fiasco, 10, 25
Betances, Ramón, 33
Bethlehem (Pa.), 186–187

Bethlehem Steel, 188
bilingual education. *See* education, bilingual
birthrate, 20
blacks, 5, 12, 19, 153, 159, 177, 187; Ameri-
    can, 42; discrimination against, 148–149;
    female-headed household formation of,
    137; female labor force participation of,
    131; from the West Indies, 13; govern-
    ment employment of, 156–157; in the
    garment industry, 128; incorporation of,
    145, 201–202; non-English speaking, 42;
    Puerto Rican, 42; Puerto Rican segrega-
    tion from, 109–115; segregation patterns
    of, 117, 118. *See also* African Americans
bodega, 152, 180
bracero program, 19, 20
brain drain, 25, 43
Bridgeport (Conn.), 190, 191, 194
Bronx, the, 124, 153, 154
Brooklyn, 153
Buffalo, 75
business acumen, 3, 30, 152

California, 15, 20, 21, 47, 131, 133, 174,
    195–196, 198
Camarioca (port of), 26
Camden (N.J.), 42, 179
Campbell Soup Company, 42, 179
capital, 37, 107, 155, 166, 181; financial, 156;
    foreign, 36; human, 9, 53, 60–66, 88, 102,
    143, 150, 200, 201; initial, 154; invest-
    ment, 150; local ownership of, 40; mate-
    rial, 9, 10; social, 40; U.S., 35
capitalism, 28, 35

Chicago, 176–177; of blacks, 104, 107, 118; of Mexicans and Puerto Ricans, 48; of Puerto Ricans, 43, 53, 138; role of, 148–149; systemic, 106; union, 128
disenfranchisement, 164
dislocation, 40, 178, 191; economic, 135
dispersion, 20, 21, 30, 45, 104, 182
dissidents, 24, 25, 28
dissimilarity index, 109–115, 116, 117
domestics, 9, 125
Dominican Republic, 5
Dominicans, 6, 118, 129, 147, 151, 161, 166, 167; compared with Puerto Ricans in New York City, 169–172
dropout rate, 65
dropouts, 64–65, 84, 86, 87, 98, 99
dual labor market, 147
dual-wage system, 17

earnings, 26, 68, 133, 135, 136, 144, 204
earnings income, 68, 69
ecological model, 107, 108, 111
economic attainment, xvii, 90
economic base, 34, 53
economic bifurcation, 67
economic dualism,151, 166
economic fluctuations, 34
economic gains, 104
economic indicators, 20, 75
economic measurements, 55
economic mobility. See mobility, economic
economic transformation, 75, 76, 78, 89, 136
economic transition, 52, 74
economic trends, 36
economic well-being, 54, 55, 78, 84
economic woes, 28
economics, xv, 20
economies of scale, 159
economy, 26, 27, 43, 52, 136, 157, 162, 171, 177; agrarian, 123; agricultural, 11; colonial welfare, 43; contracting, 157; Cuban, 22; enclave, 53, 62, 148, 155, 156; global, 162; goods, 162; greater, 11, 12; indigenous, 203; informal, 157, 164, 165; manufacturing, 67, 73, 200; middleman, 171; native, 43; New York, 158, 162, 167; of Allentown, 187; postindustrial, 42, 43, 160; on the island, 190; Puerto Rican, 35, 123; Puerto Rico's, 34; service, 67, 73, 162, 200; subsistence, 34; sugar, 34; underground, 158, 164; U.S., 20, 143; world, 34
education, xv, 80, 95, 127, 130, 136, 144,

200; African American levels of, 169; and its role in queuing, 159; as human capital, 53, 60; as important for mobility, 180, 187; bilingual, 4, 129, 130, 159; college, 149; Cuban, 22, 28; Dominican levels of, 118; higher, 133, 178; Hispanic comparisons of, 64–66; in Bethlehem, 189; in Connecticut, 194; low level of, 203; lower, 200; of New York female Puerto Ricans, 131, 132, 133; of professional immigrants, 10; poor, 177; problematic, 160; Puerto Rican regional comparisons of, 83–88; recommended policies for, 206; returns to, 98, 160, 200; underfunding of, 204
educational attainment, 60, 61, 129, 130, 157, 160, 187; Hispanic comparisons of, 64–66; Puerto Rican regional comparisons of, 64–66
educational attainment levels, 91, 98
educational benefits, 19
educational environment, 85
educational levels, 9, 129, 132, 207; Puerto Rican regional comparisons of, 83–88
el tiempo muerto, 35
Electric Boat, 190
elite, 10, 12, 25, 154, 177
employment, xiv, 138, 177, 183, 190; blue-collar, 189; contracted for, 175; Cuban, 28, 155; declining, 136; European immigrant, 144; exclusion from, 134; government, 149, 156–157, 159; Hispanic, 88; in Allentown, 187; in Bridgeport, 194; in Chicago, 178; in Milwaukee, 186; in Puerto Rico, 34, 38; lack of, 120; manufacturing, 162; of females in New York, 130; of females in Puerto Rico, 126; patterns of, 176, prospects for, 101; Puerto Rican, 157; seasonal swings in, 165; stable, 188; technical, 19
employment environment, 159
employment status, 66, 138
enclave(s), 30, 104, 206; Cuban, 155, 174; economy, 62; ethnic, 11, 149, 155–156, 171; Puerto Rican, 179
English proficiency, 66, 80, 84, 95, 97; Hispanic comparisons of, 63–64; Puerto Rican regional comparisons of, 82–83
entrepreneurs, 22, 25, 26, 151, 154, 171, 172
entrepreneurship, 149–154, 156, 157, 160, 170, 171, 180
ethnic antagonism, 177
ethnic identification, 11
ethnic networks, 166